Islam Beyond Conflict
Indonesian Islam and Western Political Theory

AZYUMARDI AZRA
State University of Islamic Studies, Indonesia

and

WAYNE HUDSON

I0894235

Routledge
Taylor & Francis Group
LONDON AND NEW YORK

First published 2008 by Ashgate Publishing

2 Park Square, Milton Park, Abingdon, Oxon OX14 4RN
711 Third Avenue, New York, NY 10017, USA

Routledge is an imprint of the Taylor & Francis Group, an informa business

First issued in paperback 2017

Copyright © 2008 Azyumardi Azra and Wayne Hudson

Azyumardi Azra and Wayne Hudson have asserted their moral right under the Copyright, Designs and Patents Act, 1988, to be identified as the editors of this work.

All rights reserved. No part of this book may be reprinted or reproduced or utilised in any form or by any electronic, mechanical, or other means, now known or hereafter invented, including photocopying and recording, or in any information storage or retrieval system, without permission in writing from the publishers.

Notice:
Product or corporate names may be trademarks or registered trademarks, and are used only for identification and explanation without intent to infringe.

British Library Cataloguing in Publication Data
Islam beyond conflict : Indonesian Islam and Western
political theory. - (Law, ethics and governance series)
1. Islamic law - Indonesia 2. Islam and politics -
Indonesia 3. Indonesia - Politics and government
I. Azra, Azyumardi II. Hudson, Wayne
340.5'9'09598

Library of Congress Control Number: 2007942639

ISBN 978-0-7546-7092-6

ISBN 978-0-7546-7092-6 (hbk)
ISBN 978-1-138-26232-4 (pbk)

ISLAM BEYOND CONFLICT

Law Ethics and Governance Series

Series Editor: Charles Sampford, Director, Key Centre for Ethics, Law, Justice and Governance, Griffith University, Australia

Recent history has emphasised the potentially devastating effects of governance failures in governments, government agencies, corporations and the institutions of civil society. 'Good governance' is seen as necessary, if not crucial, for economic success and human development. Although the disciplines of law, ethics, politics, economics and management theory can provide insights into the governance of organisations, governance issues can only be dealt with by interdisciplinary studies, combining several (and sometimes all) of those disciplines. This series aims to provide such interdisciplinary studies for students, researchers and relevant practitioners.

Also in the series

Measuring Corruption
Edited by Charles Sampford, Arthur Shacklock, Carmel Connors and Fredrik Galtung
ISBN 978-0-7546-2405-9

Re-envisioning Sovereignty
The End of Westphalia?
Edited by Trudy Jacobsen, Charles Sampford and Ramesh Thakur
ISBN 978-0-7546-7260-9

Governing the Heroin Trade
From Treaties to Treatment
Melissa Bull
ISBN 978-0-7546-7121-3

On Abuse of Idealism
Lessons from China's Cultural Revolution
Peggy Krenn (Hui-yun Chuang)
ISBN 978-0-7546-7208-1

Contents

List of Figures and Tables

Figures

Tables

Notes on Contributors

Azyumardi Azra is now Director of Graduate School, Syarif Hidayatullah State Islamic University (UIN), Jakarta, Indonesia. He was rector of this university from 1998 to 2006.

Joseph Camilleri is Professor and Director of the Centre for Dialogue, School of Humanities and Social Sciences, La Trobe University, Melbourne.

George Crowder is Associate Professor in Political and International Studies at Flinders University.

Bahtiar Effendy is Professor in Political Science at the State Islamic University (UIN) Jakarta.

Brian Galligan has been a Professor of Political Science at the University of Melbourne since 1995, and previously was a Professor in the Research School of Social Science at the Australian National University, Canberra.

Barry Hindess is Professor, Political Science Program, Research School of Social Sciences, ANU, Canberra

Wayne Hudson is a Professor in the School of Philosophy, University of Tasmania and Research Professor Australian Centre for Christianity and Culture, Charles Sturt University, Canberra.

John Kane is a Professor in the School of Politics and Public Policy, Griffith University, Brisbane.

Philip Kitley is Chair and Professor of Communications, University of Wollongong, Australia.

N.A. Fadhil Lubis is Professor of Islamic Law at the State University of Islamic Studies, Sumatra.

Ahmad Syafi'i Maarif is the head of Muhammadiyah, the second largest mass Muslim organization in Indonesia.

Graham Maddox is Emeritus Professor, Political Science, University of New England, Armidale, Australia.

Saiful Mujani is Lecturer in Muslim Politics at Syarif Hidayatullah State Islamic University, and Director of Political Research at the Freedom Institute in Jakarta.

Adnan Buyung Nasution is an Advocate with Adnan Buyung Nasution and Partners, Jakarta, and a distinguished Indonesian.

Haig Patapan is a Professor in the Department of Politics and Public Policy, and Research Member of the Centre for Governance and Public Policy, Griffith University.

Geoffrey Stokes is Professor of Politics in the School of International and Political Studies, Faculty of Arts, Deakin University, Melbourne.

Janna Thompson is Reader and Associate Professor in the School of Humanities and Social Sciences, La Trobe University, Melbourne.

Spencer Zifcak is Professor of Law in the School of Law and Management, La Trobe University, Melbourne.

Acknowledgements

The Islamic-Western Dialogue on Governance Values was a series of six workshops in Indonesia and Australia involving Australians and Indonesians from government, business, watchdog bodies and NGOs who were challenged to think more deeply about their role in governance reform in the context of globalization. The workshops were jointly convened by the Key Centre for Ethics, Law, Justice and Governance, Griffith University, Brisbane and the Centre for the Study of Islam and Society, a subsidiary institution of the State Institute for Islamic Studies, Indonesia. This project was funded by the Open Society Institute. Drawing upon both the Islamic system of thought and the Western tradition of liberal democracy, each workshop focused on a key governance value and an associated key issue. This edited collection is a product of these workshops. The editors wish to acknowledge the efforts of Robyn Lui in organizing the workshops, the advice of Julia Howell during the finalization of the manuscript, and the assistance with translation provided by Nada Ibrahim.

Chapter 1

Introduction

Azyumardi Azra and Wayne Hudson

This volume challenges the conclusions of Orientalists such as Max Weber (*Sociology of Religion*, 1963) Karl Wittfogel (*Oriental Despotism*, 1957*)* and, more recently, Samuel Huntington (*Clash of Civilizations*, 1996) and Bernard Lewis (*What Went Wrong?* 2002) who condemn Islamic societies as essentially anti-modern and anti-democratic. Until recently, however, scholars working on democratization have often overlooked political developments in Indonesia – the world's most populous Muslim country. Indeed, most literature on Islam and democracy has focused on developments in the Middle East and North Africa. Yet Indonesia has a pluralist religious tradition very different from that found in most of the Middle East, and its religious life is open to relatively high levels of accommodation and dialogue.

In seeking to address this neglect, the chapters in this volume argue that democratic nation-building in multi-ethnic Indonesia can benefit from strategic assimilations of concepts from Western political theory, especially if those concepts are approached from a basis within Islamic tradition. As many of the contributors point out, the prospects for governance reform based on Islamic principles are better than most of the existing literature suggests. It has often been argued that Western political concepts are difficult to apply to Islamic societies in so far as they imply agnostic or relativist attitudes to human affairs. Most of the contributors to this volume suggest, however, that concepts from Western political theory are compatible – to a lesser or greater degree, depending on individual interpretations – with a rational interpretation of Islamic universalism.

The first part of this volume focuses on constitutionalism and the rule of law. In Chapter 3, N.A. Fadhil Lubis explores possible foundations for constitutionalism in Islamic values and jurisprudence from an Indonesian Sunni perspective. He argues that the technicalities of Islamic jurisprudence make possible a gradual assimilation into Islam of concepts from Western political theory. However, the increasing call to incorporate and implement Islamic law into the Indonesian Constitution makes it crucial to clarify *which* constitutional values should be embodied in an Islamic state. In Chapter 4, Adnan Buyung Nasution identifies areas of potential conflict between a modern constitutional state and a state that adheres to Islamic values. He explores how Islamic values can be deployed to moderate the apparent opposition between democratic and absolute law. Nonetheless, as Brian Galligan argues in Chapter 5, Western democratic constitutionalism is not itself without ambiguities. More attention should be given, Galligan argues, to the ethical basis for law, specifically as to how it grounds the establishment and amendment of constitutional systems and provides a reference for assessing the justice of particular laws and acts of government. Galligan's approach to Western constitutionalism opens up the possibility of a dialogue with Islamic approaches to governance. Still the fact remains that in Islamic legal-political thought, God has sovereignty and the state is not recognized as an independent object of allegiance. Instead, the role of the government is to implement and enforce divine law. This role of the state leads to problems which remain to be resolved. In Chapter 6, Spencer Zifcak argues that a more developed doctrine of the rule of law needs to be developed to handle these tensions. Without clear distinctions between religion and politics, and between personal and institutional authority, the rule of law may prove difficult to establish and enforce in an Islamic society.

Democracy is the theme of the second part, with Bahtiar Effendy (Chapter 7) and Ahmad Syafi'i Maarif (Chapter 8) discussing conceptions of democracy from an Islamic perspective, and Graham Maddox (Chapter 9) and Haig Patapan (Chapter 10) examining the tensions between Eastern and Western approaches to democracy and the state. Because Islam has a number of tenets that seem in line with the general principles of democracy, many conclude that Islam is compatible with democracy. Bahtiar Effendy argues, however, that the realities are more complex, especially since Islamic tenets which contradict democratic values are often brushed aside in the standard discussions. Ahmad Syafi'i Maarif, on the other hand, argues that Indonesian Islam is well suited to engaging the challenges of governance in the twenty-first century and may serve as a model for the rest of the Muslim world. He suggests that democracy and Islam have a long concurrent history in Indonesia and, although colonial apologists attribute the arrival of democracy in Indonesia to the Dutch, Maarif points out that popular consultation and participation in decision-making were actually heralded much earlier by observance of *shari'ah* law in Islamic communities. Moreover, the case of Indonesia is distinctive because Indonesia was never involved in the philosophical and theological controversies that plagued Islam elsewhere. Graham Maddox questions, however, how far a Western conception of the state can be implemented in an Islamic society such as Indonesia, especially if robust democracy requires a secular state which can tolerate and accommodate a range of legitimate worldviews, religious beliefs and philosophical positions. Haig Patapan, in turning his attention to leadership, also questions how far Western notions of democratic leadership can be reconciled with Islamic traditions which maintain that a just ruler is one who upholds *shari'ah*. Just as Galligan notes the tensions and ambiguities in relation to democratic constitutionalism in Western political theory, so there are tensions in Western thinking, Patapan points out, between the principles of freedom and the principles of leadership which may be further aggravated in the Islamic context.

Chapters 11 to 14 examine the notion of citizenship. N.A. Fadhil Lubis argues from an Islamic perspective that there are elements in Islamic legal philosophy and jurisprudence which facilitate the development of a modern Islamic approach to citizenship. Lubis examines the question of who is a Muslim, and then deliberates on the concepts of *usul* (roots) and *qath'iyat* (absolutes) vis-à-vis *furu'* (branches) and *zanniyat* (relatives). The first two represent matters that Muslims are obliged to listen to and obey, while the latter are considered matters on which Muslims have the freedom to hold variegated opinions; or to exercise personal independent reasoning (*ijtihad*). Lubis then raises the issue of how unity and diversity are dealt with in Islamic thought, including the issue of apostasy. Geoffrey Stokes, in contrast, draws on Western conceptions of citizenship and deploys them to propose a conceptual framework for citizenship. He then argues that recent developments in the Western theory of citizenship contribute significantly towards the development of a modern Islamic conception of citizenship. From a different perspective, Janna Thompson argues that recent liberal and communitarian approaches to citizenship are relevant to Islamic societies, especially since they illumine difficult issues such as the relationship between citizens and ‘outsiders’ and the question of our duties to non-citizens. Barry Hindess is less sanguine, and insists that citizenship is too often seen as a matter of internal relations between the individual and the state. In Western discourses, he argues, the exclusionary and divisive aspects of citizenship are often overlooked. It follows, he suggests, that Islamic approaches to citizenship will need to address the negative as well as the positive aspects of citizenship.

The fourth part explores the impact of pluralism on contemporary Islamic thinking, with Azyumardi Azra asking what an Islamic pluralism would look like. Azra discusses particular challenges raised by intercultural and interfaith encounters, and concludes that the strengthening of democracy and the enforcement of law are crucial for the evolution of a democratic Indonesian state. John Kane, in contrast, argues that the question of how far pluralism can be applied to Islamic societies needs to be translated into realistic terms which recognize the tension between liberalism and nationalism in Western political theory. Liberal democratic nations embody three different political traditions – liberalism, democracy and nationalism. Although these traditions have come together at different times and in different ways, in practice their theoretical fit is imperfect and, he suggests, an Islamic version of liberalism needs to take this into account. A major challenge for Islamic societies is how far to accommodate and how far to reject Western pluralism. George Crowder clarifies this issue by arguing that Berlinian pluralism does not imply relativism or undermine personal autonomy as a universal value. Correctly interpreted, he argues, it provides a framework which may be directly relevant to an Islamic society such as Indonesia. The chapters in this section suggest, however, that any attempt to make pluralism relevant to Indonesia will need to subject existing institutions to probing scrutiny in light of both universalist and particularist principles.

In the fifth part, the contributors explore a number of dimensions of human rights and their relationship to traditional values in the context of governance reform. N.A. Fadhil Lubis proposes that traditional concepts from classical and medieval Islamic law and jurisprudence can form the basis of a contemporary Islamic approach to the theorization of rights and their enforcement, especially in the Indonesian context. Joseph Camilleri argues that human rights should not be understood as immutable or absolute but as evolving outcomes of negotiation and of consideration of civilizational diversity.

Civil society is the focus of the last section. From an Islamic perspective, Saiful Mujani argues that the democratic values, secular civic engagement and ‘Islamic’ civic engagement in Indonesia all contribute to a tolerant society in ways which significantly modify claims by Western scholars such as Bernard Lewis and Samuel Huntington which suggest that prospects for the development of civil society in

Islamic countries are poor. In the next chapter, Philip Kitley examines the role that the media plays in the construction of a public sphere in Indonesia. Kitley argues that greater attention should be paid to the unique features of civil society in Indonesia, where the intersection of civil society and the media makes it possible for Islam to play the role of a public religion in debate with other faiths and conceptions of social life. In the final chapter, the editors sum up possible convergences between Indonesian Islam and Western political theory, and conclude with some suggestions for further research.

Chapter 2

Political Modernity and Indonesian Islam: A Manifesto

Azyumardi Azra and Wayne Hudson

Indonesian Islam is essentially a tolerant, moderate and 'middle way' (*ummah wasat*) Islam, and differs significantly from the Islam found in the Middle East. In Indonesia, Islam spread peacefully, and in forms which took account of diverse ethnic, cultural and social realities of the region. Further, the vast majority of Indonesian Muslims belong to moderate mainstream organizations such as the Nahdlatul Ulama, Muhammadiyah and many other regional organizations throughout the country which support modernity and democracy, and oppose the establishment of an Islamic state.

All of these moderate and mainstream organizations are basically civil society organizations, and they play a crucial role in the development and enhancement of democracy. These organizations are also very active in the dissemination of ideas of democracy, human rights, justice and gender equality that are crucial for a modern society. It is true that there are small and fringe groups of radical Muslims which have captured a lot of media attention, such as the Islamic Defense Front (FPI), the Jihad Troops (Lasykar Jihad), the Council of Jihad Fighters (Majelis Mujahidin Indonesia), and the Party of Liberation (Hizb al-Tahrir), but these groups, which are mainly led by non-native Muslims, have limited influence in Indonesia as a whole. In these circumstances, there are reasons to believe that political modernity can be realized in Indonesia in a form which is fully compatible with Islam, especially if there is a critical reception of the main concepts of Western political thought.

Firstly, universalism can form the basis for contemporary Islamic approaches to democracy and the generation of a modern civil society. There is ample precedent for a concept of universal human rights in Islamic tradition and no justification for attempts to promote distinctive Islamic human rights. Secondly, Indonesian Islam is compatible with pluralism and actually requires it for its own self-development. The version of pluralism advocated by Isaiah Berlin is particularly relevant to the problems Indonesia faces in reconciling harmony and diversity. Berlinian pluralism is primarily about the plurality of goods, not cultures. It implies a general imperative to promote a diverse range of goods, an imperative which serves as a critical standard for the performance of particular cultures. Such a perspective is relevant to concrete situations in Indonesia and not an alien import from the West.

Thirdly, Indonesian Muslims can accept and embrace personal autonomy as a political ideal of universal application, even though this may involve some modifications of traditional attitudes. Although some argue that the personal autonomy celebrated by Mill and other liberals is not a genuinely universal good, but rather an ideal appropriate to only one kind of culture, this is not the case, and Indonesian Muslims can fully embrace the concept without in any way losing their Islamic identity. Indeed, it is arguable that a high degree of personal autonomy actually makes a Muslim's submission to God more sincere and meaningful.

Fourthly, Indonesian Islam can endorse a strong human rights regime in both traditionally Islamic and less traditional forms. International experience suggests that there may be serious problems associated with attempts to institute *shari'ah* law, and it is fair to say that an excellent modern way to institute *shari'ah* has not yet been found. However, here too Indonesian Islam can be flexible. Thus, for example, Indonesian Muslims can consider a version of *shari'ah* law based on and compatible with universal human rights. Such a regime would obviously need to protect the rights of non-Muslims. It might also be socially radical when compared with anything found in the contemporary Middle East, but it need not be identified with theocracy or with discrimination in a negative sense, even though many Western political theorists seem not to grasp this. Indonesian Islam is not incipiently theocratic, although there is a danger that less tolerant voices will be popular with mass audiences. In this context, there is a case for a 'substantification' of politics with reference to the universal values of Islam such as equality (*al-musawa*), justice (*al-adalah*), deliberation (*shura*) and tolerance *(tasamuh*), but not the supposed unity of religion (*al-din*) and the state *(al-dawlah)* demanded by traditionalists.

Fifthly, Indonesian Islam has no objection to the adoption of Western-style law over a wide area, and no problem with using Western jurisprudential principles to handle difficult issues in *fiqh*. Once the conflictual character of *fiqh* is acknowledged, there are no obstacles in the way of a genuinely modern Indonesian legal order, even if some conventional features of Islamic tradition may require amendment, including perhaps the traditional ban on Muslims converting from Islam, which made absolute sense in the time of the Prophet but now is in tension with modern conceptions of freedom of conscience.

Sixthly, there is nothing in Islamic history which compels Indonesian Muslims to uncritically accept historical ad hoc arrangements as normative for present and future political and social arrangements. Of course, it is true that historically Muslims, as subjects of the ruler, had duties defined by Islamic concepts rather than positive rights acquired as members of a political community. Nonetheless, the Islamic injunction to exercise intelligence requires Muslims to develop new arrangements when historical circumstances make them necessary and appropriate.

Seventhly, although Islam obviously has a richer understanding and practice of community than is always found in the West, Indonesian Islam is entirely compatible with a strong form of individualism, even though religious voluntarism may still sometimes be counter-factual in Indonesia, and much remains to be done to protect individual citizens both from the state and from those who demand religious group rights which they do not justify in discursive rational terms. It does not follow that Indonesian Islam has to accept a form of secularism, or that it must uncritically adopt American constructions of the public–private distinction. On the contrary, Indonesian Muslims should contextualize what they borrow from the West in every instance.

Finally, Indonesian Muslims should be resolute in defending and modernizing their Islamic heritage, especially in contexts in which it is superior to or at least a major correction to Western political thought. Indonesian Muslims should not tolerate the agnosticism or the nihilism which has shaped much of the Western tradition in political thought. They should be fearless in arguing the superiority of Islam in its commitment to justice as a universal ideal, in its insistence on the transcendence of God, and in its demand that political and social arrangements should actively promote human flourishing. In the twentieth century, Indonesian Muslims have to embrace change, along with everyone else, but there is no need for them to accept a new neo-liberal colonialism. Rather they should be independent rational thinkers, concerned to learn from other peoples and traditions, and from Western political thought in particular, in ways which promote the deepest ethical insights of Islam.

Chapter 3

Islamic Perspectives on the Rule of Law and Constitutionalism

N.A. Fadhil Lubis

Constitutionalism requires that the conduct of different organs of the state vis-à-vis citizens as well as each other be regulated by laws or rules, which may or may not be written. In this chapter, I argue that elements of a version of constitutionalism can be found in Islamic political and legal thought. My argument implies that the reception of constitutionalism in Indonesia should be contextualized having regard to precedents for constitutionalism in Islam.

Shari'ah and *Fiqh*

Muslims refer to their religion as *dīn al-islam*, a term used in the *Qur'an*. *Dīn* is established by divine institution (*wad' ilahi*) which guides rational beings, by their choosing and submitting to it, to salvation here and in the hereafter. It means 'religion' in the broadest sense. Muslims generally understand the *dīn* as covering three things: *islam* with its five pillars, *iman* with its five (some believe six) pillars, and *ihsan* (virtues). The essence of Islam, however, is *tawhīd*, the act of affirming Allah to be the One, Absolute, transcendent Creator, Lord and Master of the whole universe. *Tawhīd* is that which gives Islamic civilization its identity, which binds all its constituents together and thus makes them an integrated entity. God, in His love and mercy, revealed to humanity His will. The *Qur'an* affirms, 'Unto every people God has sent prophets to teach them the divine imperatives in their own tongue' (Q, 14:4). Reason and revelation are 'two open books' available to humanity to discern the divine imperative. Although human reasoning is fallible, yet it is trustworthy as an avenue of truth, since it can reconsider and correct its previous findings. Even if revelation is infallible, humanity's understanding of it is not free from mistakes, and therefore stands to be corrected by reason. Where errors have occurred, reconsideration by reason is the only recourse. Fortunately, it is an open, free, public, self-conscious and critical avenue.

Shari'ah originally referred to a path trodden by camels to a water source. Water is an unavoidable source of life, especially in the desert area such as Arabia in which Islam was born. Later *shari'ah* was used in the *Qur'an* to mean a straight path, as in 45:18. 'Then We put on a straight path in your affairs, so follow it and do not follow the desires of those who have no knowledge.' In Islam it is understood as the sum total of Islamic injunctions which were revealed to the Prophet and which are recorded in the *Qur'an* as well as deducible from the Prophet's divinely guided lifestyle (*Sunnah*).

For Muslims, God is the sole ultimate Law-Giver (*shari'*), and the law derives from divinely inspired sources and represents God's will for the proper ordering of all human activities. Given the absence of a living prophet, all law worthy of the name must therefore be derived from texts that contain divine revelation or possess authority grounded on that revelation. In classical Islamic jurisprudence, the letter of the prescriptive elaboration of the values of Islam was declared sacrosanct and hence absolutely unalterable, except in a few cases. The qualities of eternity and immutability belonged to the values or principles behind the prescriptive elaboration, not the legal form given them by translation of the purposes of law into legislative prescriptions. Eternity and absoluteness belonged, in the main, to the axiological postulates. With the exception of these postulates and directions, all deontological elaborations were open to reinterpretation by human beings. This openness was dictated by ever-changing conditions and situations of human life which demanded in turn a readiness on the part of the law to meet them in pursuit of its eternal objectives. *Shari'ah* was divine and eternal not in its letter, but in its spirit, just as the letter of the law was honoured because of its derivation from that which is divine and eternal.

The prime sources of Islamic law are the *Qur'an* and the *Sunnah*. For Muslims, revelation provides both the principles of laws and the mechanism for their renewal. The fundamental principles, the values, and groundwork for both the law and the methodology for its dynamic development are given by divine authority. In practice, however, Muslims invented the science of *usul al-fiqh* to systematize development of the law to meet new situations and problems, and to institutionalize the continuous adaptation of the law to historical change. It was the task of *usul al-fiqh* to distinguish between the changeable and the changeless, to develop a methodology out of the relevant principles laid down in the *Qur'an* and the *Sunnah* for governing change. *Usul al-fiqh* arose in order to establish criteria of validity for the development of new laws from the sources in the revelation. *Fiqh*, which means 'deep understanding', refers to the science of deducing Islamic laws from evidence found in the sources of Islamic law of the Prophet and has human scholars as its subject, while the subject of *shari'ah*, the *shari'ah-maker* (*al-shari'*) is ultimately God. It is under the heading of *fiqh* rather than *shari'ah* that the actual articulations of the divine characterizations by human scholars are to be placed, since these articulations represent or express the scholars' understanding of *shari'ah*. The hesitation of the Islamic tradition to identity these articulations with *shari'ah* as such arise from an acknowledgement that they are fallible, and therefore can sometimes be erroneous. The fact that the articulations of different scholars or schools can contradict each other bears testimony to this fallibility.

So do the words *shari'ah* and *fiqh* refer to the same thing? Some scholars take these two words to refer to the same entity, although with slightly different emphases. For others, the two words point to two different entities. Other scholars emphasize three differences between the two:

1. *Shari'ah* is the body of revealed 'laws' found both in the *Qur'an* and in the *Sunnah*, while *fiqh* is a body of laws deduced from *shari'ah* to cover specific

situations not directly treated in *shari'ah* law;

2. *Shari'ah* is fixed and unchangeable, whereas *fiqh* changes according to the circumstances under which it is applied;
3. The laws of *shari'ah* are, for the most part, general. They lay down basic principles. In contrast, the laws of *fiqh* tend to be specific and demonstrate how the basic principles of *shari'ah* should be applied in given circumstances.

On the whole, the better view would seem to be that the Islamic tradition distinguishes the articulation of the divine categorization by human scholars from the categorization itself.

Law and the State

In Islam there is no autonomous role for the state or the rule as such: ultimate authority is with God, who holds sovereignty but does not exercise it, and His will permeates the charismatic community (Von Grunebaum 1970, 491). Nonetheless, although the Islamic primary sources, the *Qur'an* and the *Sunnah*, have little to say on matters of government and the state, the first issue to confront the Muslim community immediately after the death of its formative leader, the Prophet Muhammad, in 632 was the problem of government and of how to select a successor (*khalifah*) to the Prophet. From the start, therefore, Muslims had to innovate and to improvise with regard to the form and nature of government, and one of the main concerns of the juristic theory of the caliphate was the issue of legitimacy. Initially, Abu Bakr and 'Umar, the first two rightly guided caliphs, had emphasized the aspect of legitimacy by resorting as much as possible to the pre-Islamic tradition but sanctioned by Islam, namely a tripartite principle of *shura'* (deliberation), *'aqd* (ruler–ruled contract), and *bay'ah* (oath of allegiance). These concepts were subsequently strengthened with the claim that the caliph is the most important instrument to implement God's will on earth.

More generally, several classical Islamic concepts traditionally facilitated the state–society relationship. These included the need for the ruler to consult with the elders of the community (*shura*), adherence to the consensus within the community (*ijma'*) on relevant legal issues, some degree of allowance for independent inquiry (*ijtihad*), and fidelity to the pact between rulers and the ruled (*bay'a*). Nonetheless, there was no body of developed constitutional theory in medieval Islam of the kind that arose in the West, partly because Islamic political and legal thought had to work with a distinctive understanding of revelation.

Sovereignty

In Islamic jurisprudence, sovereignty rests neither with the ruler nor with the *'ulama*, but with the Word of God as embodied in *shari'ah*. The ideal Islamic state is therefore not an autocracy or a theocracy, but a monocracy. The state is perceived merely as a vehicle for achieving security and order in ways conducive to Muslims attending to their religious duties. Legislation is not a function of the state, for the (divine) law precedes the state and is not one of its products. The legal process is confined to deducing detailed rules and *ahkam* (judgements) from the broader tenets of *shari'ah*. A certain element of equilibrium and balance is presumed among three powers: the caliph as guardian of the community and the faith; the *'ulama* (religious scholars) involved in the function of rendering *ifta'* (religio-legal advice), and the judges who settle disputes according to the existing laws.

The Rule of Law and Constitutionalism

The rule of law is generally understood as the largely formal or procedural properties of a well-ordered legal system (Audi 1995, 699). These properties are commonly thought to include a prohibition of arbitrary power (the lawgiver is also the subject of the laws); laws that are general, prospective, clear and consistent (capable of guiding conduct); and tribunals (courts) that are reasonably accessible and fairly structured to hear and determine legal claims. Contemporary discussions of the rule of law focus on two major questions: to what extent is conformity to the rule of law essential to the very idea of a legal system; and what is the connection between the rule of law and the substantive moral value of a legal system?

What is the meaning of 'constitutionalism' in the context of Islamic legal political thought? Constitutionalism has no readily identifiable Arabic equivalent, although some suggest the term *dusturiyyah*. In practice, however, major aspects of constitutionalism such as ruling in accordance with the law, the right to oppose unjust rule, and liberties which rulers are not permitted to infringe have long existed in Muslim legal-political thought. Constitutionalism implies the limitation of the state vis-à-vis a society and respect for a set of human rights covering not only civic rights but also political and economic rights. It also implies the implementation of a separation of powers within the state. These two ideas are closely related. According to Lane (1996, 25), the first functions as 'external principle' which restricts state power with respect to civil society, while the second functions as an 'internal principle' which ensures that no body (organ or person) in the state completely prevails over the others. But can these principles be realized in an Islamic society?

During the rule of the 'Abbasid caliphs (750–1258), Muslim philosophers and jurists, such as al-Farabi (d. 950) and al-Mawardi (d. 1058), raised fundamental questions about the relations between the ruler and the ruled and their mutual duties. In his *al-Madinah al-Fadilah*, al-Farabi set the standards by which states should be judged. Later, during the Mamluk period, one of the most important Muslim philosophers/jurists, Ibn Taymiyah (1263–1328), defined the criteria for 'just' rulers and the political and social obligations of the community. In all these instances, the positions of the ruler and the subjects were placed within Islamic principles as interpreted by the *'ulama*, the learned persons of religion.

These are loads of pure gold in less fertile ground rather than a consistent pattern of well-defined political and legal definition and argument. On the other hand, local instances show again and again that fundamental problems were acknowledged and that Muslims were often driven to the same rational considerations as Western theorists in their attempts to solve them. Thus at least one caliph, 'Umar ibn 'Abd al-'Aziz (r. 717–720), displayed an acute consciousness of the specific constraints with which any Islamic government has to come to terms:

> There could be no choice for anyone concerning God's Book and the Sunnah of God's Messenger, except acting by them, and struggling for their enforcement. When a governor is faced with a matter not dealt with in the *Qur'an* and Sunnah of the Prophet ... it is before the ruler of all Muslims that the issue should be brought and no decision should be taken without his consent (Ibn 'Abd al-Hakam 1927, 74).

First comes a *Qur'anic* ruling, and then, if there is none, the Prophet's *Sunnah.* Caliphal discretion comes only in third place. Only after exhausting the revealed verses and the received *Sunnah* with no success could the highest authority exercise its independent judgement.

The Indonesian Context

Given the fact that these precedents are often hidden in a forest of technical political and legal doctrine, it is not surprising that Indonesian Muslims did not inherit anything like fully theorized political and legal principles, let alone an explicit Islamic constitutionalism. Instead, constitutionalism was a doctrine they came round to in stages as a result of gradual accommodations of Islamic insight and Western political and legal thought.

In Indonesia, constitutionalism was not an issue when the preparatory commission for independence was designing a constitution, or when Indonesian independence was proclaimed on 17 August 1945 and the draft Constitution, with certain changes, was promulgated. Subsequently, however, the commission split into two camps, one of which strove for an Islamic state, while the other struggled for a secular state. A compromise was later reached by the special commission set up to settle the issue, and it was signed by all the members that the state is based on 'belief in God, with an obligation to observe the *shari'ah* by its adherents'. When this became an official preamble to the Constitution of the new state of Indonesia, the second half of the sentence (or what is known in Indonesia as 'the seven words') was erased.

The omission of *shari'ah* from the Constitution has not, however, prevented some Indonesian Muslims from fighting for it. When Soekarno changed the structure of the state into a more totalitarian government on 5 July 1959, by returning to the first Constitution, he made mention of the Jakarta Charter. After the fall of Soekarno, when Soeharto began to found a new constitutional government, some Muslim politicians attempted to give legal form to the content of the Jakarta Charter, but their efforts failed. On 29 June 1968, celebrations commemorating the Jakarta Charter were held in Jakarta, but the push for a more Islamic state did not succeed, and many Muslim leaders subsequently lost their political positions. The political climate changed dramatically in the mid 1980s when Soeharto sought to appease Muslims by enacting 'Islamic' laws, by strengthening the existing 'Islamic' institutions, especially the Islamic *agama* courts of justice, and by legalizing new Islamic institutions such as Islamic banks and insurance. The collapse of the New Order regime in May 1998 ushered in further hopes for the implementation of Islamic values and the application of *shari'ah* in Indonesia. Numerous Muslim groups and prominent individuals sought to grasp a golden opportunity to struggle for a fuller incorporation of Islamic values into Indonesian life. However, as time passed it became clear that political Islam was not the choice of Indonesian people at large. Islamic political parties did not do well in leading positions. On the contrary, it was the PDIP, a nationalist secular party, which gained the highest number of votes. The demands of some 'Islamic' parties to revive the content of the Jakarta Charter were also unsuccessful. This historical trajectory forms the background to contemporary debates about the extent to which constitutionalism and the rule of law should be given effect in Indonesia.

Conclusion

Although the tension between a modern nation state and political Islam continues to be important in Indonesia, the outcome of these struggles remains uncertain. On the one hand, the promulgation of legal concepts and values of Islamic origin have been increasing of late. On the other hand, the need to fully embrace modern constitutionalism and to ground it in Islamic values is widely debated. Many believe that it is possible to establish an Islamic society in which constitutionalism and the rule of law are in force, albeit in forms sensitive to and consistent with the actual religious make up of the country. This view has strong support, partly because constitutionalism has important precedents in Islamic political and legal thought, and partly because the specific political trajectory in Indonesia suggests that it is the outcome most suited to the specific circumstances of the country.

References

Abd al-Hakam (1927), *The History of the Conquest of Egypt, North Africa and Spain* (ed. Charles C. Torrey) (New Haven: Yale University Press).

Ainnurrafiq (ed.) (2002), *Mazhab Jogya: Menggagas Paradigma Ushul Fiqh Kontemporer* (Yogyakarta: Ar-Ruzz Press).

Atmasasmita, Romli (2001), *Reformasi Hukum, Hak Asasi Manusia & Penegakan Hukum* (Bandung: Mandar Maju).

Audi, R. (ed.) (1995), *The Cambridge Dictionary of Philosophy* (New York: Cambridge University Press).

Bichel, Rebecca H. (n.d.), 'Deconstructing Constitutionalism: The Case of Central Asia and Uzbekistan' (Original Publications, ICARP).

Chand, Hari (1994), *Modern Jurisprudence* (Kuala Lumpur: International Law Book Services).

Lane, Jan-Erik (1996), *Constitutions and Political Theory* (Manchester: Manchester University Press).

Lubis, Nur A. Fadhil (2000), *A History of Islamic Law in Indonesia* (Medan: IAIN Press).

Salim, Arskal and Azra, Azyumardi (eds) (2003), *Shari'a and Politics in Modern Indonesia* (Singapore: Institute of Southeast Asian Studies).

Von Grunebaum, G.E. (1970), *Classical Islam* (London: George Allen and Unwin).

Wahid, Marzuki and Wahid, Rumadi (eds) (2001), *Fiqh Mazhab Negara: Kritik atas Politik Hukum Islam di Indonesia* (Yogyakarta: LkiS).

Chapter 4

Constitutional Values and an Islamic State

Adnan Buyung Nasution

Introduction

Constitutional government is emerging only slowly in Indonesia. There was an integralist philosophy of the state (*staatsidee*) behind the 1945 Constitution which centralized the entire power of the state in the president. Soekarno called the state under such a philosophy the '*gotong-royong* State' or 'the brotherhood state', a state led by a head of state, whose soul was entwined with its people.[1] This conception of the state was arguably closer to absolutism than to democracy. Given this background, I myself argued at an early stage for *constitutionalism* as the proper basis for the development of the Indonesian state structure. Now a range of amendments to the 1945 Constitution have been implemented. To what extent do these amendments contain basic values that enable the establishment of a democratic system and principles on the basis of which *good governance* can be developed in Indonesia?

The Changes to the 1945 Constitution

Four amendments to the 1945 Constitution arguably implement elements of constitutionalism.[2] Firstly, the Majelis Permusyawaratan Rakyat (MPR) is no longer the 'manifestation of the people's sovereignty' (Article 1 paragraph (2)),[3] the stipulation that the Indonesian state is a constitutional state (Article 1 paragraph (3)) and the president is no longer the mandatary of the MPR, as in the original text

1 The ideology of a brotherhood state was reviewed by the New Order regime as of the early 1970s. First of all, General Abdil Kadir Besar, as Secretary of the MPR when it was chaired by General Nasution, brought up the concept of an integralistic state in the *White Book of the MPR*, 1972. However, such a concept already appeared in a working paper by Professor Soediman Kartohadiprodjo, Professor/Dean of the Law Faculty of the Parahiyangan University, Bandung, in the *Symposium: Indonesia as a Constitutional State*, 1966.

2 The analysis in this section draws on several sources, amongst others Harun Alrasid (2002); Asshiddiqie (2002a and 2002b); Yusuf and Basalim (2000); Arifin and Wardi (eds) (2002).

3 The amendment of Article 1, paragraph (2) reads: 'The sovereignty is vested in the hands of the people and will be executed according to the Constitution.'

of the Constitution (Elucidation of Article 3). This amendment evidences a desire to establish a presidential administration with clear limitations. The amendment stipulates that the election of the president shall be directly by the people, no longer by the MPR (Article 6A). The limitation of the presidential term of office and power is also stipulated more clearly (Article 7), so much so that the pendulum of power actually swings more toward the Parliament, in that the authority of the president is reduced and the role of the Dewan Perwakilan Rakyat (DPR) is amplified (Article 5 paragraph (1), Article 7A, 7B, 7C, Article 11 paragraph (2), Article 13 paragraph (2) and (3), Article 14 paragraph (1) and (2)).

MPR is no longer a super body, as in Article 1 paragraph (2) of the original 1945 Constitution, but constitutes the realization of a parliament with a bicameral parliamentary system, comprising the DPR as the political representative body and the Regional Representatives Council (DPD) as the representative body for the region (Article 2 paragraph (1)). For the first time, its election will take place through political parties, whereas election for the DPD will be on an individual basis. However, the election of the DPR in the Constitution is left floating and may be done either on the basis of a single member constituency or on the basis of a proportional system.

Being part of the limitation of power, the amendment also stipulates a separation (though not a division as envisaged by the original 1945 Constitution) among the three branches – executive, legislative and judicative – of the power of the state. Further, the provisional 1950 Constitution explicitly states that 'Indonesia is a constitutional state'. The principle of the independence of the judiciary, in this case the Supreme Court, in this amendment is further clarified. It is also interesting to note that nominations for the appointment of supreme judges at the Supreme Court will be made by a new institution, the Judicial Commission, and that they will be elected by the DPR (Article 248). In addition, new articles are also included regarding judicial review by the Constitutional Court (Article 7B and Article 24 paragraph (2)). In the meantime judicial review of the law under a statute will continue to be done by the Supreme Court (Article 24 A paragraph (1)).

Human rights and citizens rights have also found a place in the Constitution (Article 28 A–J). Amendment II has sufficiently adapted various basic rights from civil and political rights (Universal Declaration of Human Rights and the Covenant on Civil and Political Rights), from economic, social and cultural rights (from the Covenant on Economic, Social and Cultural Rights), and from the rights of women (from the Convention on the Elimination of All Forms of Discrimination against Women, CEDAW, which was ratified by Indonesia). As a result of this amendment, the 1945 Constitution normatively guarantees the protection of human rights.

The position and function of the State Audit Board (BPK) is further clarified (Article 23E–G) in the amendment in the context of accountability for the state's spending. Both the independence of the BPK–RI in carrying out its duties and the duty of the Parliament to follow up on the findings of its auditing results are clarified by this amendment. Aside from clarifying the position of the three state institutions in organizing the power of the state, including BPK–RI for the state finances, the emergence of other institutions such as the Constitutional Court, the Judicial

Commission and the General Elections Commission can be read as a correction of earlier deviations.

Nonetheless, the 1945 Constitution, as amended, still suffers from technical as well as conceptual weaknesses, including a lack of clarity as to how conflicts between the higher institutions of the state in the 1945 Constitution are to be resolved. As a result, the general public has not been satisfied with the results of this amendment. Nevertheless, it must be admitted that the substituting articles and paragraphs and new articles and paragraphs have already begun to adapt the elements of constitutional government, although they still need to be further clarified substantively in order to be effective.

Granted that constitutionalism is embedded in Indonesia, it remains true that a post-colonial country can only inherit constitutionalism in its own way. Indonesia was founded on the ideal of realizing a national democratic state, and this ideal was embraced by all members of the Constituent Assembly before the country was plunged into Soekarno's dictatorship of 'guided democracy' and Soeharto's 'Pancasila democracy'. Nonetheless, the tensions between Western constitutionalism and etatist traditionalist approaches to governance in Indonesia have not yet been resolved.

In addition, constitutionalism in Indonesia is now challenged by the project of an Islamic state based on the implementation of Islamic law. This project raises crucial issues about how Indonesians are to understand: (1) the concept of state, (2) their governmental systems, (3) human rights, and (4) what is implied by a constitutional state. All four are matters for academic debate as well as political practice in our country.

The Modern State versus the Islamic State

The Republic of Indonesia was set up by its founding fathers as a modern state established by a sovereign people with a mandate conferred by its citizens. The rights and the authority of the state were of a limited character, and could be revoked by the people. Further, the Indonesian state was not partial with regard to differences in ethnicity, religion, ancestry, race or other social and cultural backgrounds. The concept of an Islamic state, in contrast, assumes that the state is the realization or manifestation of the social group that adheres to the Islamic religion. The state is no longer independent, but is bound to the interests of the majority religious conviction. If such a concept were to be applied in Indonesia, then the characteristics and the ideals associated with the dream of realizing a modern state would be abandoned. The principle of equality of all citizens before the law, equal obligations under the Constitution, and the equal rights of citizens to be tried by the same public court would all have to be given up. Even though non-Muslims would still be considered and protected as citizens, their position in the social and political life of the nation would be reduced to that of second-class citizens.

To date the project of an Islamic state has not been fully realized in the state structure of Indonesia. However, there are religious courts that handle cases related to the legal interests of Muslims, and a separate religious court for Muslims, even though the enforcement of the Islamic law on marriage, divorce and reconciliation, inheritance and testament are all clearly in conflict with the modern principle of equality before the law. To some extent, the reasons for these exceptional arrangements are historical since the Dutch colonial government acknowledged the effectiveness of both *adat* law and Islamic law, including Islamic courts (Soctoprawiro 1984). But the issue is by no means a purely historical one, and the position of religious courts became stronger after the issuance of Law No. 7 of the year 1989 (Rasyid 2002).

There has also been an expansion of legislation in the field of Islamic law over the past ten years. Apart from the discriminative Law on the Religious Court, the Law on Marriage of 1974 and the Law on Tithes, the Department of Religion has prepared three further draft laws, namely the Draft Law on Islamic Marriage, the Draft Law on Islamic Inheritance and the Draft Law on Islamic *Waqf*, all of which are potentially discriminative. These developments raise the possibility that the principle of equality before the law and the principle of general judicature will not apply to all Indonesian citizens in the future. This approach is arguably already the case following the enforcement of Islamic law in Aceh Province and the formal installation of an Islamic law court. Discriminatory developments of this kind endanger the ideals of building an open and egalitarian society.

Nonetheless, the tendency to include Islamic elements in the national legal system continues to be a salient feature of our country. It can be found, for example, in the Law on Advocates regulating the education of advocates, allowing advocates to possess knowledge and expertise solely in Islamic law. Under this law, Islamic law graduates could be given the same rights and opportunities to become a public prosecutor or a judge in a general court. The situation would be even worse if Islamic law became state law. Such developments would be in conflict with the ideal of a modern state based on the national codification of law, appropriate to a democratic, open and egalitarian society in which all people and all citizens are bound by common rules of life.

Constitutional Democracy versus Caliphate Administration

In a modern state, the principles of constitutionalism, including the concept of the division of power of the state (the executive and legislative as well as the judicative branches), the supremacy of the law, and a free and impartial judiciary govern the system of government. The concept of an Islamic state, however, refers back to a model of governance under which constitutional government was not known. Under the caliphate, administrative power was vested in the king or sultan, who was simultaneously the leader of the Islamic community and the head of the state administration. The state, the head of state and the community were unified as one. This integrated pattern continues to apply in Indonesia to some degree, despite the democratic aspirations of the country. That is, the state, the head of state and the society are not separated; there is no division of the powers of the state among the executive, the legislative and the judicative branches; and there is no protection and guarantee of human rights and of the rights of the citizens of the state. In these respects, we have a long way still to go.

Universal Human Rights versus Islamic Human Rights

Most modern states have adopted the Universal Declaration of Human Rights. In Indonesia, however, the situation is more ambiguous. The Republic of Indonesia proclaimed in 1945 did not include the Declaration of Human Rights, although the founding fathers adopted the principles of universal human rights in a number of articles of the 1945 Constitution, and the Constitution of the United Republic of Indonesia (1949) and the Provisional Constitution of 1950 explicitly included all the articles of the Universal Declaration of Human Rights. During the meetings of the Constitutional Assembly from 1956 to 1959, the Islamic group in general accepted universal human rights, even though they still questioned the right to change one's religion, the right of marriage between followers of different religions, and the right of education. Further, the amendments to the 1945 Constitution include many articles on human rights that directly and indirectly refer to universal human rights. However, this is also an area in which much has still to be achieved, especially given the fact that some Islamic thinkers deny universal human rights, while others advocate particularistic Islamic human rights.

Democratic Law versus Absolute Law

The concept of law in a modern state requires that the governing law must be one that is made democratically, is applicable in general, and may change with the growth of values and needs of the society. This principle, however, cannot be applied in a state that adheres to Islamic law or that turns Islamic law into public law, because Islamic law derives its legitimacy from the sovereignty of God, not the sovereignty of the people. Islamic law refers to the provisions, values and norms that are formulated in the *Qur'an* and the *hadith* as the source of law, not the state constitution. Because it originates from divine revelation, Islamic law has an absolute character and cannot be changed in accordance with the development of society. On a strict construction, the only thing that can change is the law's interpretation. It is true that there are several countries which consider themselves Islamic states which possess a constitution, but the contents and the constitution are not permitted, at least in theory, to deviate from the *Qur'an* as the supreme source of the law.

During recent years, the voices calling for the enforcement of Islamic law in Indonesia have become stronger. Those who strongly carry such aspirations, first and foremost, are the Islamic parties of PPP, Partai Bulan Bintang (PBB) which claims itself as the heir of the Partai Islam Masyumi, Partai Keadilan, and several parliamentary seats held by other smaller Islamic parties. In addition, in several regions, regional regulations have emerged that in substance enforce Islamic law. At the same time, a movement has emerged in radical Islamic circles to establish the *shari'ah*, such as the Committee for the Establishment of Islamic Law, which has its base in Makassar. This trend contradicts the ideal of a constitutional state and endangers both the judicature and the law-making process in our country. It raises the problem of how a democracy can accommodate challenges with considerable popular support which are in direct contradiction to its constitutive principles. In Indonesia, as elsewhere, there is no consensus as to how to respond to such challenges.

Conclusion

Considerable progress towards constitutionalism has been made in Indonesia, but there are still many areas in which Indonesians have failed to choose between Islamic integralism and modern constitutionalism in a clear and convincing way. In the longer term, it is likely that Indonesians will find ways to successfully integrate Islamic values with the advances of Western political thought. However, this will be a slow and difficult process of adjustment. It will be easier, I suggest, if Indonesian Muslims are more consistent in adhering to the principles of Western constitutionalism.

References

Arafin, F. and Wardi, J. (eds) (2002), *Merambah Pembentukan Mahkamah Konstitusi di Indonesia* [Exploring the Establishment of a Constitutional Court in Indonesia] (Jakarta: Konsorsiurn Reformasi Hukum Nasional).

Asshiddiqie, J. (2002a), *Konsolidasi Naskah UUD 1945 Setelah Perubahan Keempat* [Consolidation of the 1945 Constitution Text after being Amended] (Jakarta: Pusat Studi Hukum Tata Negara FH–UI).

Asshiddiqie, J. (2002b), *UUD 1945 Hasil Amendemen & Proses Amandemen UUD; 1945 Secara Lengkap* [1945 Constitution Resulting from the Amendments & the Process of Amending the 1945 Constitution in Full] (Jakarta: Sinar Grafika).

Harman, B.K. and Hendardi (eds) (1991), *Konstitusionalisme Peran DPR Dan Yudical Review* (Jakarta: Jaringan Informasi Masyarakat and YLBHI).

Harun Alrasid, Naskah (2002), *UUD 1945 Sesudah Tiga Kali Diubah oleh MPR* [The Text of the 1945 Constitution after being Amended Three Times by the MPT] (Jakarta: UI Press).

Lev, D.S. (1990), 'Geerakan sosial, Konstitusionalisme dan Hak Asasi Manusia', in *Law and Politics in Indonesia: Sustainability and Change* (Jakarta: LP3ES).

Nasution, Adnan Buyung (2002), 'Demokrasi, Konstitusi dan Makna Pemeerdekaen [Democracy, Constitution and the Meaning of Independence] (Jakarta: Sinar Harapan).

Rasyid, Roihan A. (2002), *Hukum Acara Peradilan Agama* (Jakarta: RajaGrafindo Persada).

Soctoprawiro, Koeniatmanto (1984), *Pemerintahan dan Peradilan di Indonesia (Asal-Usul dan Perkembangannya)* (Bandung: Citra Aditya Bakti).

Soediman, Kartohadiprodjo (1966), 'Workpaper', *Indonesia Negara Hukum dan Seminar Ketatanegaraan Undang-Undang Dasar, 1945*, presented to the Symposium: *Indonesia as a Constitutional State*, University of Indonesia (Jakarta: Publisher Seruling Massa).

Taufic, Abdulla (2001), *Nasionalisme dan Sejarah* [Nationalism and History] (Bandung: Satya Historika).

Wignyosoebroto, Soetandyo (1991), 'Konstituti dan konstitusionalisme', in Benny K. Harman and Hendardi (ed.), *Konstitusionalisme Peran DPR Dan Yudical Review* (Jakarta: Jaringan Informasi Masyarakat and YLBHI).

Yamin, Muhammad (ed.) (1959), *Naskah Persiapan Undang-Undang Dasar 1945* (Jakarta: Jajasan Prapantja).

Yusuf, S.E. and Basalim, U. (2000), *Reformasi Konstitusi Indonesia: Perubahan Pertama UUD 1945* [Reform of the Indonesian Constitution: The First Change in the 1945 Constitution] (Jakarta: Pustaka Indonesia Sat).

Chapter 5

The Ambiguities of the Rule of Law

Brian Galligan

Introduction

Debates about the rule of law need to be concretized in terms of specific arrangements. In this chapter, I offer a more concretized version of an Anglo-Saxon approach to the rule of law which may be relevant to the challenges facing contemporary Indonesia.

The rule of law is one of those broad principles that is so fundamental to good governance and a decent political society that it receives virtually unanimous endorsement in Western countries. Lawyers especially are committed champions of the rule of law, perhaps because they have a more highly trained appreciation of its character and benefits, and perhaps because of a sense of professional ownership and propriety. The rule of law, however, is more celebrated than critically examined, and as a consequence its precise meaning and application are often vague and lacking in specificity. Moreover, the ownership of lawyers tends to skew the principle towards legal precepts and rules, or to bringing politics within an overarching legal domain.

The purpose of this chapter is to raise some of the difficult issues and puzzles about what the rule of law means in relation to constitutions and constitutional change. Constitutions are 'higher law' instruments that establish institutions of government and specify key practices and rules of political engagement. Hence, constitutions partake of, or are somewhat analogous to, the rule of law in setting and controlling the institutional framework of government and its operating principles and rules. If governments, leaders or organized groups persist in unconstitutional behaviour, they are also flouting the rule of law.

But constitutional systems have to be founded in the first place, which can be a radical change from what went before. To endure in changing circumstances, they probably have to change over time formally or through conventional practice. For a constitutional founding or constitutional change to be in accord with the rule of law, they must satisfy criteria of proper process and legitimacy, and be for the good, or good governance, of the people of that regime. In other words, the rule of law is not simply about the rule of existing law, but the principles of establishing systems of government that make the laws under which people live. The rule of law has as much to do with the meta-legal as the legal: with basic principles of the origin and purpose of government, legitimate processes of participation by people in designing and changing their system of government, and the ongoing issues of good government and protection of minority rights. Hence, the topic of constitutional change and the rule of law raises fundamental issues of political theory and institutional design.

In liberal democratic regimes, citizens have both freedom and equality; that is, they are entitled to choose their own way of life and have an equal say in the regime and constitutional change. Establishing inclusive and workable constitutional systems in countries where there has been exploitation and exclusion, as in South Africa, raises issues of legitimate authority and appropriate instrumentality. The people may not be habituated in, or know much about, designing an appropriate constitutional system, so will be reliant upon various political leaders and specialist elites. Determining who constitutes that group and how it should proceed might entail a robust but sensitive process of self-selection and subsequent popular endorsement or acceptance. A common way forward, followed most recently by Timor, is to have an election to a constitutive parliament which then drafts and adopts the constitution.

Often, there will be majorities and minorities, and these might reflect ethnic, cultural or class divisions, so that constitutional settlements and change might be extremely difficult, as for example in the case of accommodating Quebec in Canada. Moreover, constitutions need to be robust in handling change without having to be changed all the time, so that conventions will likely play a major part. The rule of law and constitutionalism rely heavily on habits and accustomed behaviours of elites and citizens, and these should also be acknowledged in considering the topic. Considerations of the rule of law and constitutional change need to grapple with some of the most difficult issues of contemporary politics.

The Rule of Law: What Does it Mean?

Probably the most famous definition of the rule of law was given by Aristotle as 'reason free from all passion' [350 BC] (1992). Since Aristotle's eloquent notion still has wide currency, it is worth returning briefly to his articulation. The context of Aristotle's discussion is significant: it occurs in Book 3 concerning the theory of citizenship and constitutions and in the latter chapters of this book discussing kingship. Aristotle has argued that although there is abstract merit in the claim that the absolutely best person should rule absolutely, the practical difficulties of achieving that and the adverse consequences of getting it wrong make constitutionally limited kingship preferable. Certainly where people are equal, Aristotle teaches, the offices of state cannot be vested in one man without violating basic justice. Justice for equals means their equal sharing in being ruled as well as in ruling; that involves rotation or taking turns in office; and that entails law because the arrangement providing for the turn-taking or rotation is law. Aristotle concludes this part of his analysis with the conclusion that 'The rule of law is therefore preferable … to that of a single citizen' [350 BC] (1992, 171). In other words, for there to be justice among equals, there must be equal sharing by citizens in ruling and being ruled, and that needs to be controlled by law and not dependent on the say of one person. So the rule of law in this context is not rule by some higher abstract body of law but ensuring a just sharing of citizens in holding office. It is a means to political justice and those holding office do the ruling.

Law cannot rule by itself. Aristotle's rule of law specifically allows for flexible human agency and change. As Aristotle puts it, law does the best it can: it 'trains the holders of office expressly in its own spirit, and then sets them to decide and settle those residuary issues which it cannot regulate'. It also allows them 'to introduce any improvements which may seem to them, as a result of experience, to be better than the existing laws'. Aristotle's famous peon to the rule of law follows directly after this discussion of its flexibility and creative human agency in improving the law:

> He who commands that law should rule may thus be regarded as commanding that God and reason alone should rule; he who commands that a man should rule adds the character of the beast. Appetite has that character; and high spirits, too, perverts the holders of office, even when they are the best of men. Law [as the pure voice of God and reason] may thus be defined as 'Reason free from all passion' [350 BC] (1992, 172).

But reason free from all passion does not preclude human agency or entail some supra-human order; rather it requires human actors who are reasonable and just. Even God's rule would require the intermediation of human reason to be known and human agency to be put in place. And if God's rule is separated from that of human reason, there are all the problems of restricted priestly access to such knowledge, and false or partial claims that privilege believers.

The aphorism 'Rule of law ... and yet of men' is often used to sum up a situation where human agency distorts the rule of law, as for example when judges allow their own personal preferences or biases to interfere with constitutional interpretation and decision-making. We should note, however, that there can be no rule of law without that of human beings, so the rule of law is about the principled and legitimate exercise of human agency. As Aristotle makes clear, the rule of law is about reasonable and just practices in constitutional governance and citizenship: in having agreed arrangements for the sharing in ruling that are sufficiently robust and flexible to allow those in government to decide residual issues and to introduce improvements to existing laws.

Where would one look to find supra-legal standards against which to measure existing laws, and to justify their amendment and change? Obviously, positive law cannot be its own standard, because that would entail circularity and de facto legitimacy of whatever happened to be in place. The answer must be in reason and principles of justice and morality that depend on philosophical or religious grounds. This is a realm of contention and argument, but there is no alternative unless one opts for mindless compliance with the established order just because it is established. And in opting for the established order in this way, one is invariably accepting not simply the rule of law but the rule of established rulers based upon coercion and force, or some earlier set of entrenched philosophical or religious norms.

Liberalism and the Rule of Law

All decent and stable constitutional systems must have substantial elements of the rule of law if they are to endure and retain the support of their people. Liberal systems, in particular, are based upon a strong notion of the rule of law that grounds their basic legitimacy. We can see this most clearly in the teaching of the liberal political philosopher, John Locke, who defined political power as '*a Right* of making Laws' for limited purposes – the regulation and preservation of people's lives, liberties and property; domestic law and order, and the settling of disputes; and national defence –'and all this only for the Publick Good' [1690] (1980, 308). Otherwise, according to Locke, illegitimate exercise of power by some over others is unwarranted and effectively tyranny. Such a regime should not command allegiance or respect but be overthrown and replaced by government that is properly authorized by the governed, and limited in scope to ensuring their peace and security and respecting their rights.

Law for Locke was crucial, and his understanding of law was broad and encompassing. It included natural law that could be known by reason and governed the state of nature or the pre-political; the fundamental law that established the legislative power within political or civil society; and the laws passed by the legislature to govern its day-to-day affairs. Natural law governed the state of nature, but also continued to control political society and government as the overarching or superior standard. In this view, although Locke does not use such language, the highest dimension of the rule of law was compliance of government and its laws with natural law. The legislature, properly constituted in a system of government based upon consent, is the most powerful part of government in Locke's system, but nevertheless remains bound by natural law. As Locke put it: 'The Obligations of the Law of Nature cease not in Society.' They are often embodied as declared or positive laws, but more importantly they provide a superior standard for government. According to Locke, 'the Law of Nature stands as an Eternal Rule to all Men, *Legislators* as well as others' [1690] (1980, 403).

Government must be according to 'declared and received Laws'; otherwise it is arbitrary and illegitimate. This criterion of legitimate government is closer to the modern understanding of the rule of law by lawyers. For Locke, it is a precept grounded in natural reason or the basic theory of government. Even if they eschew natural law, modern liberal theorists have a somewhat similar perspective of legitimate government being subject to standards of reasonableness and morality that are independent of government. While there is dispute about what such standards of reasonableness and moral precepts might be and how they are to be implemented in constitutional systems, there is no dispute that government – both in its fundamentals and its ongoing operation – is subject to a higher order of principle or law.

Modern liberal commentators on the rule of law, particularly liberal lawyers, are inclined to emphasize the supremacy of law over all persons and government. L.J.M. Cooray (1979) is typical when he lists the supremacy of law as the first essential characteristic of the rule of law, and the subsequent seven characteristics in fairly standard fashion: procedural justice, restrictions on the exercise of discretionary power, prospective legislation (not retrospective), parliamentary exercise of legislative power (curtailing executive power of legislating), an independent judiciary, judicial restraint, and common law methodology. Only in the ninth and last principle does he specify 'an underlying moral basis for all law'. Since this final extra-legal realm is fundamental to the whole edifice of the rule of law, I am suggesting that it should be put first and that more attention be given to establishing how it grounds the establishment and amendment of constitutional systems and provides a reference for assessing the justice of particular laws and acts of government.

Democracy and the Rule of Law

The basic principle of democracy is that individuals are politically equal and should have an equal say in affirming their constitutional system and its ongoing functioning. For much of the history of political thinking, this was considered practically impossible in anything but a small regime, an arrangement prone to turmoil and disruption because of popular ignorance and passion. If majorities ruled in a democracy they would likely threaten minorities, including the rich who would counter by insurrection and overthrow the democratic regime. Adoption of the principle of representation solved the problem by removing people from directly sharing in ruling, and this principle has produced stable democracies. Constitutional design has helped ensure the proper ordering of institutions and processes of government to prevent governing elites from abusing their delegated powers.

While a great deal has been gained by such developments in democratic institutions, there has also been a loss in the participation of citizens in political office and ruling. We have come to accept a more modest notion of democratic citizenship that is buttressed by symbol, nationalism and patriotism. In recent decades there has been a movement to enhance democratic citizenship through encouraging a more vigorous civil society, through active participation in citizenship activities and responsibilities, and notions of constitutional citizenship that endeavour to humanize the minimalist virtues of equal, but usually negative, rights and toleration for differences.

Despite all of this, there remains a deep-seated ambivalence about including the people in determining constitutional change, even in countries with long-established democratic systems. There is an important distinction to be drawn between the founding of a new constitutional system among people who are not familiar with, or practised in, democratic constitutional politics, on the one hand, and those who are habituated in a well-established system, on the other hand. Rousseau was the sharpest critic of the corruption into which people had fallen through being exploited and abused in traditional regimes based on rule from above or outside, and had to come up with a device for founding a decent regime and having the people accept it. He did this through the device of the Founder, a superior law giver and leader, who would use religion to win the support of the people. Except as a teaching model, this is an implausible and risky device. Nevertheless, practical foundings such as the American in the late eighteenth century did not include the people directly in constitution-making. Election of delegates, drafting and ratification were all done indirectly through elected legislatures and appointed conventions.

Australia was an exception in having delegates to the 1890s series of conventions that drafted the Constitution directly elected by the people of the colonies. The draft was brought back for acceptance by popular referendum, and the approved draft formally passed by the British Parliament at Westminster. Hence there was a blend of radical democratic and British imperial legitimacy in the process. Critics make much of the fact that not all women voted – they had not yet won the franchise in four of the six states – and Aboriginal people were largely excluded. Nevertheless, given the democratic constituency of the day, this was a radically democratic process.

Even today there are serious misgivings about admitting the people to constitutional referendums. 'Are the people smart enough to speak for "We the

People"?' asks Simone Chambers (2004) in a recent survey of constitutional referendums and democratic deliberation. Contrary to Bruce Ackerman's advocacy of the American people deciding constitutional matters in referendum, Chambers cites 'the spectre of majoritarian and populist abuse' that informs the view's critics. According to Philip Weiser, popular referendums lack 'the filter necessary to prevent Americans from voting away essential protections of liberty, basic civil rights, and thoughtfully entrenched institutional arrangements' (1993, 238). Chambers is concerned that constitutional issues might not fit discursive processes, with citizens being 'distracted by the end-game' (2004, 249). The critics point to the bad experience of popular referendums in the United States at the state and local level, where the hands of government have been tied unnecessarily or particular interests improperly entrenched (Mendelsohn and Parkin 2001).

Conclusion

Applying these insights to the Indonesian instance will be a complex matter, which I am not competent to address in detail. Nonetheless, it is important to refine the way in which the issues are understood by insisting that Western political thought is valuable, not so much by itself, but when it is concretized in terms of particular arrangements. In Indonesia, these arrangements will possibly include Islamic organizations such as religious courts which have not been at the heart of the Western experience. Despite the significant differences in context, however, there is reason to expect that Western political thought will provide the basis for successful institutions, provided the actual arrangements are worked through in detail. Elevated rhetoric alone will not suffice.

References

Aristotle (1992) [350 BC], *The Politics* (trans. T.A. Sinclair) (Harmondsworth: Penguin).

Chambers, Simone (2004), 'Democracy, Popular Sovereignty and Constitutional Legitimacy', *Constellations* 11, 2.

Cooray, L.J.M. (1979), *Conventions: The Australian Constitution and the Future* (Sydney: Legal Books).

Locke, J. (1980) [1690], *The Second Treatise* (ed. Thomas Peardon) (Indiana: Prentice Hall).

Mendelsohn, M. and Parkin, A. (eds) (2001), *Referendum Democracy: Citizens, Elites and Deliberation in Referendum Campaigns* (New York: Palgrave).

Weiser, Philip (1993), 'Ackerman's proposal for Popular Constitutional Lawmaking: Can It Realize His Aspirations for Dualist Democracy?' *New York University Law Review* 68.

Chapter 6

Western and Islamic Conceptions of the Rule of Law

Spencer Zifcak

Introduction

My purpose in this chapter is twofold. First, I wish to record my understanding of the idea of the rule of law from a distinctly Western perspective. Then, secondly, I want to examine some of its underlying assumptions and values in a way which will, I hope, open a dialogue between this perspective and that deriving from Islamic jurisprudence. Having said this, I enter an immediate caveat. I do not pretend to any expertise with respect to Islamic jurisprudence. Such reading as I have done in relation to it has revealed to me not only its richness but also its very great heterogeneity and complexity. It is a complexity of which I am in no way a master. The chapter therefore situates the issues I see as relevant on a very broad canvas. I seek here simply to suggest points of intersection and pose questions for discussion.

The Rule of Law: a Western Interpretation

In its classical form, the rule of law is generally understood to be comprised of a number of characteristic features.[1] Hayek, for example, believed that the 'rule of law' implied that the law must be known and certain, prospective never retrospective. No individual should be coerced except in the enforcement of a rule having these attributes. Individuals should be equal before the law. It must therefore be general rather than particular in its application. A system based on the rule of law must embody the separation of powers. This requires that the law's interpretation and enforcement be vested in judges independent of executive government. Their application of the law must be faithful, open and principled (Hayek 1960, chapter 14).

Hayek is particularly clear in setting down the ethical foundations of the rule of law. Its overarching object, he argues, is to facilitate the purposive actions of the individual. It is to ensure that the individual may make informed choices affecting

1 There is a wealth of literature on the rule of law. In developing this framework, the following books and articles were of particular assistance: Marsh (1961); Fuller (1969); Raz (1977); Dworkin (1977), chapters 2 and 3; Dworkin (1985), chapter 1; Finnis (1980), chapter 10; Hayek (1982), chapters 4 and 5; Harden and Lewis (1986), chapters 2 and 10; Allen (1993), chapter 2; Jowell (1994); Crawford (1994); Raz (1995), chapter 17; Mason (1995); Habermas (1996), chapter 4; Craig (1997); Brownlie (1998); Kay (1998); Allen (1999).

the directions of his or her life, without arbitrary interference by the state. In their interactions with the state and other entities, the rule of law ensures that individuals will be aware of the parameters within which their choices must be framed.

On a Western view, the rule of law also marks out a private sphere within which the individual's choices may be pursued. It makes it unlikely that the state will interfere too invasively in this private realm by holding it as a founding principle that laws must apply generally and equally. It is this fact, that all rules apply equally to all, including those who govern, that makes it improbable that oppressive laws will be enacted.

It is important further to remark that Hayek's conception of the rule of law does not exist in a vacuum. The thought that it might pertain in an autocracy would be anathema. He cites America's great contribution to public law as the creation of a constitution that circumscribes the powers of a democratic and therefore representative legislature in the interests of protecting the people against arbitrary action. He endorses the entrenchment of higher law, law which, possessing a greater degree of generality and proceeding from a superior authority, in turn controls the contents of more specific laws that are passed by a delegated parliamentary authority. His rule of law presumes both constitutionalism and democracy.

The principles and practices underlying the operation of the rule of law are reasonably well understood in Western legal systems, having a jurisdictionally defined, democratic and constitutional foundation. However, their concreteness tends to fracture in the fragmentation, fluidity and contingency of global interconnectedness. Given the fact of this interconnectedness, a new challenge has emerged. That is, to ascribe a new and appropriate meaning to an 'international rule of law'. To meet this challenge requires a reconsideration and reapplication of its principal ethical and institutional underpinnings in this new context. Given the polycentric nature of the global political, cultural and legal orders, this is no easy task. Yet it is one that needs to be undertaken.

In its landmark report, the United Nations Commission on Global Governance affirmed the importance of applying the rule of law in the international arena in the strongest terms:

> The rule of law has been a critical civilising influence in every free society. It distinguishes a democratic from a tyrannical society; it secures liberty and justice against repression; it elevates equality above dominion; it empowers the weak against the unjust claims of the strong. Its restraints, no less than the moral precepts it asserts, are essential to the well-being of society, both collectively and to individuals within it. Respect for the rule of law is thus a basic neighbourhood value. And one that is certainly needed in the emerging global neighbourhood (Commission on Global Governance 1995).

This statement injects into the idea of the rule of law ideas of justice and fairness that some Western academic authors may claim do not belong there (Dicey 1959; Raz 1977; Summers 1993). Nevertheless, it serves to emphasize the critical importance of translating both the rationale and value of the doctrine to the global arena.

While there are and will always be different opinions regarding the content of the core values underlying the idea of the rule of law in both the domestic and international arenas, I propose five from a Western perspective that build on Hayek's delineation and which, in my view, are worthy of particular consideration. These five are legality, equality, legitimacy, accountability and a commitment to fundamental human rights.

The value accorded to legality derives from the desire to ensure that in society we should operate under a common, articulated, general and transparent framework of rules. Within this framework, every person and organization, while respecting the constraints these rules impose, should have an equal opportunity to pursue their own ends. In global as well as national governance, legality proscribes arbitrariness. It privileges principled over particularistic decision-making. Legality as understood here also introduces the idea of equality. This concept goes further than asserting straightforwardly that the law should be general in its application. It requires that even a general law should refrain from making arbitrary or unjustifiable distinctions between peoples and among nations, thus favouring some over others. It should eschew discriminatory treatment unless the group affected accepts the discrimination proposed as legitimate. Further, equality implies equal access as well as equal treatment. Equal legal rights and entitlements are of little tangible benefit where the opportunity for their vindication before an appropriate forum is lacking.

The law must possess legitimacy.[2] While a purely formal view of the rule of law would require only that rules be known, certain and enforceable, in the international arena particularly since the end of the Second World War, it has increasingly and properly been insisted that the law be legitimate. In the Western tradition this means that it should be sanctioned democratically (Franck 1992). Again, following Hayek, it should also proceed hierarchically, with certain rules, universally endorsed by the community, and for that reason possessing constitutional standing, governing the operation of others of a more regular, legislative character.

Internationally, the UN Charter does not mention the word democracy. But as the former Secretary-General, Boutros Boutros-Ghali points out, the document is prefaced by the words, 'We the Peoples of the United Nations', thus rooting the sovereign authority of the member states and so, the legitimacy of the organization itself in the will of their peoples. Similarly, the Universal Declaration of Human Rights is also informed by a commitment to democracy, declaring that the 'will of the people shall be the basis of the authority of government', and then providing for foundational political and civil rights to underpin that authority, and so the rule of law flows from it (Boutros-Ghali 1996) .

The value of accountability is linked closely to legitimacy. General rules once adopted must be faithfully and impartially interpreted and executed. This value requires that those who exercise public power according to law be held to account for its use. Power holders in whom the community have reposed their trust should act in fidelity to that trust. Accountability demands that institutional

---

2 John Rawls puts it eloquently:

Political power is legitimate only when it is exercised in accordance with a constitution (written or unwritten) the essentials of which all citizens, as reasonable and rational, can endorse in the light of their common human reason. This is the liberal principle of legitimacy. It is a further desideratum that all legislative questions that concern or border on those essentials, or are highly divisive, should also be settled, so far as possible, by guidelines and values that can be similarly endorsed (Rawls 2001, 41).

checks and balances be created such that the exercise of public power under law be independently reviewable. The doctrine of the separation of powers, therefore, is important nationally and globally. A fundamental commitment to the creation and maintenance of independent judicial bodies to interpret and apply diverse areas of domestic and international law is essential to the law's continuing integrity.

Finally, and again since the end of the Second World War, the value accorded to fundamental human rights has become a foundational norm of all Western and many Eastern legal systems. The 'rule of law' may not stretch to the chapter-and-verse protection of every right and freedom contained in the UN Declaration and its principal Covenants. Nevertheless, it may reasonably be said that one of its primary functions is to promote the congruence of international legislation with core doctrines that underlie the international legal system. Consequently, the rule of law will embody respect for those human rights norms that are accepted as part of the backbone of international legal culture.[3]

Hayek himself argued that a bill of rights of some kind is essential to the rule of law (1960, chapter 14). A charter of this kind provides protection for significant private rights occupying a discrete private realm. In so doing, it advances the rule of law's rationale, that is, to promote the pursuit of individual human purpose and direction, and guard against its misdirection or subversion by state or society. This argument finds resonance too in more modern treatments of rights. In his recently published Harvard lectures, Michael Ignatieff, for example, argues that the fundamental idea underpinning the advancement of human rights is that their observance is an essential and non-negotiable precondition of human agency.

Such grounding as human rights requires, I would argue, is based on what history tells us: that human beings are at risk of their lives if they lack a basic measure of free agency; that agency itself requires protection through internationally agreed standards; that these standards should entitle individuals to oppose and resist unjust laws and orders within their own states; and finally, that when all other remedies have been exhausted, these individuals have the right to appeal to other peoples, nations and international organizations for assistance in defending their rights (Ignatieff 2001, 55).

To include a respect for fundamental human rights as a value underpinning an international rule of law is straightforwardly to assert that an international '*Rechsstaat*' cannot properly be said to exist where the capacity for choice that individuals should possess in determining their lives' directions may arbitrarily be constrained, withheld or abused either by the state or in consequence of its collapse.

Intersections with Islamic Jurisprudence

The idea of the rule of law delineated in the preceding section has developed in an explicitly Western context. That context is one in which the Judeo-Christian

3 On the role of rights in the rule of law domestically and internationally, see: Lauterpacht (1950); Dworkin (1985), chapter 1; Dworkin (1986), chapter 7; Laws (1993, 1995 and 1996); Kriegel (1995), chapter 2; Allen (1999); International Commission of Jurists (1999); Robertson (1999), chapter 3.

worldview has been dominant. In this tradition, the separation of religious and secular authority is both countenanced and endorsed. The Western worldview is also one in which the influence of Roman law, in particular the idea that law should be established as a universal, secular system for the resolution of conflicts, has been profoundly influential.

Shari'ah, in contrast, seems to present as a seamless web of law, religion and morality. Clearly a separation of the religious and secular spheres has emerged in practice in countries in which Islam is the dominant religion. But the deeper assumption of the Western tradition, that the source of law might rest in humanity rather than be derived from the realm of the divine, is one that is foreign to the Islamic tradition. Further, and in consequence, the idea that law should be created, as new, through secular institutions and should have a primacy over law that is divined from a reading of the holy text and the practice of the Prophet is, similarly, radically different from the Islamic conception.

Plainly a conception of law as holy law has enormously important consequences for any discussion of the meaning of 'the rule of law'. By definition, any such rule is likely to have a primarily religious rather than secular foundation. And institutionally, it will be formulated principally in and through a religious leadership rather than created legislatively by an impersonal, secular political order. These fundamental distinctions in turn appear to raise a host of consequential issues and questions. In the remainder of this chapter, I will focus on four in particular.

The Rule of Law as Contractual Agreement

It follows from what has just been said that in the Western tradition, law is regarded primarily as the product of human interaction in territorial jurisdictions. This idea is best captured by the idea of the social contract. Elaborated originally by Hobbes and given its most extensive modern interpretation by Rawls, just law is regarded as the product of the free agreement of free peoples sharing a sense of belonging in a geographical community. Law is made legitimate by the consent of those who must obey it. This consent is demonstrated in two ways: by a real or implied social contract in which each person agrees with every other to the principles of government; and by a political process through which each person participates in the making and enacting of the law. In summary, then, Western communities are held together by a political process and by the rights and duties of the citizen as defined by that process.

In the Islamic tradition, as I understand it, the source of law's legitimacy is entirely different. It is founded in the revealed will of God, as expressed in the *Qur'an* and the teachings of the Prophet. This text and teaching, in turn, is extended and given practical expression through the science of *fiqh*. This draws on two further sources, *ijma* (consensus) and *qiyas* (analogical reasoning). Two very important institutional consequences flow from this belief. First, the law is declared and given effect not through impersonal institutions such as a secular parliament, but rather through a more personalized form of religious leadership, taking a quasi-judicial form, whose task is not to make law but rather to interpret it. Secondly, it is implicit in the idea of the social contract that formal agreements are made within particular territorial jurisdictions, that is, nations, and may differ between these jurisdictions. In contrast, where law is regarded as the legal expression of divine will, no such territorial boundaries can be recognized. The law has a universal, theological foundation which is incapable of containment by geography. On an Islamic view, localities are important, not because they are the source of law but rather because they are its object.

These distinctions between the traditions have very significant consequences for the value attached to legitimacy in my initial delineation of the 'rule of law'. Whereas constitutionalism and democracy appear critical to law's legitimacy on a Western view, a question arises about the weight they need to be accorded in Islam. If the will of God is to determine society rather than be determined by it, then by what processes and through which institutions should society's laws be regarded as possessing legitimacy within a contemporary, Islamic tradition. And to what extent can the two forms of legitimacy be reconciled?

Form and Substance in the Rule of Law

Even a cursory examination of the Western idea of the rule of law discloses that it is concerned principally with legal form rather than legal substance. With the exception of the reference to fundamental human rights, the values that underlie it are predominantly procedural in nature. They relate not to what the law should contain but to the form it should take and the institutional framework through which it should be made and enforced. That this is so should not be surprising. The idea of social contract implies that the members of a geographically defined society should agree freely on the content of the laws under which they shall be governed. No such free agreement is possible if the substance of the law is determined externally in advance. The institutions and procedures of law-making then are as a machine in the hands of those chosen by the people to rule. Good law, on this view, will best be arrived at through fair procedure.

The Islamic tradition, again as I see it, differs fundamentally in this respect. It is founded on the belief that society should be organized on the basis of the *Qur'an* and the *Sunnah.* This means that the values, principles, rules and regulations contained in the *Qur'an* and the *Sunnah* should be upheld in every sphere, including the political, economic, cultural and legal. This approach does not, of course, mean that there is complete agreement in Islam upon the precise content of rules and regulations. What they should be is the subject of interpretation, and interpretations will differ according to different schools of religious and legal thought. But the essential point, that what one is concerned with here is the rule of God and not merely the rule of law, remains. Consequently, the law is necessarily infused with moral principle. The nature and content of that principle is both broadly and specifically ascertainable. And it provides an abiding code of conduct for its followers. It cannot be confined to form but flows everywhere into substance. Law, then, is founded not on a contract between people agreeing freely upon its content but on a contract between people and their Creator.

Despite this tremendous difference, however, there do appear to be grounds for movement in each tradition towards the other. It may be, for example, that the procedural values underlying the Western conception of the rule of law may be applicable to the procedural aspects of Islamic law's enunciation and interpretation. Similarly, it may be that the substantive content of Islamic law, particularly in so far as it refers to and elaborates upon fundamental human rights, may inform and enrich the Western legal tradition, particularly with respect to its emphasis upon the reciprocal relationship between human rights and human responsibilities.

The Rule of Law in the Public and Private Realm

In the Western tradition, a clear distinction is drawn between law's applicability in the public and the private sphere. The rule of law exists to facilitate human agency and, consequently, to guard individuals from any arbitrary interference by the state with their freedoms to think, believe, speak and act. It places rulers and ruled on an equal footing. It proscribes deliberate or capricious discrimination between different segments of society in the name of the underlying value of equality. In so doing, it protects the realm of thought and conscience, ordaining it as private and individual. Here again, the freedom to choose is paramount.

In Islam, however, it appears that the writ of holy law runs through all things. The idea that there should be a zone of personal freedom and experiment, protected by law purely human in origin and political in nature, is alien. Since God is the creator of all things, there is no legitimate domain of life to which His will or His laws do not apply. Legal structures apply equally in public and private. And human agency, while recognized and in many respects protected, is constrained within the limits of religious dictate. It is in this context that the significance of individual ritual is best understood. Rituals such as daily prayers, fasting, alms-giving and pilgrimage are all acts of worship and are each prescribed. The content of individual faith is also framed jurisprudentially. The ways of the faith may differ, but it is faith that gives personal life its meaning and sets its broad course.

Two implications would appear to follow from this contrast. First, in the Western tradition, the rule of law, with the value it places upon equality, provides an institutional foundation for protection against individual oppression and encouragement for individual thought. In the Islamic tradition, however, I conclude, tentatively, that this protection and encouragement must be sought in the content of the law itself and in the benevolence of its administration and interpretation. This appears a shakier foundation. Secondly, because *shari'ah* is a law governing only its adherents, the status of other communities within the territorial boundaries of an Islamic state is uncertain. How far the value of equality under law extends to them, therefore, is a question upon which I would value further dialogue and clarification.

The Rule of Law and the State

In the Western tradition, the state, expressed through its legislative and administrative institutions, is foundational in determining the form and content of law. It is through these institutions that the social contract is constructed and given effect. Consistent with the injunction against arbitrariness and the requirement of procedural due process, in theory at least, the state's institutions are constructed so that its systems will operate for the benefit of the people, regardless of the virtues or vices of its leaders.

In law, such institutions are given a corporate personality which differs from and transcends that of the individuals of whom they are comprised. The idea of legal personality is equally influential in the commercial sphere. Further, the Western corporation commands a special kind of loyalty that, importantly, transcends ties of kinship and other forms of essentially personal allegiance. Its existence and form, whether in the public or the commercial sphere, may also have a profound effect on the behaviour of its individual members.

State institutions embody no particular faith or ideology. Instead, they are the institutional machinery through which the popular will may be made manifest. Just as importantly, they provide the mechanism through which the rule of law's requirement of accountability may be given effect. So, the separation of powers is regarded as a cardinal constitutional doctrine, and judicial independence in particular is valued as a critical means through which those who hold power do so according to law and, in that way, remain faithful to the trust reposed in them by their constituents.

The situation with Islam appears to be different. In Islamic political theory, sovereignty belongs ultimately to God as expressed in divine law. An Islamic society is one in which this sovereignty is accepted. In principle, therefore, no recognition is given to the distinction between religion and politics, since every sphere of life is subjected to moral principles derived from religion. A good society is one in which the values fundamental to Islam are permitted to flourish not only individually but also collectively.

Crucially, Islam does not recognize the state as an independent object of loyalty. Nor in Islam is there any secular conception of government, similar to that which Christianity inherited from Roman law. The state is a necessity to be tolerated rather than an earthly, positive expression of a divine ideal. It is almost incidental to the primary relationship which each individual has to their God. This relationship, in turn, is not mediated by institutions of government. The mediating role is reserved for religious leadership and is expressed in juridical form. Further, the concept of corporate personality has no equivalent in *fiqh*. Leadership vests firmly in persons rather than corporate entities. In Islamic political theory, the role of government is always limited and subordinate.

These differences would appear to bear on the value that the rule of law accords to accountability in a number of ways. In the Western tradition, accountability is conceived of primarily in institutional rather than personal terms. In the Islamic tradition, the opposite would seem to be the case. In Islam, the direction of the accountability of both religious and political leadership would appear to be primarily upwards towards God. In the West, accountability moves downwards, with institutions accountable to the people for the effective performance of their constitutional tasks. In the West, those who legislate and lead do so with the polis in mind. They are almost entirely unconstrained by the moral prescriptions of religion or religions. In Islamic societies, those who lead, whether in the political or juridical realms, do so in the consciousness that they are constrained by a closely defined religious, moral and ethical principle, having its foundation in the *shari'ah*.

Conclusion

My discussion suggests that the rule of law may need to be applied to Indonesia in ways which draw upon both Western and Islamic traditions. If, however, sufficient accommodations to context and culture can be made and honest institutions can be put in place, then the prospects for the rule of law in Indonesia may be brighter in the long run than some commentators suggest.

References

Allan, T.R.S. (1993), *Law, Liberty and Justice* (Oxford: Clarendon Press).
Allan, T. (1999), 'The Rule of Law as the Rule of Reason', *Law Quarterly Review* 115, 221.
Boutros-Ghali, B. (1996), *An Agenda for Democracy* (New York: The United Nations).
Brownlie, I. (1998), *The Rule of Law in International Affairs* (The Hague: Martinus Nijhoff).
Commission on Global Governance (1995), *Our Global Neighbourhood* (Oxford: Oxford University Press).
Craig, P. (1997), 'Formal and Substantive Conceptions of the Rule of Law: An Analytical Framework', *Public Law* 467.
Crawford, J. (1994), *Democracy in International Law*, Inaugural Lecture (Cambridge: Cambridge University Press).
Dicey, A. (1959), *An Introduction to the Study of the Law of the Constitution*, 10th Edition (London: Macmillan).
Dworkin, R. (1977), *Taking Rights Seriously* (London: Duckworth).
Dworkin, R. (1985), *A Matter of Principle* (Cambridge: Harvard University Press).
Dworkin, R. (1986), *Law's Empire* (London: Fontana Press).
Finnis, J. (1980), *Natural Law and Natural Rights* (Oxford: Oxford University Press).
Franck, T. (1992), 'The Emerging Right to Democratic Governance', *American Journal of International Law* 86, 46.
Fuller, L. (1969), *The Morality of Law* (New Haven, Conn: Yale University Press).
Habermas, J. (1996), *Between Facts and Norms* (Cambridge: Polity Press).
Harden, I. and Lewis, N. (1986), *The Noble Lie: The British Constitution and the Rule of Law* (London: Hutchinson).
Hayek, F. (1960), *The Constitution of Liberty* (London: Routledge).
Hayek, F.A. (1982), *Law, Legislation and Liberty* (London: Routledge).
Ignatieff, M. (2001), *Human Rights as Politics and Idolatry* (Princeton: Princeton University Press).
International Commission of Jurists (1999), 'Globalisation, Human Rights and the Rule of Law', *The Review, International Commission of Jurists*, Special Edition, 61.
Jowell, J. (1994), 'The Rule of Law Today', in J. Jowell and D. Oliver (eds), *The Changing Constitution*, 3rd Edition (Oxford: Oxford University Press).

Kay, R. (1998), 'American Constitutionalism', in L. Alexander (ed.), *Constitutionalism: Political Foundations* (Cambridge: Cambridge University Press).

Kriegel, B. (1995), *The State Under the Rule of Law* (Princeton: Princeton University Press).

Lauterpacht, H. (1950), *International Law and Human Rights* (London: Butterworth).

Laws, J. (1993), 'Is the High Court the Guardian of Fundamental Constitutional Rights?', *Public Law* 59.

Laws, J. (1995), 'Law and Democracy', *Public Law* 72.

Laws, J. (1996), 'The Constitution: Morals and Rights', *Public Law* 622.

Marsh, N. (1961), 'The Rule of Law as a Supra-National Concept', in A.C. Guest (ed.), *Oxford Essays in Jurisprudence* (Oxford: Oxford University Press).

Mason, K. (1995), 'The Rule of Law', in P. Finn (ed.), *Essays on Law and Government*, vol. 1 (Sydney: Law Book Co).

Rawls, J. (2001), *Justice as Fairness: A Restatement* (Cambridge, Mass: Harvard University Press).

Raz, J. (1977), 'The Rule of Law and its Virtue', *Law Quarterly Review* 93, 197.

Raz, J. (1995), *Ethics in the Public Domain: Essays in the Morality of Law and Politics* (Oxford: Oxford University Press).

Robertson, G. (1999), *Crimes Against Humanity: The Struggle for Global Justice* (London: Allen Lane, The Penguin Press).

Summers, R. (1993), 'A Formal Theory of the Rule of Law', *Ratio Juris* 6, 127.

Chapter 7

Democracy and Islam

Bahtiar Effendy

Is Islam really compatible with democracy? To what extent are they compatible? The answers to these questions vary. Some argue that Islam is congruent with democratic principles. On the other hand, there are those who believe that Islam is not democratic, thus making what constitutes Islamic democracy an unclear or ambiguous theme. Few Muslims, at least in Indonesia, are willing to be characterized as undemocratic, given the ramifications that opposition to democracy carries – authoritarianism, totalitarianism, fascism, absolutism, indecency, dictatorship, non-competitiveness and so forth. But not many Muslims have actually thought through the relationship between democracy and Islam.

Those who believe that Islam is compatible with democracy usually base their argument on several Islamic precepts that are congruent with democracy. These normative ideals include the principles of justice (*'adl*), consultation (*shura*), egalitarianism (*musawah*), trust (*amanah*) and freedom (*hurriya*) in the *Qur'an*. These are the very principles which Muslims are obliged to exercise and implement in their socio-cultural, economic and political activities. In fact, these principles were applied and demonstrated vigorously in the political tradition of early Islam, particularly during the Prophet's time. Because of this, many argue that Muhammad's city-state of Medina 'embodied a form of equalitarian participant nationalism' (Bellah 1991, 151) best expressed in Muhammad's *mitsaq al-madina* (Constitution of Medina). This Constitution was the governing formula which regulated the socio-political relationship among members of the Medinan community, at which time the single political community described by Muhammad as an *Ummah* constituted a number of different religious groups, such as Muslims, Jews and tribal pagans.

In short, it suffices to say that the high culture form of Islam, in the words of Ernest Gellner, is 'endowed with a number of features – unitarianism, a rule ethic, individualism, scripturalism, puritanism, an egalitarian aversion to meditation and hierarchy, a fairly small load of magic – that are congruent, presumably, with requirements of [political] modernity or modernization' (Gellner 1989, 307). In the view of Samuel Huntington (1996), who often puts Islam in a hostile position vis-à-vis the West, these features 'are generally congruent with the requirements of democracy' (Gellner 1989, 307).

What has been presented earlier does not paint the whole picture of Islam. Islam is certainly more than a set of principles covering the notion of justice, egalitarianism, consultation or any other principles which resemble or form a part of democratic values. Islam, being a divine instrument to understand the world, is also construed as the total way of life. The embodiment of this is expressed in Islamic law (*shari'ah*).

This has led many Muslims to believe in the complete and holistic nature of Islam. Thus, Islam 'encompasses the three famous Ds (*dīn*, religion; *dunya*, life; and *dawla*, state)' (Ayubi 1996, 63).

This intellectual preference emphasizes the inseparability of Islam from the various aspects of worldly life. Instead of limiting themselves to the principles of justice, consultation, egalitarianism and so forth in their socio-economic and political activities, the advocates of this now propose that Islam be the sole governing formula. Thus, instead of democracy, the state should be based on Islam; *shari'ah* ought to be adopted as the state constitution. For them, political sovereignty rests in the hands of the Divine.

Islam, however, also rejects any distinction between the religious community and the political community. Hence, there is no equipoise between Caesar and God, and political participation is linked to religious affiliation. Fundamentalist Islam demands that in a Muslim country the political rulers should be practising Muslims, *shari'ah* should be the basic law, and *'ulama* should have a 'decisive vote in articulating, or at least reviewing and ratifying, all governmental policy' (Huntington 1991, 307). The theological sources of this intellectual tradition include the *Qur'anic* verses: *innal hukm illa* – the decision rests with Allah only; *wa man lam yahkum bima anzala Allahu fa ulaaika hum al-dhalimum* – who so judge not by that which Allah had revealed, such are wrong doers; *athiu Allah, wa ar-rasul* – obey Allah and the messenger. On the other hand, some portions of Islamic tenets seem to be inimical to democratic values. For example, the concepts of *ahldhimmi*, however benign its motivation, can be viewed as an indication that Islam supports the idea of second-class citizens, as does the principle of *Qur'anic* Islamic inheritance by which sons inherit twice as much as daughters. Indeed, in some circumstances, this particular regulation seems to contradict the very notion of justice. Because of this, many have argued that the 'Islamic concept of politics differs from, and contradicts, the premise of democratic politics' (Huntington 1991, 307). However, it is by no means clear that Islam is inimical or antithetical to democracy (Beinin and Stork 1997).

Huntington is probably correct when he suggests that 'Islamic doctrine contains elements that may be both congenial and uncongenial to democracy' (1991, 307). And yet some have argued that what makes Islam congenial or uncongenial to democracy is a matter of how someone interprets its doctrine. Different intellectual inclinations – whether the motive is to recover the true meaning of the doctrine as literally expressed in the text, or to find out the general principles of the doctrine beyond its literal or textual expression – may lead to different interpretations of a particular doctrine. The former may give birth to an understanding of Islam which contradicts the politics of democracy, while the latter has the potential to make Islam congenial to democracy.

But, even if the amicability of Islamic doctrines with democratic values is established, an intellectual endeavour which had not been undertaken seriously enough,[1] this does not necessarily mean that the compatibility of Islam with democracy is resolved. The congeniality of Islam to democracy does not rest solely in the realm

1 Presumably by campaigning for a more tolerant, inclusive or liberal Islam. See Kurzman (1998).

of religious doctrines. It is also closely related to the belief of many Muslims that democracy really represents 'the end of history'. Hence, democracy has become – to borrow Serif Mardin's terminology – 'the dream of Muslim societies' (1995, 278).

However, given the compatibility of Islamic doctrines with democracy, why has no Islamic country sustained a fully democratic political system for any length of time? Huntington has indicated that, with the exception of Turkey, where Mustafa Kemal Ataturk explicitly rejected Islamic concepts of society and politics and vigorously attempted to create a secular, modern, Western nation state, the 'experience with democracy has not been an unmitigated success'. He then goes on to say that:

> Elsewhere in the Islamic world, Pakistan attempted democracy on three occasions, none of which lasted long. Turkey has had democracy interrupted by occasional military interventions; Pakistan has had bureaucratic and military rule interrupted by occasional elections. The only Arab country to sustain a form of democracy, albeit of the constitutional variety, for a significant period of time was Lebanon. Its democracy, however, really amounted to consociational oligarchy, and 40–50 percent of its population was Christian. Once Muslims became a majority in Lebanon and began to assert themselves, Lebanese democracy collapsed (Huntington 1991, 307–8).

Thus Indonesia, the biggest Muslim country on earth, has only been able to undergo democratic practices for a very short period of time (1950–57/59) (Feith 1962). This is one reason why the Muslim world was excluded from the recent study of democratization. Indeed, as is argued in Larry Diamond, Juan Linz and Seymour Martin Lipset's (1989) four-volume study of democratization in Asia, Africa and Latin America, with the exception of perhaps Egypt, Lebanon and certainly Turkey, the Islamic countries of the Middle East and North Africa generally lack democratic experience, and most appear to have little prospect of transition even to semi democracy.[2] Muslims' social capital – cultures, values, norms and so forth – need to be taken into account in the effort to reconcile Islam with democracy.[3]

Given such a perspective, the tendency to encourage Islam to adjust itself to democracy is unfortunate. Mutual adjustment has rarely been the case in the development of the discourse of Islam vis-à-vis democracy. Democracy is part of the dream of the Western world and it was born in Europe. This point of origin is not simply a matter of birthplace. Quite significantly, it refers to the socio-economic, cultural and political circumstances which influenced and shaped the concept of democracy. Whether such a product is exportable or transferable to different socio-cultural, economic and political backgrounds remains an interesting puzzle in today's nearly borderless world. Some have suggested that, even with some luck, the exportability of democracy is somewhat limited. Thus George Kennan saw democracy as:

> a form of government which evolved in the eighteenth and nineteenth centuries in northwestern Europe, primarily among those countries that border on the English Channel

2 Compare with Esposito and Voll (1996).

3 For the Indonesian case, a pioneering endeavour has been undertaken by, among others, Robert Hefner (1998).

> and the North Sea (but with a certain extension into Central Europe), and which was then carried into other parts of the world, including North America, where peoples from that northwestern European area appeared as original settlers, or as colonists, and laid down the prevailing patterns of civil government (Kennan 1977, 41–3; cited in Huntington 1991, 298–9).

Based on such a historical perception, democracy actually has 'a relatively narrow base both in time and space'. And because of that, Huntington concludes that 'democracy is appropriate only for north-western and perhaps central European countries and their settler-colony offshoots' (Huntington 1991, 299). In the same spirit, Islam has been singled out as a cultural obstacle to democracy in developing nations.

Yet, as indicated by the recent worldwide democratic resurgence, it may be correct to argue that there are some universal values which are shared by all citizens of the world. And some of those values might be democratic in nature. However, if the idea of the transferability of democracy beyond Western contexts is to be pursued, then certain caveats are in order. First, it is imperative that Western constructions of civil society be adjusted for non-Western contexts. Muslims might then indeed move between or even shop around for new identities (Hall 1995, 26). Second, the idea of democracy needs to be placed in a certain structural and cultural plateau. Unless democracy is contextualized, it will always be seen as a product of Western traditions, attitudes, values and beliefs with which the Muslim world has little to do.

The history of Indonesia's struggle to achieve a synthesis of Islam and democracy does not escape the above predicament. After the collapse of the New Order regime, amidst 30 long years of tireless effort to promote the notion of substantive as opposed to formalist Islam, the idea of 'political Islam' is still very important to our country, including demands that the state adopt the Jakarta Charter. This suggests that the question of Islam and democracy has not been entirely resolved. Contrary to many Western accounts, this issue is not so much about how to synthesize Islamic doctrines with democratic values, but how to adapt to Indonesia's Muslims' socio-cultural fabric. Future research on Islam and democracy in Indonesia should be geared in this direction if there is to be any real prospect of success.

References

Ayubi, N. (1996), *Political Islam: Religion and Politics in the Arab World* (London and New York: Routledge).

Beinin, J. and Stork, J. (eds) (1997), *Political Islam: Essays from the Middle East Report* (Berkeley and Los Angeles: University of California Press).

Bellah, R.N. (1991), *Beyond Belief: Essays on Religion in a Post-Traditionalist World* (Berkeley and Los Angeles: University of California Press).

Diamond, L., Linz, J. and Lipset, S.M. (eds) (1989), *Democracy in Developing Countries* (Boulder, Colorado: Lynne Reinner Publishers).

Esposito, J. and Voll, J. (1996), *Islam and Democracy* (New York and Oxford: Oxford University Press).

Feith, H. (1962), *The Decline of Constitutional Democracy in Indonesia* (Ithaca: Cornell University Press).

Gellner, E. (1989), 'Up Form Imperialism', *The New Republic*, 22 May, 35–6.

Hall, J.A. (ed.) (1995), *Civil Society: Theory, History, Comparison* (Cambridge: Polity Press).

Hefner, R. (1998), 'A Muslim Civil Society?: Indonesian Reflections on the Conditions of Its Possibility', in R. Hefner (ed.), *Democratic Civility: The History and Cross-Cultural Possibility of a Modern Political Ideal* (Somerset, NJ: Transaction Publishers).

Huntington, S. (1991), *The Third Wave: Democratization in the Late Twentieth Century* (Norman and London: University of Oklahoma Press).

Huntington, S. (1996), *The Clash of Civilizations and the Remaking of World Order* (New York: Simon and Schuster).

Kurzman, C. (ed.) (1998), *Liberal Islam: Source Book* (Oxford: Oxford University Press).

Mardin, S. (1995), 'Civil Society and Islam', in J.A. Hall (ed.), *Civil Society: Theory, History, Comparison* (Cambridge: Polity Press).

Chapter 8

Islam and Democratization in Indonesia

Ahmad Syafi'i Maarif

Introduction

The relationship between Islam and democratization in Indonesia is often misunderstood. In this chapter I argue that democracy has been central to Indonesian aspirations since independence and that Islam has played a major part in the achievement of democracy in Indonesia through its part in the actual processes by which democracy has been realized. My discussion reads a well-known record somewhat differently, and in a way that has implications for the political future of the country.

Muslims and Majority Rule

Muslims supported majority rule even before Indonesia declared its independence on 17 August 1945. Indeed, the Islamic movement known as Muhammadiyah put the majority's right of electing its top leadership in its first Constitution of 1912 (Badawi 1998, 2–3, Articles 6, 10, 11), even though the word 'democracy' was not part of the political vocabulary of educated Indonesians at that time. The founder of Muhammadiyah, Ahmad Dahlan (1868–1923), probably gained the idea of the right of the majority from the *Qur'anic* doctrine of mutual consultation or *shura* (*Qur'an* III, 159 and XLII, 38), which deals with the equal right of people to actively participate in the decision-making process. He was not trained in any Western educational system. This suggests that practices of democracy have been deep-rooted in Indonesian Islam's political culture for a long time. Consistent with this, Muhammadiyah has been consistent in practising the principles of *shura*, not only when electing leaders, but also in the process of writing programmes and agendas in regular meetings and congresses at all levels of its organization. Other major Muslim organizations such as Nahdhatul Ulama have also implemented the principle of *shura* in running their socio-religious activities from the very beginning of their history. This suggests that it is misleading to discuss democracy as a Western idea which needs to be introduced into Indonesia in the face of Islamic opposition.

Unlike many countries in the Arab world which still maintain the view that democracy is not compatible with Islam, Indonesian Muslims have accepted and defended the political democratic system in light of their understanding of the Islamic teachings for decades. According to Indonesia's first vice president, Mohammad Hatta (1945–56), democracy in Indonesia has three main sources: the Western idea of socialism advocating the principles of humanism, the Islamic teachings on God's justice and the need to establish universal brotherhood, and the knowledge that Indonesian society is based on collectivism. If these influences are harmoniously combined as interdependent ingredients, then democracy in Indonesia has a strong chance of survival, despite its ups and downs in different periods of contemporary Indonesian history (Hatta 2000, 435).[1] As the leading Indonesian historian, Taufik Abdulah, notes, democracy was one of the ideals of the Indonesian struggle for independence, and democracy is a national ideal which has more and more become a consensus.[2] The founding fathers of the Indonesian republic understood that a modern state needed to take the form of a republic with a commitment to the rule of law, and their democratic aspiration has remained central to the national historical conscience. Indeed, belief in democracy has never died out in Indonesia, and this is in part to be explained by the character of Indonesian Islam.

Difficult Histories

On the other hand, it cannot be denied that the dream of setting up a strong and healthy democracy has encountered serious obstacles, partly because most Indonesian political leaders were not democrats in practice. Once again the history of these obstacles is instructive.

The emergence of various political parties with different and contradictory ideologies, starting from the second decade of the twentieth century, strengthened and solidified the foundations of democracy in colonized Indonesia, though the Dutch were always watchful of their activities. Three competing ideologies operated in Indonesia before independence: Islam as a political ideology, Marxism/socialism, and nationalism. Though the leaders of the political parties were mostly Muslims, devout or otherwise, the ideologies they adopted were quite far apart. This situation led Soekarno as early as 1926 to write an article under the title 'Nationalism, Islamism, and Marxism' in an attempt to bridge the divisions between the political parties, given that the Dutch colonial system remained diehard and totally opposed to Indonesian independence (Soekarno 1965, 1–23). Soekarno was convinced that Indonesians would only be able to force colonialism to leave the archipelago if Indonesian political leaders were united, but his Romantic nationalism arguably delayed the emergence of democracy in the country.

Democracy in Indonesia is a story of general elections through which the people learnt what democracy was in principle and also in stages what it might be. I believe that Islam was crucial in facilitating the first genuine elections in Indonesian history:

---

1 'Demokrasi Kita' first appeared as an article in Panji Masyarakat, May 1960, as Hatta's response to Soekarno's authoritarian political system called 'Guided Democracy' which only survived from 1959 to 1966. With the collapse of this system, Soekarno's political career gradually but surely came to an end in 1968, succeeded as president by his stubborn army general Soeharto, who ruled until 1998.

2 Taufik Abdullah (2001), *Nasionalisme dan Sejarah* [Nationalism and History] (Bandung: Satya Historika). In particular, see Chapter 1, 'Democracy. History and Cultural Interpretation', and Chapter 2, 'Historical Reflection on the National Awakening'.

the general elections of 1955, 1999 and 2004, through which the dream of democracy became an enacted reality for most of the population. The first general elections were held in September and December 1955 under the Burhanuddin Harahap government, ten years after the declaration of independence. Originally the elections were to be held six months after independence, but the Dutch, aided by British troops, launched brutal attacks on the new-born state in order to continue their colonial system after the defeat of Japan. These attacks prevented Indonesia from realizing one of the pillars of democracy: to have elections very soon after the declaration as required by the Constitution. Consequently, Indonesia was forced to defend itself from the attacks of colonial troops which lasted more than four years. The Dutch forces in Jogjakarta arrested President Soekarno, Vice President Hatta, and some other cabinet ministers, and these arrests lasted for around seven months. Fortunately, under the leadership of Sjafruddin Prawiranegara an emergency government was established in Sumatra to defend the existence of Indonesia as an independent nation.

The 1955 elections under the umbrella of the 1950 Constitution were peaceful, democratic, clean, and not a single drop of blood was spilled in the midst of heated ideological conflict. This fact assured the people that democracy was the right alternative for the future of Indonesia. Four political parties were the winners in the elections: the nationalist PNI, the modernist Muslim Masyumi, the Muslim traditionalist NU and the communist PKI. However, when the new cabinet was formed under the Premier Ali Sastroamidjojo, Soekarno was unhappy because of the exclusion of the communists. Subsequently Soekarno reluctantly agreed with Ali's cabinet composition without the inclusion of the communists. This cabinet was known as ARI's (Ali-Roem-Idham) cabinet, representing the elements of PNI, Masyumi, and NU, and was the first real democratic government installed in the modern history of Indonesia. Soekarno, however, did not like this new political coalition and he cooperated extensively with the PKI because he needed their support at the grass-roots level.

The 1955 elections aimed to form two constitutional bodies: a parliament and a constituent assembly. The latter had the obligation to write a permanent constitution. This assembly had worked hard and almost completed its task, except for its work on the philosophical basis of the state, which remained contested. About this crucial matter, the assembly was divided into three factions: the first group proposed Pancasila to be the basis of the state; the second proposed Islam; and the third was for a socio-economic basis for the state. When voting failed to resolve these differences, Soekarno and the army became impatient and proposed a return to the 1945 Constitution. Unfortunately, the ARI cabinet only survived for a year before Soekarno used its internal divisions to consolidate his own power.

Indonesia now entered a critical transitional period leading to the creation of Guided Democracy (1959–66), based on Soekarno's decree of 5 July 1959. The communists supported this decree, while the other parties just adjusted themselves to this new undemocratic political arrangement. Two parties opposed the new system: Masyumi under the leadership of Prawoto Mangkusasmito, and PSI (Indonesian Socialist Party) under the leadership of Sutan Sjahrir. At the end of 1960, Soekarno outlawed the two parties on the pretext that they were involved in the regional rebellions in 1958. The truth actually was that some former leaders of the parties joined the rebellions in their effort to force Soekarno to return to the 1950 Constitution. Both parties themselves had legally no connection with the rebellions.

The failure of ARI's government to survive dragged Indonesia into the prison of Guided Democracy. Natsir, one the Masyumi's top leaders, commented on this new system: '... that everything will be found in the Guided Democracy, except democracy' (Maarif 1996, 75). As an experienced democrat and politician, Natsir was correct to criticize this system because the grave of democracy now appeared right in front of his eyes. With the coming of Guided Democracy, real democracy was killed for a while until the system finally collapsed as a result of a communist coup on 1 October 1965.[3] With this coup, Soekarno's career also started to fade away. The only benefit contributed by this system to the nation was Soekarno's success in his effort to include West Papua as part of Indonesia. Meanwhile, the nation became almost totally bankrupt, with the inflation rate reaching 650 per cent in 1966. Ironically, on 12 March 1966, the PKI was banned by General Soeharto, a newcomer in Indonesian politics.

The coming to power of General Soeharto was not a major improvement. Participation by the people in the process of decision-making was initially part of Soeharto's agenda, but under his regime the people had no right to define the mode of their participation. The ruler defined everything, while the people were only permitted to implement government policy. Once General A.H. Nasution, who had proposed Soeharto to replace Soekarno as president, was sidelined, Soeharto followed his predecessor by killing democracy on behalf of Pancasila Democracy. Consistent with this approach, the elections under Soeharto's regime were not real elections from a democratic stand-point. Though Soeharto claimed to have created a democracy based on the principles of Pancasila, his regime, known as the era of *Demokrasi Pancasila* (Pancasila Democracy), or the era *Orde Baru* (New Order), was really a continuation of the previous Guided Democracy. It was not easy for either Soekarno or Soeharto to accept a democracy in which the principle of equal status before law among citizens was fully assured by the constitution, since their outlook was shaped by a political sub-culture which was happy for centuries to live under the umbrella of a feudal or semi-feudal political system. Both of them preferred ruler's sovereignty (*daulat tuanku*) to people's sovereignty (*'daulat rakyat*).

This situation lasted for 32 years. If the monetary crisis had not suddenly happened in 1997–98, resulting in the unpredictable 'free fall' of Indonesian currency, Soeharto's regime would probably have survived even longer. As long as they were not hungry, the issue of democracy was not of primary importance for the ordinary people. However, when the acute monetary crisis paralyzed the Indonesian economy fundamentally, and the nation's per capita income dropped dramatically, Soeharto

---

3 For around four decades, the communist coup of 1 October 1965 was controversial among some leftist observers. But with the two recent works by Fic (2005) and Dake (2005), the political map of the coup has made it clear that the communists were those most responsible for that bloody tragedy. Of course, we have to be critical when reading their works, since there are still many controversial issues in them. Among other things, there is the possible role of Soekarno in the coup. On this, a more serious discussion among experts is badly needed; otherwise people will remain in the situation of political uncertainty.

had no other choice but to resign, and B.J. Habibie, as vice-president, took his place as third Indonesian president on 21 May 1998. It was Habibie who opened the door for genuine democracy after its slumber for almost four decades under Soekarno and Soeharto. Habibie successfully held the second real and peaceful general elections in 1999, but failed to win the majority votes in the MPR (People's Consultative Assembly) to continue his term, which only lasted for 17 months.

The third fair general elections on 5 July 2004, under President Megawati, marked a turning point for Indonesian democracy because they produced a significant change in the electoral rules. Henceforth the people not only elected the legislative members, but also the president and vice president were elected directly, something new in Indonesian politics. Susilo Bambang Yudhoyono and Muhammad Yusuf Kalla finally won the presidential election with a landslide of over 60 per cent of the total vote. All commentators, domestic and abroad, praised highly the democratic process of the 2004 elections. Former US President Carter, who observed these elections directly, concluded that they demonstrated that Islam was not anti-democratic (see Carter 2004). This was an over-optimistic verdict in some respects. Obviously peaceful and fair elections are not enough. Honesty is also needed for good and effective government. Under Yudhoyono, Indonesian politics is still characterized by pervasive corruption, and democracy may fail if this corruption is not defeated.

Conclusion

This short political history signals the fragility of democracy in our country. It certainly implies that democracy is compatible with Indonesian Islam, but it gives little basis for confidence that Indonesian institutions are mature enough to guarantee that a democratic system will be fully realized, at least in the short run. On the other hand, the fact that democracy in Indonesia emerged in a difficult colonial context, and then survived decades of dictatorial misrule, gives grounds for hope. The commitment of Muslim institutions to not only the theory but also the practice of democracy has been vital to the emergence of democracy in Indonesia, and is another ground for hope; and, contrary to some interpretations found in Western texts, it suggests that Islam will be of overwhelming importance for the survival of democracy in the foreseeable future. The real and dangerous enemies of democracy in Indonesia in the present era are not the people's lack of belief in the system or opposition to democracy from the side of Islam, but irresponsible politicians and self-interested conglomerates whose primary concern is not the welfare of the nation. Islam, on the other hand, is a positive force for democracy, through which people acquire values and ways of life which receive a fuller and more authentic expression when democracy is achieved even to a limited extent within the national political life.

References

Badawi, M. Djaldan (1998) (ed.), *Anggaran Dasar dan Anggaran Rumah Tangga Muhammadiyah: 1912–1985* [The Statute and Regulation of Muhammadiyah] (Jogjakarta: PP Muhammadiyah).

Carter, J. (2004), 'Surprisingly Fair Elections in Indonesia', *International Herald Tribune*, 15 July.

Dake, Antonie C.A. (2005), *Berkas-berkas Soekarno 1965–1967: Kronologi Suatu Keruntuhan* [Soekarno's File 1965–1967: Chronology of a Downfall] (Jakarta: Aksara Karunia).

Fic, Victor Miroslav (2005), *Anatomy of the Jakarta Coup: October 1, 1965* (Jakarta: Yayasan Obor).

Hatta, Mohammad (2000), 'Demokrasi Kita' [Our Democracy], *Karya Lengkap Bung Hatta* [Complete Work of Bung Hatta], 10 volumes (Jakarta: LP3ES).

Maarif, Ahmad Syafii (1996), *Islam dan Politik: Teori Belah Bambu Masa Demokrasi Terpimpin, 1959–1965* [Islam and Politics: A Theory of Splitting Bamboo in the Era of Guided Democracy, 1959–1965] (Jakarta: Gema Insani Press).

Sastroamidjojo, Ali (1974), *Tonggak-tonggak di Perjalananku* [Milestones in My Journey] (Jakarta: Kinta).

Soekarno (1965), *Di Bawah Bendera Revolusi* [Under the Banner of Revolution] (Jakarta: Panitia Penerbit Di Bawah Bendera Revolusi).

Chapter 9

Islam and the Claims of Democracy

Graham Maddox

At the end of the Cold War, a surge of triumphalism swept over the West. As the communist countries went down like dominoes, some authorities were ready, perhaps prematurely, to pronounce the final victory of democracy. In 1989, Francis Fukuyama first launched his speculative proposition that the end of the Cold War meant 'the universalization of Western liberal democracy as the final form of human government' (Fukuyama 1989), and in 1990 Paul Hirst wrote: 'There are no credible forces seeking to overthrow Western politics' (Hirst 1990, 1). Eight years later, Ulrich Beck published his *Democracy Without Enemies* (Beck 1998). More recently John Dunn's sober assessment was that democracy has 'won the global struggle for wealth and power' (Dunn 2005, 20), but at the expense of submerging its traditional freedom ideals of equality and freedom beneath the 'order of egoism' (Dunn 2005, 124).

The Universal Claims of Democracy

It is not yet established whether democracy is a specifically Western construct. It is almost impossible for us to disentangle the democratic idea from the history of the West. If we were able to observe the Athenian democracy without subsequent encumbrances, however, we could appreciate an experiment without antecedents which was designed to address universal problems such as poverty and human dignity. It is a paradox of history that the first democracy emerged as a by-product of aristocratic faction-fighting, but we can hardly take the silence of the sources to determine that when the aristocratic Cleisthenes of Athens 'attached the demos to his faction' (Herodotus 5, 66), there was not some canny bargaining with unknown representatives of the demos to produce a constitution favourable to them. The institutions and practices of the democracy bespeak this approach with unmistakable clarity.

In all discussions of the Athenian democracy, we have first to dispose of those features to which the modern democrat takes exception. Athenians accepted the institution of slavery, which, however mild its practice may have been by comparison with the African slave trade of the seventeenth and eighteenth centuries, nevertheless represented a contradiction of human dignity which the ethos of the democracy generally upheld. The enfranchised citizens of Athens were the free, adult *males* who were eligible to serve in the military forces. Even in times of peace, the democracy was organized as though prepared for war. Finley tells colourfully how the democratic mind was concentrated when a decision to go to war taken in the morning in the Assembly would mean that the very men who had voted would be in the field in the afternoon (Finley 1983, 60–61). So the Assembly never contained women who, although they were bearers of Athenian citizenship, could not vote, and neither could the many foreign residents, some of whom may have contributed as much to the culture as did the alien Aristotle.

Within these limitations, more objectionable to the modern mind after centuries of political philosophizing than to the ancient, the original democracy was a remarkable and radical institution. (The canonical philosophers objected to democracy on quite other grounds.) For those who were citizens, it required of them nothing more than that they had reached their majority to qualify them to take a share in decision-making equal to that of the greatest in the land. Abject poverty was no barrier to participation. Neither was a lack of education or literacy – witness the extraordinary story of the ostracism of Aristeides the Just (Hansen 1991, 312). For the first time, the dignity of the ordinary human was asserted for no other reason than that he was a mature adult. Of course, in this example, we must acknowledge that we are speaking of the Athenian adult, but this is no obstacle to acceptance of the principle of adult maturity and autonomy.

Democracy, therefore, draws its universal claim from the proposition that the adult individual, as a mature and autonomous being, has the ability and responsibility to make rational decisions concerning the conduct of his or her life. Thomas Hobbes addressed the problem of universal liberty, which requires that there be political organization to arbitrate between conflicting exercises of adult autonomy. His solution was not democratic and he excoriated the self-important 'democratical gentlemen' of the House of Commons (Hobbes 1969, 26–44, as in Dunn 2005, 60), but the modern democrat has to take into account the need for government as an arbitrator between competing interests. It is important in this context to affirm that democracy is a form of government and not just the impossible ideal that Rousseau despaired over. Yet democracy, in its various guises, articulates the principle that each adult person should have as much autonomy as possible, and should share in the collective exercise of power by the community as far as possible. This is not necessarily to privilege those political theories which seek to reduce the power of government in the name of democracy, nor to accept those interpretations of democracy which characterize it as 'elite rule'. On the basis of a universally shared humanity, these principles of adult autonomy and the sharing of collective authority can be construed as universal principles, not confined to any one nation or cultural tradition.

It is at this point that we encounter those arguments which seek to confine democracy to its Western origins and to exclude it from certain other traditions. This was powerfully asserted, for example, in respect of the anti-democratic coup that took place in Fiji in 1987. The coup ringleader, Sitiveni Rabuka, when accused of 'raping' democracy, said that 'Fiji was being judged according to European standards, European cultures and European ways of thinking'. He did not seem to appreciate the contradiction when he justified his action in terms of loyalty to the British Crown or in defence of the Christian religion. His Christianity was of the Methodist variety (ironically the same practised by the ousted Prime Minister, Timoci Bavadra), firmly rooted in the Church of England and the British and American evangelism of John Wesley.[1] The real fear of the coup supporters was the political rise of the Indian community in its coalition with Bavadra's party. This rejection of democracy really meant a disenfranchisement of the sizeable Indian population (Lawson 1991). Similar views about 'Western' democracy have emerged from Zimbabwe recently.

It is important to dissociate democracy from the defence or promotion of any religion. While there have been powerful arguments linking the rise of modern democracy with Christianity, these can only apply to the provenance of the modern democratic idea, and perhaps to its inauguration, but not to its continuing operation. Fundamental to the foundation of democracy is the separation of church and state, enshrined in the American Bill of Rights. In the Western tradition, secularization does indeed stem from religious sources, and it is salutary to recall that the campaign for the separation of church and state in America was led by the Calvinist Baptists Roger Williams and John Clarke (James 1999). The doctrine may be traced ultimately to the two cities of Augustine, or indeed to the dichotomous history of ancient Israel, in which Brueggemann discerned two 'trajectories' of covenant theology, the royalist represented by the court, and the theocratic represented by the foundational figure of Moses, the judges and the prophets (Brueggemann 1979). Some modern republicans have drawn much sustenance from the virulent anti-king literature in the *Book of Judges*, and in the Samuelic crisis concerning the transition of Israel from direct theocracy to a monarchy (I Samuel 8, 11–18; Buber 1967). The paradigm case for the continuing struggle between the two ideas is the confrontation between Nathan the prophet and the sinning King David. This pericope concerning David and Bathsheba was central to Leo Strauss' case in his famous 'Jerusalem and Athens' (Orr 1995).

Augustine generalized the two streams by dividing all humanity between those who truly loved God and those who were worldly. The importance of this dualistic approach emerged with the theory of Martin Luther, a friar of Saint Augustine, who did not divide humanity after the manner of Augustine, but postulated a two-regime theory: the realm of the spirit and the realm of temporal things. While both realms were subject to God's sovereignty, the methods of conduct were widely divided. The world of the spirit – the inner world of conscience – was to be ruled only by persuasion, by the effect of the Word, by the moving of the Spirit. This realm had nothing at all to do with physical coercion or punishment. It was the work of the devil to allow physical coercion to have a part in the persuasion of the spirit. On the other hand, we all also live in the temporal order, where brigands and pirates and other miscreants can interfere with the orderly conduct of our affairs. It is they who must be curbed by legitimate force, and indeed we all need correction from time to time. In this realm, the ruler wears a sword and administers the prison. Never should the functions of the two realms be confused. It was a prostitution of the church that it should ever use coercive methods to compel adherence or belief (Thompson 1984).

This formulation was taken seriously by all the Protestant political theorists who succeeded Luther. Hobbes' secular polity was appropriate to the time since the 'second Fall', when Israel repudiated the direct rule of God by adopting an earthly

1 In another mood, he could have evaluated his own religion by European standards, European cultures and European ways of thinking. Mr Bavadra might have thought of it as universal.

kingship and fell repeatedly into anarchy (Pocock 1973). Most influential were the teachings on toleration by Roger Williams in Rhode Island (Williams 1644) and John Locke in England (Locke 1689). Locke pointed out that the magistrate should have no part in the religious beliefs and practices of the people, and that forced belief was no belief, coerced worship no worship. It was to protect the free exercise of worship that constitutional provisions saw to the separation of church and state. People were to be free to assemble and to worship as the spirit moved them, while the sword of the magistrate had no more to do than to clear and keep safe a public space for them.

It would not be too long before people saw the reciprocal benefits of the separation of church and state. It was just as important to see that the state remained free from the control of religious fanatics willing to impose their morality on an unwilling people. There was even more to it than this. The state was the one association which had to embrace people of all persuasions and accommodate the several ends they might hold for their lives. The search for cultural or ideological homogeneity was a disaster, as the puritans discovered to their cost. The democratic state is a somewhat fragile flower, and needs to be protected from the righteousness of those who can see no other possible truth than their own (Stout 2004, 188). Rawls wished to protect the liberal state from the ravages of 'comprehensive doctrines' (Rawls 1971). More recently, others such as Stephen Carter and Robert Kraynak have believed that the state and the courts system in America have gone too far in the secularization of public life, leaving little room for public expressions of faith or publicly observed prayers (Carter 1993; Kraynak 2001). Indeed, these types of opinions are shared by the present US administration, where foreign affairs are prosecuted under a rhetoric of righteousness and a dualistic assignment of virtue to friends and evil to enemies. Implicit in much of the advice that the President receives is a qualitative differentiation between the world's great religions, and a striving for ideological homogeneity quite inappropriate to a democracy. Many have seen President Bush's domestic 'faith-based initiative' as a direct assault on the separation of church and state doctrine and an attempt to evangelize the nation (Maddox 2003).

A resilient democracy requires a secular state which can tolerate and, where appropriate, accommodate the whole range of legitimate philosophical and vocational positions which allow personal autonomy to all adult citizens within its purview, so long as their liberties do not interfere with the like liberties of others. Such a state must be secular in the religious sense and neutral as far as ideologies are concerned. This last consideration raises problems about the structures of certain 'democratic' states which tend to enshrine certain ideological positions, while outlawing other, equally legitimate, positions. None of this is to imply that religious morality should have no part in public life. Indeed, the general level of morality accounted for in most legal systems, such as the outlawing of murder and stealing, could be traced to religious teachings such as the Ten Commandments. Robert Kraynak argues that the whole edifice of the liberal state rests on substructures of morality taught for centuries in the West by the Jewish and Christian religions. He deplores such liberal teaching that would cut the religious foundations from liberal ethical understandings with a trenchant atheism (Kraynak 2001). It is important that such teachings from the Jewish and Christian traditions as were so highly valued by Leo Strauss should continue to influence the liberal state. Yet, they should do so only in so far as they are accepted at a general level as being reasonable by the general bulk of the community. That is to say, their inputs are tested and refined through the objective mechanisms of the secular state. In any case, democracy accepts that policy solutions are at best interim, since no government, no policy, is good enough to persist in permanence. Democracy is a mechanism for perpetual revision.

Democratic Control of the Military

The idea of secularization can be extended to embrace institutions within a state which may develop their own quasi-religious ethos. The role of the military in any state is of paramount importance, yet its significance should never be misapplied in order to give that ethos priority in political decision-making. The importance of the military is that it actually defines the first function of the state, that is, to protect its citizens. As Aristotle wrote, the state came into being to preserve life, and this function requires the instrumentalities of both a police force for internal security and a military force for external defence. Since *salus reipublicae suprema lex* there is clearly a temptation for military officers to regard their own protective function as outweighing all other considerations, and they themselves to be the best judges of when the safety of the state is under threat. In Latin America there has been a tradition of a de facto designation of the military as a fourth branch of government, where sometimes the military has taken onto itself the function of 'judicial review with bayonets'. There is a parallel between the position of the armed forces and religious institutions. They are both clothed in elaborate ceremonial, with fanciful costumery and distant echoes of sanctity. The military hallows its war dead like saints, and endues their sacrifice with mystery. The military tradition is entitled to be viewed as an ideology (if not a theology) in itself. As with religious bodies, it is necessary that there be no political interference in the internal conduct of the armed forces, which must be run on military efficiency, with promotion on merit alone. There was a belief among members of the US armed forces that the Vietnam War was lost because of too close interference in the military objectives of the war on the part of political leaders. At least a screen of separation (if not a wall) should divide the military from the political.

There the parallel ends. The military always remains an instrument of government in a way in which religious bodies can never be in a secular state. It is the state, not the service, which controls the means of coercion, and these only as subject to democratic control. It is therefore an absolute principle of democracy that the military be controlled by the government. This approach implies the right of the government to appoint those officials of the army who must be answerable directly to the government. Any interference with appointments down the line would seriously undermine the morale of the forces, interrupt the efficiency of a system based on merit, and introduce political factionalism into a service in which cohesiveness is a necessity. Moreover, maintaining a military force is a hugely expensive business, which requires financial sacrifice on the part of the citizenry. It is vital that this expenditure be seen as community expenditure, that is, government expenditure subject to the same democratic controls (through supply measures) as all the other expenses of government.

Military Solutions to Political Problems

Just as under a democracy the armed forces are required to act entirely under the restraint of orders from the civilian government, so too must governments exercise the enormous power given to them with a restraint engendered by their responsibility to the electorate. The safety of the country is of prime concern to the government, but it also places in their hands the means to oppress their own community. Finding the balance between maintaining a force sufficiently strong to ensure protection but not too great as to endanger the civilian nature of government is a delicate business. The ancient Romans understood the dangers of enormous power by making it a matter of law and sacred duty that a general was required to demobilize his troops before entering the city. Now that we consider democracy to be a universal good, rhetorically reinforced by the American President's declared determination to bring democracy to other countries, similar restraint needs to be extended to other nations and peoples who, by the claims of international democracy, deserve the respect given to internal constituents (Barber 2003). The matter is now hugely complicated by the new realities of international politics.

There is no doubt but that international terrorism, much of it from 'fundamentalist' Islamic sources, is the preoccupation of contemporary politics: 'The world is not the same since 9/11.' The response of the American President and his international allies has been to answer with overwhelming force. Clearly, however, the elusive terrorist makes no easy target for overwhelming force. As Benjamin Barber has suggested, George W. Bush is tied to an older and no longer appropriate version of gunboat diplomacy by seeking a nation state to hold to account for the attacks on America (Barber 2006). His response was understandable in terms of domestic politics, since the electorate would believe that if we are under attack, someone identifiable must be made responsible. Moreover, since it is the first function of the state to provide security for its citizens, then it must appear to be doing something actively for their protection. The United States, as its successive leaders proclaim, is the most powerful nation the world has ever seen, making it beneath its dignity to suffer attack from 'rogue' elements. The whole swathe of propaganda surrounding Bush's polemic against the state of Iraq was to link it to terrorists by endless repetition of the mantra, 'weapons of mass destruction'. The idea was to link 'the enemy' to the production and retention of weapons that could be supplied to terrorists. That neither weapons nor provable links to terrorists were found served nothing to blunt the acerbity of the President's anti-Iraq rhetoric. Many suspected that the assault on Iraq was a surrogate for an assault on Islam itself; indeed, many of the Christian 'right' saw it that way, and applauded. Although Bush himself refused to denigrate Islam itself, pointedly calling it a 'religion of peace', his designation of two Islamic countries, Iraq and Iran, together with an old-style communist one, North Korea, as an 'axis of evil' (Bush 2002) reawakened the currents of religious sectarianism. No one could mistake the tone of righteous contrast with the evil ones.

Enough sober voices have now enjoined upon the President, and his most loyal allies Tony Blair and John Howard, that one cannot defeat terrorism by attacking one country with overwhelming force, and that one cannot establish essential accommodations with Islam by punishing Islamic countries. You cannot make people democrats by killing them. A *Lancet* study has estimated that up to 650,000 civilians (or 2.5 per cent of the population) have been killed in the war (Burnham et al. 2006). That civilians would be killed in an attack characterized by 'shock and awe' was obvious from the start. The morality of that assault from a democratic viewpoint was dubious to say the least. The pain and insult inflicted upon an entire population prepares a breeding ground convenient for terrorists. Ironically, there are now estimated to be many terrorists in war-torn Iraq, whereas there were few or none before the invasion. As some sardonically suggest, Middle East terrorists are grateful that the Americans have brought their targets closer within range in the form of American troops, construction workers and businessmen.

Islam and Democracy

It is now surely evident to everyone, except perhaps the American President, that you do not simply create democracy by destroying a regime and replacing it, under external pressure, with another. One must even question Bush's intention of 'rolling back terrorism' (Dunn 2005, 140) through the spread of democracy. When elections were held in Iraq, he welcomed the onset of 'democracy', but at the beginning of 2007 his barely veiled threat to remove the elected Prime Minister of Iraq, Mr al-Maliki, if he did not live up to the President's 'benchmarks' (Bush 2007) rather gave the lie to democratic intentions. Many of Bush's supporters would believe that democracy is not possible under Islamist ideology (Maddox 2003, 402–3). Their fear and loathing of Islam stands at the latest point of a long history of Christian denigration of Islam, which began as a defensive reaction to Muslim conquest in the Middle East, Africa and Spain, but which burgeoned into a full-scale damnation often marked by deliberate misunderstanding and misrepresentation (Daniel 1993). Slandering the Prophet himself has been central to this misrepresentation, and has continued to this day. None of this is likely to induce accommodations between Islam and 'the West', nor to dissuade terrorists from their endeavours. Yet, Christians could learn from a moderate of their own tradition. As Thomas Aquinas advised, it was necessary to look 'for moral and philosophical arguments acceptable to Muslims, for it is clearly pointless to cite against them authorities which they do not accept' (Daniel 1993, 255).

Taking Aquinas's advice, and so acknowledging the centrality of a 'mainstream' Christian tradition to any dialogue, would be a good move. To counterpoise the discussion between Islam and 'the West' is a confusion of categories, and if Huntington's provocative 'clash of civilizations' argument did nothing else, it correctly formulated the 'clash', which we here prefer to designate 'dialogue', in religious terms (Huntington 1993). It is futile, and vaguely insulting, to talk to the representatives of a world religion in the smugly superior, rationally 'secular', voice of the objectified 'West'. It is perfectly true that Western secular democracies are not

'Christian', nor could they be, but the position of interlocutor should be adopted from the standpoint of the major world religion that has predominated in the formation of 'the West'.

This being said, a major modification is required in the Christian attitude to Islam. Those Christians who declare that God wishes them 'to take dominion' (Benen 2001, 4) need to be reminded of the humility that defines the very nature of original Christianity. The Constantinianism that for centuries portrayed Christianity as a doctrine of enforced rule is easily demonstrable as an aberration from Christian teaching (West 2004, 148–9; Kee 1982). The Jesus whose birth stories present an unequivocal picture of lowliness, and whose life ends as 'God crucified' (Moltmann 1974), lived out a ministry of 'good news to the poor' and of healing for the afflicted. When bombs are raining on innocent Iraqi children and their civilian parents, it is unthinkable that Jesus should be identified with anyone but the suffering, 'Christian' or 'Muslim' regardless. Christian triumphalists should recollect the humility and powerlessness of Christ, and of his message of infinite compassion and justice for the oppressed. If the American President ever believed that God had instructed him to invade a country with force of arms (as was sometimes reported), his lines of communication must have been hopelessly tangled.

Secondly, Christians need to encounter Muslims with a great deal more respect. In the eighteenth century, the founder of Methodism, John Wesley, when campaigning for the abolition of slavery, was shocked to discover that African Muslims showed a great deal more concern for human life, and a great deal more compassion for their fellow men, than did their 'Christian' captors. Many of those taken into slavery were already deeply religious, gentle persons of the Muslim faith (Wesley 1998, 88).

Saying that Islam is an eirenic religion is a good start, but President Bush and his advisers and followers need to elaborate on this basic understanding and articulate how it is that democracy may come to Muslim countries without the use or threat of armed force and external imposition. First, much more needs to be made of the accommodation which countries that are overwhelmingly Muslim have made with secular government, as in Turkey, Indonesia, Malaysia or Pakistan. Secondly, the most staunchly liberal of our democrats need to recognize that secularized government does not require atheism. Indeed, religious argument needs to be welcomed into democratic discourse before a genuine dialogue can be opened up with peoples of Muslim faith. To talk with committed Muslims, liberals need at least to admit of the possibility that some people genuinely believe in a sovereign God. Cornel West quotes the salutary advice of Khaled Abou El-Fadl on tolerance in Islam:

> A case for democracy presented from within Islam must accept the idea of God's sovereignty: it cannot substitute popular sovereignty for divine sovereignty, but must instead show how popular sovereignty – with its idea that citizens have rights and a correlative responsibility to pursue justice with mercy – expresses God's authority, properly understood. Similarly, it cannot reject the idea that God's law is given prior to human action, but must show how democratic law-making respects that priority (West 2004, 138–9).

It is not only imprudent to dismiss such views as irrational, but also untrue to the history of democracy in the West. *Vox populi vox Dei* is a familiar expression. It now needs to be recast as *vox Dei vox populi*: God is heard through the voice of his creatures. Even in pagan democratic Athens, the foundations of the democratic state rested on the basis of a higher authority than that of the members of the community themselves. The embryonic constitutionalism of that community rested on the oaths that citizens took to respect the laws and to refrain from using the seemingly unlimited power of the assembly to erode the liberties of fellow citizens (Dillon 1995, 146). When democracy re-emerged in the West in the seventeenth century, it was largely under the religious conviction that the human person should enjoy freedom and equality under God's providence. The secularization that democracy underwent came at the expense of attempts to keep religiously founded communities doctrinally pure – an impossibility once trade and commerce became part of the necessities of sustenance and preservation. The separation of church and state was pressed by deeply religious people who required freedom to worship as the spirit moved them (Carter 1993).

Whatever pride and gratitude Westerners may invest in democracy, there is something vaguely imperialist in the attempt to bring democracy to non-democratic countries, let alone to implant it from outside. This is not to diminish the universal value of democracy, which should be apparent to all reasonable people (Sen 1999). Yet it is not merely arrogant, but also impractical, to seek to introduce democracy from external sources. The entire history of democracy shows how it takes root in the practices and ethos of an entire people (Stout 2004) and is maintained because they themselves recognize its worth. The best the West can do to retail democracy is to demonstrate its worth to the neighbours of the older democracies by their example. This would require treating them with forbearance and dignity. However the current conflict in Iraq turns out (and at present it is difficult to see how sectarian civil war can be avoided), democrats need to acknowledge that violent invasion is the worst possible example. The rhetoric that links 'democracy' to foreign occupation and the continued use of force must be repudiated in unequivocal terms.

References

Barber, B. (2003), 'Startling Gap between Democracy Rhetoric and Invasion Policy', *Los Angeles Times*, 3 December.

Barber, B. (2006), 'The Clash of Cultures and American Hegemony', *American Political Science Association Annual Meeting*, Philadelphia, September.

Beck, U. (1998). *Democracy Without Enemies* (Munich: Ludwig-Maximilian University).

Benen, S. (2001), 'Fall from Grace', *Church and State* 54, 6.

Brueggemann, W. (1979), 'Trajectories in Old Testament Literature and the Sociology of Ancient Israel', *Journal of Biblical Literature* 98.

Buber, M. (1967), *Kingship of God* (trans. R. Scheiman), 3rd Edition (London: Allen and Unwin).

Burnham, G., Lafta, R., Doocy, S. and Roberts, L. (2006), 'Mortality after the 2003 Invasion of Iraq: A Cross-sectional Cluster Sample Survey', *The Lancet* 368: 9545, 1421–8.

Bush, George W. (2002), 'The President's State of the Union Address', 29 January.

Bush, George W. (2007), 'Address on Iraq', televised 11 January.

Carter, S.L. (1993), *The Culture of Disbelief. How American Law and Politics Trivialize Religious Observance* (New York: Anchor).

Daniel, N. (1993), *Islam and the West: The Making of an Image* (Oxford: Oneworld).

Dewey, J. (1916), *Democracy and Education* (New York: Macmillan).

Dillon, M. (1995), 'By Gods, Tongues and Dogs: The Use of Oaths in Aristophanic Comedy', *Greece and Rome* 42: 2, 135–51.

Dunn, J. (2005), *Democracy: A History* (New York: Atlantic).

Finley, M.I. (1983), *Politics in the Ancient World* (Cambridge: Cambridge University Press).

Ford, P. (2001), 'Why Do They Hate Us?', *Christian Science Monitor*, 27 September.

Fukuyama, F. (1989), 'The End of History?', *The National Interest*, Summer.

Gregor, A.J. (2001), *Giovanni Gentile: Philosopher of Fascism* (Somerset, NJ: Transaction).

Hansen, M.H. (1991), *The Athenian Democracy in the Age of Demosthenes. Structure, Principles and Ideology* (Oxford: Blackwell).

Herodotus (1920), *The Histories* (trans. and ed. A.D. Godley), Book 5, Chapter 66 (London: W. Heinemann).

Hirst, P. (1990), *Representative Democracy and its Limits* (Cambridge: Polity).

Hobbes, T. (1969), *Behemoth, or the Long Parliament* (ed. F. Tönnies), 2nd Edition (London: Frank Cass).

Huntington, S.P. (1993), 'The Clash of Civilizations?', *Foreign Affairs* 72: 3, 22–49.

James, S.V. (1999), *John Clarke and his Legacies: Religion and Law in Colonial Rhode Island 1638–1750* (ed. T.D. Bozeman) (University Park, PA: Pennsylvania State University Press).

Kee, A. (1982), *Constantine versus Christ: The Triumph of Ideology* (London: SCM Press).

Kraynak, R.P. (2001), *Christian Faith and Modern Democracy: God and Politics in the Fallen World* (Notre Dame, IN: University of Notre Dame Press).

Lawson, S. (1991), *The Failure of Democratic Politics in Fiji* (Oxford: Oxford University Press).

Lindsay, A.D. (1940), *I Believe in Democracy* (London: Oxford University Press).

Lindsay, A.D. (1943), *The Modern Democratic State* (London: Oxford University Press).

Locke, J. (1689), *A Letter Concerning Toleration* (London: A. Churchill).

Maddox, G. (2003), 'The Crusade Against Evil: Bush's Fundamentalism', *Australian Journal of Politics and History*, 49: 3, 398–411.

McCormick, J.P. (1999), *Carl Schmitt's Critique of Liberalism. Against Politics as Technology* (Cambridge: Cambridge University Press).

Moltmann, J. (1974), *The Crucified God: The Cross of Christ as the Foundation and Criticism of Christian Theology* (trans. R. Wilson and J. Bowden) (London: SCM Press).

Orr, S. (1995), *Jerusalem and Athens: Reason and Revelation in the Work of Leo Strauss* (Lanham, MD: Rowman and Littlefield).

Pocock, J.G.A. (1973), *Politics, Language and Time* (New York: Athenaeum).

Rawls, J. (1971), *A Theory of Justice* (Oxford: Oxford University Press).

Sen, A. (1999), 'Democracy as a Universal Value', *Journal of Democracy* 10: 3, 3–17.

Stout, J. (2004), *Democracy and Tradition* (Princeton: Princeton University Press).

Thompson, W.D.J. Cargill (1984), *The Political Thought of Martin Luther* (Brighton: Harvester Press).

Wesley, J. (1998) [1774], 'Thoughts Upon Slavery', in G. Maddox (ed.), *Political Writings of John Wesley* (Bristol: Thoemmes).

West, C. (2004), *Democracy Matters. Winning the Fight Against Imperialism* (New York: Penguin).

Williams, Roger (1848) [1644], *The Bloudy Tenent of Persecution* (ed. Edward Bean Underhill) (London: J. Haddon).

Chapter 10

Democratic Leadership

Haig Patapan

Countries in transition to democracy face numerous obstacles and challenges. Securing democratic institutions and the new principles of representation, accountability and the rule of law are perhaps the most obvious. The more subtle and complex concern the attempts at accommodating and reconciling powerful traditions, rich cultural heritage and religious beliefs with democratic practices. Indonesia, in transition to democracy, has certainly confronted many of these difficulties and, due to prudent leadership, is successfully negotiating a stable transition. What may be less evident to countries in transition to democracy, however, is that the leadership that facilitates such transitions may have to redefine itself in a democracy; put differently, that democracies mandate a unique democratic form of leadership. But what is this form of democratic leadership? In posing this question, we are struck by the fact that although there is an extensive scholarship on democracy and on leadership, *democratic leadership* has received little scholarly attention (see Kane, Patapan and Wong 2008; Burns 1978; 2003; Mughan and Patterson 1992; Kellerman 1986; Edinger 1976; Elcock 2001; Ruscio 2004; and Miroff 2000). One reason for this is that those scholars who took leadership seriously, the so-called 'elite' theorists, indicated the fundamentally undemocratic consequences of leadership in democracy (see, generally, Pareto 1935; Mosca 1939; Michels 1962). That leadership was necessary but necessarily undermined democracy explained, in part, the reluctance of other democrats to confront directly the theme of leadership. The response by democratic scholars to these elite theorists has been to ignore leadership altogether, suggesting that different forms of democracy – deliberative, participative, associational, and so on – do away with the need for leadership in democracies.[1] Thus between a scholarship that emphasizes the impossibility of democratic leadership, and another that implicitly claims that leadership is not necessary provided 'true' democracy is instituted, the very serious and the important topic of democratic leadership has not been addressed.

If leadership is important in democracies, what sort of leadership is made possible by democracy? What types of leaders does it favour? How does it shape and limit its leaders? These are the questions that we explore in this chapter. We do so not

---

1 For an analysis of this scholarship, see Kane and Patapan (2008) and, more generally, the literature on direct democracy (Pateman 1970; Barber 1984; Held 1996); associative democracy (Hain 1983; Hirst 1994; Cohen and Rogers 1995; Giddens 1998); deliberative democracy (Elster 1998; Cohen 1989; Dryzck 1990; 2000; Habermas 1987; 1996; Guttman and Thompson 1996; 2004).

simply because these are pressing questions for countries that are in transition to democracy, but also because of the larger theoretical significance of these questions, both to the study of good leadership, and of democracy.[2] Our examination of the nature of democratic leadership is warranted by the ubiquity and moral authority of democracy.[3] That democracy is the only standard for judging regimes, and that all regimes claim democratic credentials, makes it difficult for us to realize that historically democracy is a late-comer. If anything, history favours monarchy and empire as the seemingly natural forms of political association. Moreover, the modern dominance of democracy tends to discourage reflection on those other regimes that vied with democracy for authority – regimes based on excellence (aristocracy), honour (timocracy), wealth (oligarchy). Thus in asking the question of democratic leadership, we are also retrieving a philosophical tradition that understood politics in terms of regimes rather than contractual settlements.[4]

What are those fundamental aspects of democratic regimes that have significant implications for leadership? Here, it is necessary to distinguish between classical democracy and modern democracy. In classical political thought the core feature of democracy, its primary animating principle or idea, is freedom. This idea of freedom, however, is fundamentally political, based on the notion of who belongs to the city or the idea of citizenship. Thus in classical political thought, the 'free-born' of the city (as opposed to those vanquished in wars and therefore the enslaved) claimed freedom to be the pre-eminent good, defining democracy as the best regime for those who were by nature free.[5] Because democracy is founded on freedom, it is open to the various political claims made by the other regimes (based, for example, on the idea of wealth or honour). Thus democracy does not instruct its citizens the way other regimes impose their principles – freedom in democracy allows room for those principles that define other regimes. Consequently, democrats will claim the right to enjoy their own pleasures and desires, opinions and judgements, habits and conventions. The democrat, according to Socrates in Plato's *Republic* (561c-d):

---

2 On the importance of elites in democratic transitions, see O'Donnell, Schmitter and Whitehead 1986; Karl and Schmitter 1991. For attempts to combine both structural and agency perspectives, see Diamond 1993; Linder and Bächtiger 2005.

3 In what has been called the 'third wave' of democracy of the late twentieth century (Huntington 1991), the spread of democratic government has been quite remarkable. For example, in 1974, 39 countries (26.9 per cent of all) were electoral democracies; by 1997 the number was 117 (61.3 per cent) (Diamond 1999, 25).

4 For democracy as a 'regime' rather than the form of the executive (per Hobbes and modern social contract theorists), see the classical formulations of Plato, Aristotle, Cicero and its modern variants in the works of Montesquieu, Tocqueville and Bryce. For a recent example of scholarship that employs the concept of regime, see McCarthy (2006).

5 See, generally, Plato, *Republic* Book VIII (Plato 1968); Aristotle, *Politics* Books 1, 4 (Aristotle 1984).

> ... lives along day by day, gratifying the desire that occurs to him, at one time drinking and listening to the flute, at another downing water and reducing; now practicing gymnastic, and again idling and neglecting everything; and sometimes spending his time as though he were occupied with philosophy. Often he engages in politics and, jumping up, says and does whatever chances to come to him; and if he ever admires any soldiers, he turns in that direction; and if it's money-makers, in that one. And there is neither order nor necessity in his life, but calling this life sweet, free, and blessed he follows it throughout.

This freedom appears noble because it is a type of independence and self-sufficiency. Importantly, it is this freedom, permitting and sustaining a variety of views, lives and regimes, that makes democracy particoloured and beautiful.

Modern democracies, in addition to the principle of political freedom, are founded on the idea of natural rights.[6] Consequently, the classical understanding of freedom coexists in modern democracies with the idea of liberty and liberalism, of freedom not founded simply on political considerations (such as citizenship) but on transpolitical foundations such as autonomy and dignity. An important implication of this for our discussion is that, although freedom is the animating principle of both classical democracy and modern liberal democracy, the way democracy understands and defines leadership will differ, based on the differing sources of the notion of 'freedom'.

'We the People'

The beauty and nobility of democracy – the diversity and variety it fosters – has significant consequences for rule and leadership. At best, the freedom encouraged by democracy results in an ambivalence regarding the merits of political life – politics is no different from the other choices, of idleness and pleasure, money-making or honour-seeking. In addition to a certain ambivalence, democratic freedom may also lead to a rejection of politics because it is an imposition upon one's independence and therefore a limitation on freedom. Thus democrats will be suspicious of those who seek political office, judging them as opportunists who will exploit public funds or as potentially dangerous oppressors.[7] In this light, one can argue that the animating principle of modern democracy is in profound tension with political life, and in particular, rule and authority – that at the core of democratic politics is an ambivalence, or indeed a distrust, of political rule and leadership.[8] Put in other words, the principal problem of leadership in democracies is its very legitimacy.

---

6 As Tocqueville (2000) notes in *Democracy in America*, this notion has its source in the theological debates that introduced dogmatism into politics.

7 This accounts for two aspects of modern democracies – the low regard people generally have for politicians (see, for example, Inglehart 1997; Putnam 2000; Gidengil et al. 2004), and the extraordinary public concern with misuse of even small amounts of public funds (see, for example, the recent enactment of 'codes of conduct': Fleming and Holland 2001).

8 One can argue that democracy is the exception, that the other regimes implicitly adopt a principle of rule and therefore are more open to leadership. For example, oligarchy

How can the principles of freedom and leadership be reconciled? The democratic answer to this problem of articulating freedom as a political principle is to turn to a different principle, equality. This is a natural move because the logic of equality lies at the core of the principle of freedom. In classical democratic thought one can almost say that equality is contemporaneous with the claims for freedom – 'equality' is the first claim of the democrat. In liberal democracies the argument is well known: if I respect freedom then I must respect it in others who may exercise their freedom differently from me. Thus my endorsement and defence of freedom demands that I, at the very least, mute my criticism of the choices made by others. More generously, it requires that I concede the equal worth of those choices. Thus democratic freedom leads to democratic equality, as a matter of principle (all freedom must be defended), and as a matter of liberal prudence (such compromise will also assure my freedom).

Freedom, and now equality, become the animating, though not simply harmonious, principles of democracy. More specifically, freedom and equality are of necessity the theoretical foundation for all democratic leadership. But the need to introduce equality to implement freedom compromises it, thereby challenging and undermining the legitimacy of all leadership in democracy. Leadership thus has a curious place in democracies. It is always questionable yet always necessary. This tension can be seen in two democratic attempts to solve the problem of rule and leadership – direct rule and ruling in turn.

The one obvious way to preserve freedom is to have all rule – direct democracy seems to be the most democratic solution to the problem of freedom. It solves the problem of leadership by making all leaders, assuming all are equally capable of rule. It soon becomes clear, however, that all cannot rule. There are practical reasons for this: all cannot dedicate all their time to rule; some, not all, need to bring matters on for consideration, shaping the agenda; all will not always speak with a united voice. The democratic compromises of a parliament (that reconvenes rather than being in continuous authority), appointment of executives who will convene and dissolve parliament as well as initiating motions (for review by all), and majority rule (however 'majority' is defined) undermines the legitimacy of direct rule and of those 'leaders' who facilitate the will of all.[9] Importantly, rule by all as a solution to the problem of democratic leadership mandates small democracies, leading to instability and insecurity.[10]

The other pre-eminently democratic solution to the problem of leadership is the principle of ruling in turn. Ruling in turn solves a number of problems we discern in direct democracy by acknowledging them as strengths. Ruling in turn defends the

---

favours rule that endorses the principle of wealth – the best money-maker or the wealthy are entitled to rule according to the principles of that regime.

9 For the most sophisticated analysis of this problem, see Rousseau's *Social Contract* (1978) where he attempts to preserve the will of all without compromising individual freedom.

10 See the discussion in *The Federalist Papers* (Hamilton, Madison and Jay 1982) regarding representative democracy as a major modern innovation in republican thought that overcomes the dangers and instability of ancient small republics.

freedom and equality of all by allowing all to rule, not at the same time but serially, appropriating and overcoming what appeared to be a problem in direct democracy, the executive. Ruling in turn concedes the democrats' general ambivalence about the merits of politics by sharing the burden of office and letting others rule. Finally, ruling in turn makes possible representative government and therefore large democracies. Though resolving a number of problems, this solution to democratic leadership raises a range of new concerns. Ruling in turn is clearly only an approximation or compromise of people ruling for themselves, ironically something democrats do not want to do. That another will lead me, albeit for now, and until I take over, points to representative democracy.[11] Representative democracy introduces the considerable theoretical problems of representation, such as consent, agency and mandate, and reveals the uneasy status of leaders in such democracies. Is my leader my agent or trustee? Do I authorize or mandate all or only some of my agent's decisions? If trustee, do I accept that some are superior in leadership and thereby question the principle of ruling in turn? Accordingly representative democracy, in conceding the need for leadership by a few of the many, makes possible the idea of superior leadership, implicitly challenging the democratic principles of freedom and equality. Ruling in turn justifies democratic leadership but it is an uneasy, tenuous justification precisely because it seems to challenge those principles that animate democratic politics.

These reflections point to important aspects of democratic leadership. Leadership, at tension with the democratic principle of freedom, tends to be addressed in democracies as a matter of process rather than substance – rotation and representation are procedural means for resolving the problem of who should rule. As a consequence most debates on leadership in democracies are less about the merits of the leader or the action proposed and more on whether the process is suitable; for example, is it 'transparent'? Is it inclusive? And so on. Process tends to replace substance because the substance – rule – is an intractable democratic problem.

Moreover, the coexistence of the principles of freedom and of equality and the willingness of democrats to 'see' equality more clearly than freedom poses a problem that is a continuing theme of political thought: democratic egalitarianism is as open to direct democracy as it is to rule by one. The potential of democracy to fragment into tyranny, in the classical sense, or in the modern Tocquevillian sense of bureaucratic soft-despotism, is due primarily to the compromise of freedom with equality.

Finally, the many attempts to implement freedom as a political principle, and their varied though ultimately unsuccessful outcomes, point to an unavoidable fact about leadership in democracy: it is fundamentally prone to accusations of illegitimacy. That there is no democratic solution to the problem of leadership – all such attempts compromise democratic freedom – accounts for the perennial democratic political debates concerning participation, consultation, populism, strong leadership and elitism.

---

11 On the extensive literature on these themes, see, for example, Pitkin (1967); Manin (1997).

Democratic Leadership

The discussion above is intended to show the important ways in which democracy defines and shapes its leaders. In addition to the foundational question of the legitimacy of any leadership, democratic politics has significant implications for leadership in a number of important areas. It is not possible to do justice to the complexity of these themes in this context. It is useful, however, to sketch the more important ways in which democracy defines leadership. These include the problem of law and bureaucracy, commerce, ethics and international relations.

Bounded Leaders and Administrators

The questionable status of leadership and authority in democracy gives rise to two divergent tendencies regarding democratic leadership. One acknowledges the need for leadership, and even argues that leaders have special skills and talents that may require significant discretion in the exercise of authority. In conceding these principles, democracy demands that such authority be held responsible or accountable. The 'bounded leader' is the natural consequence of this concern. Leadership is bounded principally by law, specifically by the rule of law, constitutionalism, separation of powers, and ideas of fundamental rights and freedoms.[12] The 'legalization of politics', that includes judicial politics as well as an evolving international legal regime, points to the unique democratic demands placed on modern leadership (see Montesquieu 1989; Hamilton, Madison and Jay 1982; Russell and O'Brien 2001; Zifcak 2005). At the same time, the democratic ambivalence regarding leadership tends to relegate the leader to no more than a bureaucrat, reducing politics to nothing more than technical administration. Leadership as administration means that technical, incremental and bureaucratic solutions leave little room for individual leadership, discretion and prudence, reducing the leader to a sort of social scientist who uses the modern sciences of statistics, demographics and related disciplines to order the regime.[13] The dynamic tension between these two tendencies contributes, in part, to the contested nature of leadership in democracies.

Chief Economist

Freedom provides the link between democracy and commerce. The freedom that is the foundational principle of the regime inevitably justifies economic as well as political freedom. Combined with the observation that the desires of the many in democracy are those that can largely be satisfied by money, it soon becomes clear that democracy tends towards commercial freedom. The significance of this for leadership can be seen more clearly when we note that the equality and individualism that is a major part of modern democracies makes desire for well-being intense

---

12 We cannot explore in this context the extent to which these measures may be said to be different for classical and liberal democracies.

13 For an examination of the problem of prudence in modern managerial reforms, see Kane and Patapan (2006).

and permanent. The painful realization of unequal wealth and the importance of 'this-worldly' prosperity justify a competition for comforts that appears to have no obvious end point. This frantic competition defines the nature of success – financial rather than political – and elevates commerce, making it the measure of politics. This has important implications for leadership. The depreciation of the political in democracies has the serious consequence of making the people even more unpolitical. Thus the democratic leader, who is now judged in economic terms and has to speak to the people as an economist, finds it difficult to engage the people politically.[14] At the same time, the people who eschew politics as unprofitable judge it as a sort of business, but demand that the leader not profit from office. Democratic leadership becomes a competition based on promises of prosperity and accusations of financial mismanagement. Budgeting becomes the new political accountability.

Moral Leader

There is of course another form of accountability in democracies: the democratic leader has to be an ethical and moral leader (see, generally, Kane 2001). But what are the precise contours of this form of accountability? The foundational principle of freedom defines morality in democracies – we are free to make moral choices. This understanding tends to dismiss arguments based on necessity as excuses by the weak, lazy or corrupt. It accounts for the indignation – the moral fevers and demonizations – that sometimes afflict democracies. Thus democracies tend to high moralism in political matters, expecting their leaders to represent, and be, the 'best'.

The best for democrats is understood in terms of individual morality; it is personal morality that is the measure of politics in democracies.[15] In not distinguishing between the personal and the political, democrats gauge and evaluate political action in terms they understand – truth-telling, fidelity, consistency, sacrifice, compassion, generosity, even piety.[16] Importantly, freedom, and the dignity of free moral choice, demands that persuasion, not fear, is the basis of democratic politics. Democratic leaders need to argue, debate, even cajole but never threaten citizens. Taken together these demands impose a very high personal standard on the democratic leader that is generally at odds with political life, where lies, compromises and changing of alliances is political currency. The distance between these two worlds necessitates a sort of politics of hypocrisy (Grant 1997), where the democratic politician continues to be political while attempting (or seeming) to rise above the fray.

These considerations become acute when a democratic leader has to negotiate international relations. The unsavoury, albeit necessary, aspects of international

14 See, in this respect, Putnam's attempt, applying Tocqueville, to revive 'social capital' in democracies (Putnam 2000).

15 This may be at tension, of course, with the liberal notion that demarcates politics between the 'private' and 'public'. Therefore certain standards of morality may not apply to public figures if they can show that the relevant matter was in some sense 'private'. In this context, consider, for example, the failed attempt to impeach President Clinton.

16 The piety is not simply 'religious' – it can refer to 'sacred limits' concerning, for example, the honouring of parents, treatment of the dead.

relations, ranging from spying to the possibility of pre-emptive war, challenge the tendency of democracy to favour peace, stability and virtuous rule.[17] In his *Discourses on Livy* (Book I, chapter 59), Machiavelli (1992) commends the 'slow motion' and honesty of the many when he recounts the proposal put to the Athenians by Themistocles. Themistocles told Aristides, the people's representative, that the entire Greek fleet, which they held in good faith, could easily be gained and destroyed, making the Athenians all-powerful. Aristides reported to the people that Themistocles' policy was 'very useful but very dishonest'. On this basis the people refused it. That democratic politics is fundamentally 'moral', imposing considerable demands and requirements on its leaders, suggests that in international relations a different rhetoric is demanded of the democratic leader, one that will have to negotiate the moral and the useful.

Leadership in Democracies

The discussion above is no more than an indication of the important ways in which the democratic leader is different from leaders in other regimes. We have not examined, for example, the greater powers enjoyed by democratic leaders, and significantly, the unique problems faced by leaders in regimes in transition to democracy. Transitional democracies confront many obstacles – institutional, traditional and religious – in their attempts to adopt democratic practices. What we have suggested in this chapter is that in confronting these formidable and sometimes intractable difficulties, it may be easy to overlook fundamental tensions within democracy itself. To the extent that leadership is important in the transition to democracy, then the problem of democratic leadership is one of these foundational problems that need to be confronted and understood. The power, legitimacy and authority of democracy is now conceded by all. An understanding of the unique demands and requirements which it imposes on its leaders is only now being recognized as essential for both promoting and sustaining democracy. The need to explore the realities of leadership is even more pressing in the case of Indonesia, which has relied so significantly on its leaders in the transition to democracy. Importantly, the nature of democratic leadership in Indonesia is complicated by the powerful demands of religion; the democratic leader in Indonesia will have to reconcile and accommodate the legitimate claims of religion, without sacrificing the core demands of democratic governance. Whatever the basis of such reconciliation, it is evident that a clearer appreciation of the character of leadership in democracies is an important starting point for securing both stable democratic rule and prudent statesmanship.

References

Aristotle (1984) [350 BC], *Politics* (trans. with introduction, notes and glossary) (Chicago: University of Chicago Press).

17 Note, however, that the democratic tendency to favour democratic regimes impels it towards an international political agenda that demands it abandon simple pacifism.

Barber, B. (1984), *Strong Democracy* (Berkeley: University of California Press).

Burns, J.M. (1978), *Leadership* (New York: Harper Colophon).

Burns, J.M. (2003), *Transforming Leadership* (New York: Atlantic Monthly Press).

Cohen, J. (1989), 'The Economic Basis of Deliberative Democracy', *Social Philosophy and Policy* 6: 2, 25–50.

Cohen, J. and Rogers, J. (1995), *Associations and Democracy* (New York: Verso).

Diamond, L. (ed.) (1993), *Political Culture and Democracy in Developing Countries* (Boulder: Lynne Rienner Publishers).

Diamond, L. (1999), *Developing Democracy: Toward Consolidation* (Baltimore: Johns Hopkins University Press).

Dryzek, J.S. (1990), *Discursive Democracy: Politics, Policy and Political Science* (New York: Cambridge University Press).

Dryzek, J.S. (2000), *Deliberative Democracy and Beyond: Liberals, Critics, Contestations* (Oxford: Oxford University Press).

Edinger, L.J. (ed.) (1976), *Political Leadership in Industrialized Societies* (Huntington, NY: R.E. Krieger Publishing).

Elcock, H. (2001), *Political Leadership* (Cheltenham, UK: Edward Elgar).

Elgie, R. (1995), *Political Leadership in Liberal Democracies* (London: Macmillan).

Elster, J. (ed.) (1998), *Deliberative Democracy* (Cambridge: Cambridge University Press).

Fleming, J. and Holland, I. (eds) (2001), *Motivating Ministers to Morality* (Aldershot: Ashgate Publishing).

Giddens, A. (1998), *The Third Way: The Renewal of Social Democracy* (Malden, MA: Blackwell).

Gidengil, E., Blais, A., Nevitte, N. and Nadeau, R. (2004), *Citizens* (Vancouver: UBC Press).

Grant, R. (1997), *Hypocrisy and Integrity: Machiavelli, Rousseau and the Ethics of Politics* (Chicago: University of Chicago Press).

Guttman, A. and Thompson, D. (1996), *Democracy and Disagreement: Why Moral Conflict Cannot Be Avoided and What Can Be Done About It* (Harvard: Harvard University Press).

Guttman, A. and Thompson, D. (2004), *Why Deliberative Democracy?* (Princeton, NJ: Princeton University Press).

Habermas, J. (1987), *The Theory of Communicative Action* (trans. Thomas McCarthy) (Boston: Beacon Press).

Habermas, J. (1996), *Between Facts and Norms: Contributions to a Discourse Theory of Law and Democracy* (Cambridge, MA: MIT Press).

Hain, P. (1983), *The Democratic Alternative: A Socialist Response to Britain's Crisis* (Harmondsworth: Penguin).

Hamilton, A., Madison, J. and Jay, J. (1982) [1788], *The Federalist Papers* (ed. G. Wills) (New York: Bantam).

Held, D. (ed.) 1996), *Prospects for Democracy* (Cambridge: Polity Press).

Hirst, P. (1994), *Associative Democracy: New Forms of Economic and Social Governance* (Cambridge: Polity Press).

Huntington, S.P. (1991), *The Third Wave: Democratisation in the Late Twentieth Century* (Norman: University of Oklahoma Press).

Inglehart, R. (1997), *Modernization and Postmodernization: Cultural, Economic and Political Change in 43 Countries* (Princeton: Princeton University Press).

Kane, J. (2001), *The Politics of Moral Capital* (New York: Cambridge University Press).

Kane, J. and Patapan, H. (2006), 'In Search of Prudence: The Hidden Problem of Managerial Reform', *Public Administration Review* 66: 5, 711–24.

Kane, J. and Patapan, H. (2008), 'The Challenge of Dissident Democratic Leadership', in J. Kane, H. Patapan and B. Wong (eds), *Dissident Democrats: The Challenge of Democratic Leadership in Asia* (New York: Palgrave).

Karl, T.L. and Schmitter, P. (1991), 'Modes of Transitions in Latin America, Southern Europe and Eastern Europe', *International Social Science Journal* 128, 269–84.

Kellerman, B. (1986), *Political Leadership: A Sourcebook* (Pittsburgh, PA.: University of Pittsburgh Press).

Linder, W. and Bächtiger, A. (2005), 'What Drives Democratisation in Asia and Africa?', *European Journal of Political Research* 44, 861–80.

Machiavelli, N. (1992) [1513–17], *Discourses On Livy* (trans. Harvey C. Mansfield Jr and Nathan Tarcov) (Chicago: University of Chicago Press).

Manin, B. (1997), *The Principles of Representative Government* (Cambridge: Cambridge University Press).

McCarthy, S. (2006), *The Political Theory of Tyranny in Singapore and Burma* (London and New York: Routledge).

Michels, R. (1962) [1915], *Political Parties: A Sociological Study of the Oligarchical Tendencies of Modern Democracy, with an introduction by Seymour Martin Lipset* (trans. Eden and Cedar Paul) (New Brunswick, NJ: Transaction Publishers).

Miroff, B. (2000), *Icons of Democracy: American Leaders as Heroes, Aristocrats, Dissenters, and Democrats* (Lawrence, KA: University Press of Kansas).

Montesquieu (1989) [1752], *The Spirit of the Laws* (trans. and ed. Anne M. Cohler, Basia C. Miller and Harold S. Stone) (Cambridge: Cambridge University Press).

Mosca, G. (1939), *The Ruling Class* (trans. H.D. Kahn) (New York: McGraw-Hill).

Mughan, A. and Patterson, S.C. (eds) (1992), *Political Leadership in Democratic Societies* (Chicago: Nelson-Hall).

O'Donnell, G., Schmitter, P.C. and Whitehead, L. (eds) (1986), *Transitions from Authoritarian Rule–Comparative Perspectives* (Baltimore: Johns Hopkins University Press).

Pareto, V. (1935), *Mind and Society* (trans. A. Livingston) (New York: McGraw-Hill).

Pateman, C. (1970), *Participation and Democratic Theory* (Cambridge: Cambridge University Press).

Pitkin, H.F. (1967), *The Concept of Representation* (Berkeley: University of California Press).

Plato (1968) [360 BC], *Republic* (trans. Allan Bloom) (New York: Basic Books).

Przeworski, A. (1998), 'Deliberation and Ideological Domination', in J. Elster (ed.), *Deliberative Democracy* (Cambridge: Cambridge University Press).

Przeworski, A. (2000), *Democracy and Development: Political Institutions and Well-*

being in the World, 1950–1990 (New York, NY: Cambridge University Press).

Putnam, R.D. (1993), *Making Democracy Work: Civic Traditions in Modern Italy* (Princeton: Princeton University Press).

Putnam, R.D. (2000), *Bowling Alone: The Collapse and Revival of American Community* (New York: Simon & Schuster).

Rousseau, Jean Jacques (1978) [1762], *On the Social Contract with Geneva Manuscript and Discourse on Political Economy*, (ed. R. Masters and trans. J. Masters) (New York: St Martin's Press).

Ruscio, K. (2004), *The Dilemma of Democratic Leadership* (London: Edward Elgar).

Russell, P.H. and O'Brien, D.M. (eds) (2001), *Judicial Independence in the Age of Democracy: Critical Perspectives from Around the World* (Charlottesville: University Press of Virginia).

Tocqueville, A. de (2000), *Democracy in America* (trans. and ed. H.C. Mansfield and D. Winthrop) (Chicago: University of Chicago Press).

Yeltsin, B.N. (2000), *Midnight Diaries* (trans. C.A. Fitzpatrick) (New York: Public Affairs).

Zifcak, S. (ed.) (2005), *Globalisation and the Rule of Law* (London: Routledge).

Chapter 11

Islamic Perspectives on Citizenship and Statehood

N.A. Fadhil Lubis

It is now widely agreed that comparative studies of Islamic and Western traditions on citizenship may help to bridge the differences between us. However, some key concepts need to be clarified before a fruitful dialogue can start. My discussion in this chapter is from the perspective of the Sunni tradition, and I draw on the chief judge and influential figure of the late Abbasid dynasty, al-Mawardi, in particular for my exposition. The substance of my argument is that the four classical sources of Islamic law, namely the prophetic traditions (the *Qur'an*, the *Sunnah*), consensus (*Ijma'*), and analogical reasoning (*qiyas*) provide indications from which an Islamic account of citizenship can be constructed. Apart from traditional materials pertaining to membership of a community, however, critical use can also be made of positive regulative frameworks clarifying the relationship between citizenship and the state.

Ummah: Muslim Community

Often translated as 'Muslim community', the term *ummah* occurs 64 times in the *Qur'an*. Most studies of the *Qur'anic* concept of *ummah* assert that the term designates a people to whom God sends a prophet, or a people who are objects of a divine plan of salvation. According to these studies, the term *ummah* refers to a single group sharing some common religious orientation. In *Qur'anic* usage, however, the connotations of community and religion do not always converge, and the word has multiple and diverse meanings.

In several instances, *ummah* refers to an unrestricted group of people. Verse 28:23, for example, reads: 'And when he (Moses) came to the water of Madyah, he found on it a group of people (*ummah min al-nas*) watering.' The term can also mean a specific religion or the beliefs of a certain group of people (43:22–23); or an exemplar of faith, as in the reference to Abraham as an '*ummah*, obedient to God' (16:120). *Ummah* also refers to the followers of prophets: 'For every *ummah* there is an apostle' (10:470); to a group of people adhering to a specific religion: 'To each one of you We have appointed a law and a pattern of life. If God had pleased He could surely have made you all a single *ummah*' (5:48); to a smaller group within the larger community of adherents: 'They are not all alike; among the people of the Book is an upright *ummah*' (3:113); to the followers of Muhammad who are charged with a special responsibility: 'And thus We have made you a medium *ummah* that you may be the bearers of witness to the people and that the Apostle may be a bearer of witness to you' (2:143); or to a sub-group of these followers: 'So there be an *ummah* among you who may call to good, enjoin what is right and forbid the wrong, and these it is that shall be successful' (3:104).

Ummah often denotes a misguided group of people: 'Were it not that all people would be a single *ummah,* We would certainly have allocated to those who disbelieve in the Beneficent God (to make) of silver the roofs of their houses and the stairs by which they ascend' (43:33); or a misguided party from among the followers of a prophet: 'And on the day when We will gather from every *ummah* a party from among those who rejected Our communications, then they shall be formed into groups' (27:83); or 'Then We sent Our apostles one after the other; whenever there came to an *ummah* their apostle, they called him a liar, so We made one follow the other (to its dooms)', and 'We turned them into bygone tales' (23:44). Finally, *ummah* could mean a period of time: 'And if We hold back from them the punishment until a stated *ummah*/period of time, they will say' (11:8); it can also mean an order of being: 'And there is no animal that walks upon the earth nor a bird that flies with its two wings but they are an *ummah* like yourself' (6:38).

The rudimentary concept of the *ummah,* however, is complemented by the narrower concept of the *ummah* of believers. This is the 'medium *ummah*' (2:143), which is further qualified in the *Qur'an* as: 'the best *ummah* evolved for mankind, enjoining what is good, forbidding what is wrong, and believing in God' (3:110) (see also 4:41 and 16:89). This specific *ummah,* or the followers of Muhammad, is further differentiated from the followers of earlier messengers and prophets; whereas the latter's sphere of influence is restricted to particular peoples, the former scope is all humanity. When referring to prophets before Muhammad, the *Qur'an* says, 'to every *ummah* we have sent an apostle (saying) Worship God' (16:36) (see also 10:47). In reference to Muhammad, however, the *Qur'an* adds, 'Say O men, I am verily the apostle of God to you all' (7:158). In this way the universality of Muhammad's mission was asserted, and the 'medium *ummah*' took on the central role in the fulfilment of this mission after him.

The Constitution of Medina

With respect to citizenship, classical judgement by and large reflected the pattern evidenced in the Constitution of Medina or the agreement between the Prophet and the various groups living in the city. Under this Constitution, the Muslims and those who followed them, joined them and laboured with them were regarded as one community to the exclusion of others. The Jews of Medina were said to constitute a distinct community with their own religion. They were 'protected' by the Muslims in the sense that they were free to follow their own sacred texts and laws, within limits indicated by the security needs of the Muslims.

The occasional rift between the civil and religious notions of *ummah* in *Qur'anic* usage has parallels in the *hadith* literature. In several traditions, Muhammad is said to use 'my *ummah*' to mean the group related to him by lineage rather than by religion. It is the *hadith* literature, however, that provides the concept of *ummah* with its precise and focused meaning. Besides the *Qur'an*, the earlier extant source available is a set of documents written by Muhammad shortly after his arrival at Medina. These documents, commonly referred to in modern scholarship as the Constitution of Medina, comprise several practical provisions designed to regulate social and political life under Islam. Most scholars agree that the main purport of the Constitution was political, and not religious. It defined treaty relations between the different groups inhabiting Medina and its environs, including the Muslim tribes of Medina, Muslims who emigrated from Mecca, and Jews.

The Constitution starts with the pronouncement that all these groups constitute 'one distinct community (*ummah*) apart from other people'. In the 47 clauses of the Constitution, the term *ummah* appears in only one other instance, when the Jews of Banu 'Awf are said to constitute 'an *ummah* with the believers'. The same clause goes on to state that the Jews have their religion and the Muslims have theirs. The meaning of the term *ummah* in the Constitution is clearly not synonymous with religion. The Constitution also delineated relations of mutual aid among the different constituent tribal groups, actions to be taken against those who violate the terms of the agreement, and actions to be taken against the criminals belonging to the incipient community in Medina. Rather than supplanting or abolishing tribal bonds, the Constitution regulated relations among tribes, and between them and the outside world, on the basis of the higher order of the *ummah.*

While the Constitution of Medina seemed to sanction diversity within the Islamic *ummah*, the *Qur'an* sanctions differentiation among various *ummahs* as a norm decreed by God. *Qur'anic* verse 10:19 reads: 'People were once a single *ummah*; but they differed (and followed different ways). Had it not been for the word proclaimed by your lord before, their differences would have been resolved.' (See also 2:213, 5:48, 11:118, 16:93, and 42:8.) There is a sense, therefore, in which the concept of the *ummah* refers to an ideal state, an original all-encompassing unity that is always invoked but never completely recovered. In Islam, sovereignty belongs to God, and in Islamic history the caliph/sultan ruled over the Islamic community in accordance with *shan'a*, based on the *Qur'an* and the *Sunnah* (the traditions of the Prophet Muhammad).

Ideas dealing with equality of Muslim and non-Muslim subjects and the protection of rights in return for specific obligations to the state were clearly expressed by some Muslim intellectuals, such as Rifa'ah al-Tahtawi and Mehmed Sadik Rifat Pasha. Al-Tahtawi, in *Manahij al-Albab al-Misriyah fi Mabahij Adab al-'Asriyah* [Methods for Egyptian Minds on the Joys of Modem Manners], outlined the citizens' duties toward their country (Egypt) as well as their rights. He assigned an active role to the members of the political community. Said Rifat Pasha, in his monumental book, *Muntehabat-i 'Ast* [Selected Works], made frequent use of the term *hulk* (the people) and discussed the rights of subjects to liberty.

Islam also developed the general notion of a just ruler from very early on. A just ruler is one who first and foremost upholds the Islamic law (*shari'ah*), which for all practical purposes functions as the constitution of the Islamic state. In addition, the ruler is expected to defend the community, collect taxes, supervise the conduct of war, consult with leaders of the community and administer judicial and executive regulations. There are no clear-cut provisions for dismissing a ruler who violates these norms, however. In fact, concern with order is so strong that classical jurists had even rationalized tyrannical rule at times and judged it to be superior to chaos, and social and political disorder. However, such a view has not stopped frequent overthrows of political leaders and dynasties or the onset of upheavals, riots and revolutions. There has not often been a conjunction of theory and practice in this matter.

Community and State

Several classical concepts have traditionally facilitated the state–society relationship for Muslims. These include the need for the ruler to consult with the elders of the community (*shura*), adherence to the consensus within the community (*ijma'*) on relevant legal issues, some degree of allowance for independent inquiry (*ijtihad*), and fidelity to the pact between rulers and the ruled (*bay'a*). The meaning and relative importance of these concepts have been conditioned by historical and sectarian specificities. On the whole, however, they have had some degree of continued relevance to state–community relationships in Islamic societies.

In the Islamic worldview, a vibrant community needs the state in order to allow for full participation in public life. It is the state that provides protection, maintains legal order and safeguards the rights of individuals and groups. Traditionally Islam has been preoccupied with order and overwhelmingly fearful of chaos (*fitnah*). The mutual dependency of state and society is also well recognized in Islam, and a believing Muslim citizen is also expected to be involved in civic matters.

Citizenship

The Islamic approach to citizenship is more complex, and there are Islamicists such as Takfir wa l-Hijrah who exclude Muslims, rulers and otherwise, who do not fully share the Islamist's view on the organization of the polity. Even al-Mawardi, in his much-quoted book, *AI-Ahkam al-Sulwniyyah* [The Ordinance of Governance], does not devote a single sub-heading to citizenship. The first chapter is dedicated to discussing the head of state. The second is for ministers, followed by chapter three on provincial governors. The fourth chapter is on the commandant of the armed forces. The following chapters are on police, *qadhi* (*shari'ah*-based court), *mazhalim* (noble court of complaints), and the leaders of public prayers. It is very top-down.

The discussion on citizenship and statehood in the perspective of Islam may be better discerned through important concepts and terms used in Muslim tradition. There are two terms which especially pertain to the relationship between the ruler and the ruled. Those terms are *uli al-amri*, meaning one who manages the affairs, which is found in the *Qur'an*. The verse reads: 'O believers, obey God, obey the Prophet and those who manage affairs.' *Qur'anic* exegetes construe the verse as referring to *'ulama* (learned persons), *umara'* (army generals), sultan (secular kings) and as implying the priority and importance of each focus of loyalty. The first is loyalty to God which is absolute, secondly to the Prophet, in the sense of obeying his orders and avoiding his prohibitions. One may observe that for these two loyalties, the verse repeats the word *athi'u* (Be loyal/obey), while for the third, *uli al-amri*, it was only affixed by a preposition 'and', showing a less significant loyalty, compared to the first two. The structure of the verse gives an understanding that one may not follow a human leader if it means going against the loyalty to God and His Apostle. It gives a right of 'rebellion' to a sinful ruler, a ruler who orders his subjects to commit sin to his Creator.

The second term is *ahl al-hill wa al-'aqdi* (those who loose and bind), meaning the leaders of the community or the notables in any grouping. According to al-Mawardi, it is this *ahl al-hill wa al-'aqdi* who have the responsibility to appoint *uli al-amri.* This interpretation is closer to the modern idea of representative democracy, in which members of a community directly or indirectly appoint their leaders, and the leaders subsequently choose the top leader. According to al-Mawardi, these representatives of *ahl al-hill wa al-'aqdi* must fulfil at least three requirements: (a) possess personal credibility or uprightness *(al-' adalah)*; (b) have sufficient knowledge; and (c) be wise. Meanwhile, those who are appointed to be candidates for the head of state must fulfil at least seven requirements:

1. Be *Al-'adalah*, someone who does not commit *zhulm* (cruelty) and *fasiq* (big sins);
2. Have sufficient and relevant knowledge and skills;
3. Have fully functioning five senses;
4. Have no serious physical handicaps;
5. Have good vision;
6. Be courageous;
7. Be descendants of the Quraish tribe.

Modern Muslim scholars have interpreted the last requirement to mean anyone who has the capabilities of the Quraish tribe. In principle, the members of the Islamic community, the *ummah*, were all equal without deference to race, colour or ethnic background. In practice, however, from very early in Islamic history, during the rule of the Umayyad dynasty (661–750 CE), for instance, more than one class of subject emerged. The *mawali* (singular, *mawla*), or Muslims who were non-Arabs or not a full member by descent from an Arab tribe, did not receive equal economic and social benefits and were not fully accepted by the Arab aristocracy.

In later Islamic history it is harder to find a single authoritative pattern. During the rule of the 'Abbasid caliphs (750–1258), the practical social order of the Muslim *ummah* was central to the philosophy of the state. Nevertheless, Muslim philosophers and jurists, such as al-Farabi (d. 950) and al-Mawardi (d. 1058), raised fundamental questions regarding the relations between the ruler and the ruled and their mutual duties. In his *al-Madinah al-Fadila* [The Ideas of the Citizens of the Virtuous City], al-Farabi set the standards by which states should be judged. Later, during the Mamluk period, one of the most important Muslim philosopher/jurists, Ibn Taymiyyah (1263–1328), defined the criteria for 'just' rulers and the political and social obligations of the community. In all these expressions, the positions of the ruler and the subjects were placed within Islamic principles as interpreted by the *'ulama*, the learned, and membership in the *ummah* recognized no geographical boundaries.

A degree of pluralism was a prominent feature of Islamic governance in some periods. As is well known, in the Ottoman Empire (c. 1300–1918) from the mid-fifteenth century the population was organized into millets, legally recognized religious-communal organizations. The four millets, Greek Orthodox, Armenian, Jewish and Muslim, were differentiated according to their ecclesiastical affiliations, and not according to their ethnic and linguistic differences. With privileges granted by the ruler, the millets under religious leadership assumed a number of social and economic responsibilities. The leaders of the millets thus also had fairly extensive civil authority over the membership, including matters related to internal organizations, education and personal status. The millet system continued long into the nineteenth century – a period of intensive educational, military and administrative reforms commonly referred to as the Tanzimat (reorganization) era. With two major reform edicts in 1839 and 1856, the Ottoman government recognized and reaffirmed equality among its subjects and their rights to security of life, honour and property, preconditions to the modern concept of citizenship. The Ottoman subjects, however, at this time still identified themselves as members of the millets.

During the nineteenth century, various nationalist tendencies emerged in the Ottoman territories, and Islamic doctrine developed in order to respond to them. In 1869, the Ottoman government, in its efforts to provide a viable ideology for the unity of the Empire and to curb the interference of European powers and Russia in its domestic affairs, issued the law of nationality and naturalization. Article 1 of the law stated that all individuals born to an Ottoman father and mother, or only to an Ottoman father, are Ottoman subjects. Article 2 provided that all individuals born in Ottoman territories to parents of foreign nationality can, at the age of majority, claim Ottoman nationality. Other aspects of the law were in accordance with the principles of international conventions. For the remainder of the nineteenth century, Ottoman intellectuals, notably Namik Kemal (1840–81), discussed the nature of the political system and the individual's role within it. They recognized certain natural rights for citizens and argued for their preservation. Consistent with the Western liberal political tradition, these writers emphasized 'people's will' and the people's right to exercise sovereignty. At the beginning of the twentieth century, similar arguments were heard among Egyptian intellectuals, the nationalist Young Tunisians, and members of the Young Algerian movement.

From the early decades of the twentieth century, as modern nation states emerged, specific citizenship regimes were set up for Muslims and Islamic governments which defined the rights and duties of their citizens. In Turkey, the National Assembly, established in 1920, during the war of independence, by the nationalist government under Mustafa Kemal (later Ataturk), declared that 'sovereignty unconditionally belongs to the people', thus establishing a de facto republic before its official declaration in 1923. The deposition of the last Ottoman sultan in 1922 and the abolition of the caliphate in 1924 eliminated any legal basis for a challenge to a people's exercise of political will. The extension of full and equal franchise to women in 1934, permitting them to vote and stand for election, and giving them full political rights and duties, allowed all Turkish citizens to become active participants in the political process.

The Anglo-Egyptian Treaty of 1936 recognized Egypt's independence. As other Muslim countries gained their independence – for instance, Indonesia (1945), Transjordan (1946), Libya (1951), Tunisia and Morocco (1956), Algeria (1962) – each country established its own criteria for citizenship, based on its own political ideology, historical experience and social customs. Although some countries provided their citizens, men and women, Muslims or non-Muslims, with extensive political and social rights (for example, Egypt, Iraq and Indonesia), others (for example, Kuwait and Saudi Arabia) limited the privileges of citizenship. In Kuwait, two classes of citizenship are still in effect: first-class citizens, whose forebears lived in Kuwait before 1922; and second-class citizens, who belong to families that came to Kuwait between 1922 and 1945. Those individuals who arrived after 1945 are not considered for citizenship at all. Women who are Kuwaiti citizens are also disfranchised. In all instances, however, citizenship in Muslim countries is now defined with specific reference to national boundaries, not with regard to membership of the *ummah*.

This admixture of learned precedents and actual regulation means that the Islamic approach to citizenship is still relatively underdeveloped, especially with respect to areas which were not within the purview of theorists in the classical period. Muslims have a wealth of indications to draw upon, but they still have a great deal of work to do.

Conclusion

One of the most dynamic aspects of the Islamic revival during the past two centuries has been the rethinking of Islamic political thought. If one looks at the rich classical heritage of Islamic thought, especially in the field of Islamic legal tradition, Islamic sources, especially the *Qur'an* and the *Sunnah*, have sufficient principles plus a rich legacy of literature dealing with problems faced by Muslim communities. My point is that the classical literature arguably provides sufficiently rich sources for contemporary Indonesian Muslims to coherently respond to a significant range of problems. However, while it is important for Indonesian Muslims to approach the reinterpretation of Islamic teaching on the basis of divinely inspired and highly regarded Islamic sources and methodology, their work also needs to be enriched by insights and ideas from other traditions, especially the tradition of Western political thought. To strengthen our Islamic inheritance by learning from the West is not contrary to Islam. On the contrary, the Prophet explicitly encouraged his followers to seek knowledge even as far as China.

References

al-Farabi, *Abu Nasr* (1985) [870–950], *al-Madina al-Fadila [The Virtuous City]*, (trans. R. Walzer) [*Al-Farabi on the Perfect State: Abu Nasr al-Farabi's Mabadi' Ara Ahl al-Madina al-Fadila]* (Oxford: Clarendon Press).

al-Mawardi, Imam (2000), 'AI-Ahkam al-Sultaniyyah wa al-Wilayat al-Diniyah' [The Ordinance of Governance], in Terj. A.I. Kattani and Wafaa H. Wahba (eds), *Hukum Tata Negam don Kepemimpinan dalam Takamn Islam* (Jakarta: Gerna Insani).

Dallal, Ahmad S. (1995), 'Ummah', in John L. Esposito (ed.), *The Oxford Encyclopedia of the Modem Islamic World* 4, 267–70 (Oxford: Oxford University Press).

Donohue, John J. and Esposito, John L. (eds) (1982), *Islam in Transition: Muslim Perspectives* (Oxford: Oxford University Press).

Hashmi, Sohail H. (ed.) (2002), *Islamic Political Ethics: Civil Society, Pluralism, and Conflict* (Princeton: Princeton University Press).

Weber, Max (1976), *Politics as a Vocation* (trans. and ed. H. Geerth and C. Wright Mills) (New York: Oxford University Press).

Chapter 12

Towards a Conceptual Framework for Citizenship

Geoffrey Stokes

This chapter aims to provide a conceptual framework for discussing citizenship. It offers a brief account of various dimensions of citizenship that may be used as a guide to understanding the evolution of Western ideas and forms of citizenship, as well as contemporary problems with them. The chapter considers citizenship as a legal status, as an administrative category, as a political practice and as an ideal to be attained.[1] It also considers the sites or domains in which citizenship is or ought to be practised. Each of these dimensions raises questions that citizens, non-citizens and governments have asked over the centuries and that still provoke debate.[2] Nonetheless, the chapter makes no claim to be comprehensive and, for the sake of brevity, its generalizations may not be sufficiently sensitive to the many variations and peculiarities of Western concepts and practices of citizenship.

Citizenship as a Legal Status

Citizenship may be understood as a way of allocating and distributing civic rights and responsibilities. In the Western tradition, to be a citizen is first to be a member of a political community – real or imagined – in which one has access to particular resources (legal, material, symbolic), through the possession and exercise of rights, and in which one also has obligations to the polity. To be a citizen is to have an official legal status. Those without that status are denied certain kinds of rights and generally do not have to take on the same public responsibilities. This legal emphasis provides the foundation of the current, dominant, official, Western conception of citizenship whose origins lie in the ancient Roman republics. According to Pocock (1998, 37), a citizen of Rome 'came to mean someone free to act by law, free to ask the law's protection, a citizen of ... a legal community, of ... legal standing in that community'. Initial questions for this dimension are: Who is or can become a citizen? Who is excluded and why?

Over a long period of time, Western democracies have gradually expanded the categories of individuals allowed to become full citizens, usually indicated by the award of the vote. Where suffrage was originally granted to property holders, now

1 These terms are based upon a brief schema in Hudson and Kane (2000a, 5) and my own reflections.

2 For an application of this model to deliberative democracy, see Stokes (2006).

the working class, women and indigenous people are included. The growing numbers of asylum seekers and refugees around the globe have provoked much debate over criteria for inclusion. To be granted official citizenship status, individuals have often had to show that they meet certain qualifications or criteria, such as language proficiency, education levels, and so on. Such criteria are also often the grounds on which immigrants are allowed entry into countries, which may then enable them to gain full citizenship at a later date.

Whereas the dominant stories of citizenship tend to celebrate the triumphs of democratic inclusion over previous discriminations, inequities and injustices, other more critical accounts point to the complexity of the outcomes. Civic inclusion can mean incorporation into the routines of state, rather than political agency. The process of inclusion can also mean that the citizen relinquishes their previous cultural identities and values. Expanding regimes of citizenship often function to regulate and discipline the populations of states.

Citizenship as an Administrative Category

Citizenship is also an administrative category in which those individuals accorded the legal status of citizenship are ranked and ordered, and various rights, responsibilities and resources allocated to them. These tenets too are usually authorised by law. Whereas in the Roman republics the right to certain basic freedoms was central, in the contemporary Western world, these are almost taken for granted among citizens, and rights to different kinds of material support become important. In modern liberal democracies, for example, there exist complex administrative regimes that allow for the claiming of different kinds of rights to social security benefits and allowances (unemployment, single parents, child care, education) depending upon the assessed needs of the claimant. Often, differential responsibilities are also imposed. One of the most longstanding responsibilities of citizenship has been that of bearing arms to defend the nation state. Such rights and responsibilities are subject to political struggles over attempts to expand or curtail them. (Different administrative regimes apply also to those who are not citizens, but who may be granted permanent residence, or in the Australian case, where asylum seekers are given 'temporary protection visas'.) This account gives rise to key questions such as: What rights can be claimed by citizens? What are their obligations?

Here the work of T.H. Marshall is relevant. Marshall portrays the historical evolution of citizenship in the West and its extension into areas beyond the formally legal and political. He writes that, by the mid twentieth century, citizenship had come to comprise three parts, namely the civil, the political and the social (Marshall 1994 [1950], 173). The civil element refers to those basic legal rights 'necessary for individual freedom – liberty of the person, freedom of speech, thought and faith, the right to own property and to conclude valid contracts, and the right to justice'. Equality before the law and due legal process are crucial to the civil element. He takes the political element to mean 'the right to participate in the exercise of political power, as a member of a body invested with political authority or as an elector of the members of such a body'. Marshall's contribution is to draw attention to the social element, by which he means 'the whole range from the right to a modicum of economic welfare and security to the right to share to the full in the social heritage and to live the life of a civilized being according to the standards prevailing in the society'. Marshall sees the emergence of 'social citizenship' through the institutions of the welfare state as vital for political citizenship. Without the resources provided by education, health and social welfare, the poor are unlikely to be effective citizens in exercising their legal or political rights.

Although Marshall's historical generalizations have been contested, his categories do indicate a few of the areas in which expanding claims to citizenship rights have been made over the twentieth century. We may now add other kinds of citizenship to Marshall's categories, such as 'multi-cultural citizenship' in which ethnic minorities and indigenous peoples claim rights to retain culture, language and heritage (see Kane 2002). There is also widespread advocacy of an 'ecological citizenship' that focuses upon our responsibilities towards the environment (van Steenbergen 1994c, 142). It is now argued further, given the diversity of citizenship claims, that there can be no unified civic identity (Hudson 2000) and that 'differential citizenship' must be recognized within nation states.

Citizenship as a Political Practice

The foregoing examples suggest that citizenship denotes more than a legal status or administrative category: it is also a political practice, or a mode of participation in public life (van Steenbergen 1994b, 2). That is, citizenship is not so much defined by law as by how one conducts oneself in public affairs and in politics. For the ancient Athenians, politics in their small city-state was the activity of ruling and being ruled, and this activity was thought to be a good in itself, not just a means to the public good (Pocock 1998, 34). Nevertheless, to be a citizen was to be a male head of household who was free to participate in politics because his private, domestic responsibilities were carried out by women and slaves. As we have seen, in modern Western countries, the history of democracy has generally been a history of inclusion where exclusions simply based upon sex or race is no longer supported officially.

Paradoxically, as more categories of people have been recognized as citizens, the possibility for effective, direct political participation has tended to decrease. Given the size and complexity of modern mass liberal democracies, most citizens restrict their official participation in politics to voting in periodic elections. The main task of a citizen is that of electing representatives who will then vote along party lines to install political leaders and governments. Where low levels of citizen participation are seen as problematic, debates have occurred on how to increase participation and over what forms this should take. For example, the programmes of civic education and the advocacy of 'active citizenship' among Western governments in the 1990s were attempts to overcome the apparent deficiencies of 'passive citizenship'.[3]

3 See, for example, Civics Expert Group (1994), Advisory Group on Citizenship (1998).

Normative Dimensions of Citizenship

The issues considered above press us to acknowledge that the quality of political practice is significant. Discussions of citizenship therefore include a normative dimension concerning how citizens ought to behave. Different conceptions of citizenship may advocate different visions of an ideal civic identity and forms of political conduct. Key questions arising from this account include: What is the good citizen? What capacities and competencies are required to be a good citizen? Depending upon the answers given to such questions, different theories of citizenship become 'expressions of political possibility and imagination that transcend current practices' (Stokes 2002, 24). Normative conceptions of citizenship typically provide a source of critique of existing political, legal and administrative arrangements. Ideal civic values and identities can be invoked to suggest what is right or wrong or capable of improvement about current laws and practices of citizenship.

The normative force of most Western theories of citizenship usually derives from political theories of democracy, such as those based upon liberal, civic republican, developmental or deliberative principles (Stokes 2002, 27). That is, the ideals of citizenship will vary according to the theory of democracy in which it is located. The dominant model of democracy in the West is a liberal one that requires minimal citizen participation. Civic republican, developmental and deliberative theories, however, have posed practical challenges to liberal democracy by requiring more, and different kinds, of participation. This approach has meant that, to varying degrees, liberal democracies have incorporated different aspects of other theories. For example, in addition to liberal democratic political institutions, modern democracies maintain a welfare state inspired by developmentalist principles. Civic republican (Oldfield 1990) and deliberative values (see Uhr 1998) are also evident in both public debate and institutional practice.

Nevertheless, since the key civic activity of governing and being governed may be undertaken in democratic and undemocratic contexts, it is open to question about the form that the links with democracy may take and whether citizenship is necessarily democratic. Clearly, individuals under authoritarian regimes may be given the official legal status of citizenship, hold certain civic rights, and be bound to undertake civic duties. But the limits placed on political participation and expressions of consent and dissent would mean that this kind of citizenship could not be called democratic. Under such circumstances, democratic citizenship might be a political aspiration and guide to reform.[4]

Domains of citizenship

Ideas of consent, dissent and participation are necessarily linked to particular political sites, forums or domains in which citizenship can be claimed and practised. The first demarcation usually made is that between the public sphere and activities in private or personal moral life, though the former may have implications for the latter, and the boundaries may be difficult to draw. The language of citizenship is also traditionally

4 See the argument in Stokes (2004).

expressed with reference to the nation state or sub-national units within it. Since at least the work of de Tocqueville (1988, 189–93), however, it has increasingly been extended to other areas, such as civil society. Membership and participation in non-governmental organizations (NGOs) such as churches, voluntary service clubs and social movements are considered to be acts of citizenship.

In the context of historical struggles for industrial democracy, a vigorous form of industrial citizenship can be discerned that goes beyond the rights of workers to join unions and engage in collective bargaining for higher wages and improved conditions of work. Here, industrial citizenship is expressed by workers asserting their rights to manage and control aspects of their workplace. A more radical extension of this idea envisages workers jointly owning the corporation.[5] From within the business world itself, the term 'corporate citizenship' has emerged to describe the voluntary tendency among some corporations to undertake social and ecological responsibilities, as well as those to make profits (Moon, Crane and Matten 2005).

The discourse of citizenship has increasingly been applied to activities that include, but also reach beyond, the nation state. We can speak about nation states being bound by the norms of 'good international citizenship' (Williams 2002). This type of transnational citizenship is expressed by the participation of nation states in international institutions created to promote international principles, such as those of human rights and free trade. Another type of transnational citizenship arises when individuals are called upon to become 'global citizens' (Hutchings and Dannreuther 1999; Stokes 2000a). Self-ascribed 'citizens of the world' do not usually feel constrained primarily by the laws of their nation state, but obligated to higher principles of duty towards humankind. Global citizens may be motivated to action, for example, because they see their states failing to abide by international principles to which they are committed by membership in the United Nations. In this vein, 'ecological citizens' may believe that their first duty is to protect the earth as a sustainable ecosystem. The pursuit of citizen activism beyond the state raises issues about the shifting boundaries of the public sphere, and the limits of politics within it. Accordingly, we are led to ask: in what sites or locations can citizens act with effect?

Such a question inevitably requires us to canvass reservations expressed about the achievements of citizenship in the West. For all the educational initiatives, there is little evidence that citizens are more interested or active in formal party politics, though they may be participating more in non-party political activities or social movements. Despite being crucial to the conduct of democratic politics, legal and civil rights are never sacrosanct, and have to be constantly defended. In times of war, or crises of national security, such as in the so-called 'war on terror', the civil rights of citizens and non-citizens are routinely suspended. Conservative critics suggest that the growth of social rights has created greater welfare dependency, rather than the conditions for active political engagement.

For other critics, there is little possibility of achieving one of the fundamental objectives of citizenship, which is for them to make or influence political decisions. Barry Hindess (2000) has pointed out that the traditional language of citizenship

5 See, for example, Dahl (1985).

is exceedingly limited. This is because of its misleading assumptions about the capacities of modern states to manage their affairs, but also because of the limited and inaccurate view it promotes of the relations between governments and citizens. The activities of governments are not always visible, nor are they always able to be held to account through public debate and elections. Yet, Hindess (2000, 73) still thinks that the language of citizenship is an important resource for promoting free political debate, campaigning against the arbitrary decisions made by government, and for attempting to protect politically weak minority groups.

Conclusion

This chapter has sought to indicate the various conceptual dimensions of citizenship in the Western tradition. On the account given above, the history of citizenship may be understood, not only in terms of shifts in emphasis among the different dimensions, but also through the different answers given to the questions arising out of each dimension. As we have seen, ideas of citizenship can provide the basis for critical debate over political values and institutions, as well as social and economic organizations. Disputes over citizenship regularly derive from the normative aspirations of reformers who seek to change the empirical constraints imposed on them by governments, corporations, religions, and cultures.

These conclusions may have considerable relevance for contemporary Indonesia. A focus on citizenship suggests that discussions of governance need to extend beyond issues of efficient and effective management to take account of broader civic values. Not least of these are the values of *democratic* citizenship. In this context, paying due attention to citizenship can help strengthen democracies. If issues of political legitimacy and trust in government are to be addressed, then neither improving representation in the nation state or its governance will be sufficient. Consideration must also be given to enhancing citizen participation and deliberation in a variety of forums. Implemented properly, a democratic governance attentive to citizenship concerns would be an innovative, if somewhat challenging, political strategy. Nonetheless, it would be one that would go part of the way to addressing central problems in Indonesian democracy.

References

Advisory Group on Citizenship (1998), *Education for Citizenship and the Teaching of Democracy in Schools – Final Report* (London: Qualifications and Curriculum Authority).

Carter, A. (2001), *The Political Theory of Global Citizenship* (London: Routledge).

Carter, A. and Stokes, G. (eds) (2000), *Democratic Theory Today* (Cambridge: Polity).

Civics Expert Group (1994), *Whereas the People: Civics and Citizenship Education in Australia* (Canberra: Australian Government Publishing Service).

Dahl, R.A. (1985), *A Preface to Economic Democracy* (Berkeley: University of California Press).

de Tocqueville, A. (1988), *Democracy in America* (ed. J.P. Mayer, trans. G. Lawrence) (New York: Harper Perennial).

Hindess, B. (2000), 'Limits to Citizenship', in W. Hudson and J. Kane (eds), *Rethinking Australian Citizenship* (Cambridge: Cambridge University Press).

Hudson, W. (2000), 'Differential Citizenship', in W. Hudson and J. Kane (eds), *Rethinking Australian Citizenship* (Cambridge: Cambridge University Press).

Hudson, W. and Kane, J. (eds) (2000a), *Rethinking Australian Citizenship* (Cambridge: Cambridge University Press).

Hudson, W. and Kane, J. (2000b), 'Rethinking Australian Citizenship', in W. Hudson and J. Kane (eds), *Rethinking Australian Citizenship* (Cambridge: Cambridge University Press).

Hutchings, K. and Dannreuther, R. (eds) (1999), *Cosmopolitan Citizenship* (Houndsmill: Macmillan).

Kane, J. (2000), 'Democracy and Group Rights', in A. Carter and G. Stokes (eds), *Democratic Theory Today* (Cambridge: Polity).

Kane, J. (2002), 'Communitarianism and Citizenship', in W. Hudson and J. Kane (eds), *Rethinking Australian Citizenship* (Cambridge: Cambridge University Press).

Marshall, T.H. (1994), 'Citizenship and Social Class', in P.B. Clarke (ed.), *Citizenship* (London: Pluto).

Moon, J., Crane, A. and Matten, D. (2005), 'Can Corporations Be Citizens? Corporate Citizenship as a Metaphor for Business Participation in Society', *Business Ethics Quarterly* 15: 3, 427–51.

Oldfield, A. (1990), *Citizenship and Community: Civic Republicanism and the Modern World* (London: Routledge).

Pocock, J.G.A. (1998), 'The Ideal of Citizenship Since Classical Times', in G. Shafir (ed.), *The Citizenship Debates: A Reader* (Minneapolis: University of Minnesota Press).

Stokes, G. (2000a), 'Australia and Global Citizenship', in W. Hudson and J. Kane (eds), *Rethinking Australian Citizenship* (Cambridge: Cambridge University Press).

Stokes, G. (2000b), 'Democracy and Citizenship', in A. Carter and G. Stokes (eds), *Democratic Theory Today* (Cambridge: Polity).

Stokes, G. (2002), 'Global Citizenship', in W. Hudson and J. Kane (eds), *Rethinking Australian Citizenship* (Cambridge: Cambridge University Press).

Stokes, G. (2004), 'Transnational Citizenship: Problems of Definition, Culture and Democracy', *Cambridge Review of International Affairs* 17: 1, 119–35.

Stokes, G. (2006), 'Critical Theories of Deliberative Democracy and the Problem of Citizenship', in Ethan Leib and Baogang He (eds), *The Search for Deliberative Democracy in China* (New York: Palgrave Macmillan).

Uhr, J. (1998), *Deliberative Democracy in Australia: The Changing Place of Parliament* (Melbourne: Cambridge University Press).

van Steenbergen, B. (ed.) (1994a), *The Condition of Citizenship* (Thousand Oaks, CA: Sage).

van Steenbergen, B. (1994b), 'The Condition of Citizenship: An Introduction', in B. van Steenbergen (ed.), *The Condition of Citizenship* (Thousand Oaks, CA: Sage).

van Steenbergen, B. (1994c), 'Towards a Global Ecological Citizen', in B. van Steenbergen (ed.), *The Condition of Citizenship* (Thousand Oaks, CA: Sage).

Williams, J. (2002), 'Good International Citizenship', in N. Dower and J. Williams (eds), *Global Citizenship: A Critical Reader* (Edinburgh: University of Edinburgh Press).

Chapter 13

Liberal and Communitarian Approaches to Citizenship

Janna Thompson

Introduction

In this chapter, I will analyze Western liberal and communitarian approaches to citizenship and then suggest three challenges that they raise in the context of Indonesian Islam. Those who take these approaches differ on many issues, but they agree that citizens ought to be regarded as equals. The equal status of citizens does not mean that they have to be treated alike or that their responsibilities are exactly the same. But it does require an equality of respect – above all, equal rights and equality before the law. This presumption of equality motivates views about rights of citizens. But it also poses problems – particularly in respect to treatment of outsiders.

Citizenship is not merely a status – a matter of possessing certain rights and responsibilities. It is also an identity, 'an expression of membership in a political community' (Kymlicka and Norman 1994, 369). The political community to which a citizen belongs is generally assumed to be a national state. The notion of citizen, as it is usually understood, thus presupposes the existence of outsiders – those who are citizens of other nations or those who do not accept or fulfil all of the requirements of citizenship. In this chapter, my aim is not only to outline some contemporary philosophical views about the meaning of citizenship but I also want to explain the implications of these views for relationships between citizens and outsiders. In doing so, I will explore some ideas about how citizenship can transcend national boundaries.

The Liberal View of Citizenship

Liberals have been traditionally concerned to define and defend the rights of citizens. Freedom of individuals to pursue their own good is a predominant liberal value, and in discussions of citizenship this priority is translated into a concern for civil liberties: the right of citizens to worship as they please, the right of free speech, free association, and so on. Democratic rights – the right to vote, for example – are conceived by most liberals as political means for defending individual rights and interests.

Liberals differ among themselves about what rights individuals possess as members of a polity. Some believe that citizens have economic or welfare rights as well as civil rights. Others disagree.[1] But liberals have traditionally agreed that citizens' rights are the political realization of universal human rights – rights that all individuals have just because they are human. The equality of citizens is justified by reference to the equality of humankind.

Liberal ideas about citizen identity follow from their views about rights. States or associations of other kinds have value only in so far as they serve the interests of individuals and protect or promote their rights as individuals. If individuals live in a state that generally protects their rights, then they have an interest and a duty to defend it and maintain it. But apart from this, they have no reason to value or identify with the state that they belong to.[2]

Motivated by a philosophy of individual equality, liberal ideas about the rights of citizens have played a radical role in the history of many political societies. They have been used to oppose slavery and discrimination based on race, religion or ethnicity. They have led to the recognition of women as equal citizens. They have been used as reasons for extending the right to vote. Most people have now accepted these reforms. But in respect to outsiders, the radical implications of liberalism go far beyond what people in liberal states are (now) prepared to accept.

Liberal ideas about equality and non-discrimination are in tension with the common assumption that states are entitled to limit immigration and put restrictions on trade for the sake of national interest. If it is wrong to discriminate against people because of their race or religion, then it seems equally wrong to discriminate against them because of where they were born. For a liberal, national borders have no inherent moral significance. A liberal can justify restrictions on trade and immigration which are necessary to protect the security of citizens and their rights. But it is doubtful that liberals can justify restrictions imposed with the intention of protecting the high standard of living of themselves and their compatriots, their jobs or their culture, especially when outsiders are in desperate need.

In general, global poverty and inequality pose a problem for liberals. If all humans are equal, then liberals should not tolerate social or economic relationships which disadvantage some groups of people. Whether these people are fellow citizens or outsiders should make no moral difference. Some liberals have indeed argued that people in wealthy countries should be doing much more to help the poor of the world than they do; others argue that people who benefit from the present state of affairs should be participating in constructing global institutions which are just for everyone (Singer 2002; Moellendorf 2002).

What this requires is not clear, but these ideas about duty go beyond what most citizens of liberal states are prepared to accept.

1 Two liberals who take very different views of this matter are Rawls (1973) and Nozick (1974).

2 For example, the liberal philosopher Simmons (1979) argues that there is no rational basis for the patriotic bias that many people have for their own state.

The Communitarian View of Citizenship

There are two criticisms of liberal ideas about citizenship which have received attention in recent years. The first is that liberalism's universalist assumptions cannot be universally justified. Most philosophers have had to acknowledge that liberal justifications for rights cannot persuade people who do not accept liberal premises or liberal ways of arguing. In fact, liberal ideas about rights of human beings and citizens are not shared by everyone in the world – or, for that matter, by everyone in liberal states.

This criticism seems to me to be less serious than many people think. First of all, there may be more agreement among the world's people about basic moral matters than critics of liberalism suppose. The widespread popularity of ideas of human rights suggests that this might turn out to be true. Second, an agreement about basic principles does not require an agreement in justifications or ways of arguing. Rawls points out that people with different comprehensive views about moral and philosophical matters may be able to arrive at an overlapping consensus about rights using arguments from their own traditions (Rawls 1979). In a liberal political order, according to his view, this consensus is the basis for citizenship and not the particular philosophical doctrines of traditional liberals. And there is no reason why an overlapping consensus cannot also be the basis for a theory of global justice.[3]

The second criticism of liberalism is that it does not adequately account for the relationship of citizens to each other and to their polity. It does not explain why people often identify with their political community and are willing to make great sacrifices in order to defend and preserve it. This is the primary criticism of those thinkers who have been labelled 'communitarian'.[4]

Communitarians think that citizens identify with their community or the people in it, that this identity is important to their lives and thus has to be regarded as morally important. Some communitarians simply take the fact that most people regard membership in community as morally important as a reason for assuming that it is morally important.[5] Communitarians are in a better position than liberals to justify beliefs and practices that are part of the meaning of citizenship as many people understand it. They can explain why citizens are entitled to be patriotic – why it is reasonable for them to care about the well-being of their particular state (and not just the abstract principles of right that it promotes). They can explain why borders are morally important – why it is justified for citizens to think that they have duties to each other that they do not have to outsiders. They can justify restrictions that states put on immigration and trade – at least those that are designed to protect the heritage of a state, its traditions, culture and the values it stands for.

Communitarianism has often been criticized for its uncritical acceptance of common views about membership. The fact that people are inclined to favour people of their own country does not mean that they are justified in doing so. Whether

---

3 As Rawls argues in *Law of Peoples* (1999).

4 MacIntyre (1988), Walzer (1983) and Taylor (1992) are among those philosophers identified as communitarians.

5 Miller (1995) argues in this way about nationalism.

the communitarian view of citizenship is acceptable depends on its implications for the world as a whole. Its plausibility also depends on the account it gives of what citizens should identity with. There are two main possibilities. One is that they should identify with their cultural tradition and the ideas of the good that come out of this tradition. The other is that they should identity with their institutions of state and their political history. But both ideas about the meaning of citizenship are problematic.

The first is problematic because most modern states are multi-cultural. They contain within their borders people from many (or at least more than one) cultural tradition. But this implies that citizenship cannot mean the same for all citizens of a political society. If people of the majority culture adopt policies that favour their traditions and ideas of the good, then the minority is likely to suffer. Even if their civil rights are not violated, they will not be able to identity with the predominant idea of the good, and the institutions and policies which embody this good. They will become outsiders in their own country, alienated from its political affairs. This situation is not compatible with equal citizenship – particularly from a point of view which regards identity as essential to citizenship.

An idea of identity which focuses on the political institutions and political values that citizens of a particular state are supposed to share seems much more promising. This form of identity is purely political and as such is supposed to transcend ethnic and religious divisions among the population. One problem is that in practice it is unlikely to do so. Political institutions are the product of a particular historical development and are likely to embody the cultural values and understandings of the majority religious or ethnic group. But even if institutions of state could be purged of their cultural or religious content, this would not overcome all of the difficulties. For it is not likely that all members of the population would accept this political identity – or at least regard it as having overriding importance. Some people might be more inclined to identify with other members of their religious or ethnic community or with others in their region. Historically speaking, states that have attempted to unite their population around a political identity have often had to adopt repressive measures in order to undermine or subordinate other communities of identification – and these measures have not always worked. But whether successful or not, repression is not a justifiable means for communitarians whose moral case depends on the identifications that people regard as important to their lives.

Communitarians present themselves as opponents of liberalism. But if they are to deal with the problems associated with multi-cultural, multi-religious societies, it seems inevitable that they adopt some of the ideas and strategies associated with liberalism. One possible solution is a federal state in which citizens reach an overlapping consensus, so far as this is possible, about basic rights and responsibilities, but are otherwise free to maintain the communities with which they identify.

Citizenship in such a federal society would have a complex meaning and there would be differences of opinion about how these meanings should be reconciled – how, for example, the rights of individuals should be reconciled with the rights of communities. Some people believe that conflict about this matter or conflicts of interest between communities are likely to spell the doom of any federal system – that the centrifugal force resulting from the demands of communities for more independence would tend to shatter a federation into many pieces, and the identification of citizens with their federation would not be strong enough to resist this tendency.

In my view, the prospects for federation as a solution to the problem of citizenship in a multi-cultural political society depend on global as well as national developments. In an interdependent world society, even large states have no prospect of an independent self-sufficiency. The centrifugal tendencies created by demands for independence are countered by the need for new forms of cooperation. Members of communities have pragmatic reasons for cooperating with outsiders on a national, regional and even global scale. Cooperation requires the development of a common politics, however tentative and contested, and this could be the first step toward the development that Rawls describes in his account of the creation of an overlapping consensus. Relationships and institutions which are at first no more than a *modus vivendi* – a political means of solving common problems – can become imbued in the course of time with moral significance and generate a binding force sufficient to draw together a population with different interests and allegiances. The development of multi-cultural federations, national or regional, might be able to follow this path. If so, they will be the basis for citizenship which transcends nationality.

Cosmopolitan Citizenship

The liberal tradition, motivated by its universalist idea of rights, also developed an idea of 'cosmopolitan citizenship'. The philosopher Kant used this notion in anticipation of an evolution toward a peaceful world society of law-abiding states in which all individuals would enjoy their rights. Kant's idea of cosmopolitan citizenship, though still popular, seems inadequate for a world society in which global institutions and relationships have an effect on so many people's lives. Some philosophers have suggested that cosmopolitan citizenship in an interdependent world society will involve membership in a complex web of institutions. Thomas Pogge offers the following picture:

> Persons should be citizens of, and govern themselves through, a number of political units of various sizes, without any one political unit being dominant and thus occupying the traditional role of state. And their political allegiance and loyalties should be widely dispersed over these units: neighbourhood, town, county, province, state, region and world at large. People should be politically at home in all of them, without converging upon any one of them as the lodestar of their political identity (Pogge 1992, 58).

This idea is compatible with the federalist conception of citizenship outlined in the last section – an idea of citizenship which does not require that individuals have one community identity. But how such a decentralized world order could be brought into being, whether it is feasible at all, depends on a lot more than the reasoning of philosophers.

Conclusion

These Western political concepts raise challenges in the context of contemporary Indonesian Islam. In particular, it may be important to ask how far Indonesian Muslims can accept a liberal conception of citizenship in which individuals are free to pursue their own good. In the same way, Indonesians will need to decide how far their commitment to community is compatible with high levels of pluralism or with pluralist option-taking in controversial areas. Finally, Indonesian Muslims might find a federalist conception of citizenship especially valuable. There may be tensions between such a conception of citizenship and Indonesian nationalism, as well as problems stemming from a strong sense of common religious identity. In the longer term, however, Indonesian Muslims may need to moderate Islamic social holism in order to achieve a society which can cope with the plurality and difference that the contemporary world appears to favour.

References

Kant, I. (1970), 'Perpetual Peace', in Hans Reiss (ed.), *Kant's Political Writings* (Cambridge: Cambridge University Press).

Kymlicka, W. and Norman, W. (1994), 'Return of the Citizen: A Survey of Recent Work on Citizenship', *Ethics* 104, 352–81.

MacIntyre, A. (1988), *Whose Justice, Which Rationality*? (Chicago: University of Notre Dame Press).

Miller, D. (1995), *On Nationality* (Oxford: Clarendon Press).

Moellendorf, D. (2002), *Cosmopolitan Justice* (Cambridge, MA: Westview Press).

Nozick, R. (1974), *Anarchy, State and Utopia* (Oxford: Blackwell).

Pogge, T. (1992), 'Cosmopolitanism and Sovereignty', *Ethics* 103, 48–75.

Rawls, J. (1973), *A Theory of Justice* (Oxford: Oxford University Press).

Rawls, J. (1979), 'Constitutional Liberty and the Concept of Justice', in D. Lyons (ed.), *Rights* (Belmont, California: Wadsworth).

Rawls, J. (1987), 'The Idea of An Overlapping Consensus', *The Oxford Journal of Legal Philosophy* 7.

Rawls, J. (1999), *Law of Peoples* (Cambridge: Cambridge University Press).

Simmons, A.J. (1979), *Moral Principles and Political Obligation* (Princeton: Princeton University Press).

Singer, P. (2002), *One World: The Ethics of Globalisation* (Melbourne: Text Publishing).

Taylor, C. (1992), *Multiculturalism and the Politics of Recognition* (Princeton: Princeton University Press).

Walzer, M. (1983), *Spheres of Justice* (New York: Basic Books).

Chapter 14

Problems with Citizenship

Barry Hindess

Citizenship is commonly regarded as a matter of internal relations between individuals and the state to which they belong and between those individuals themselves. Standard accounts of its modern development describe it as appearing first, along with the modern state itself, in parts of Western Europe, and subsequently developing both to incorporate a range of civil, political and social rights and to include within its reach all but a small minority of the state's population. It is seen as developing elsewhere as the modern system of states expanded to rule over the greater part of humanity. Citizenship in this sense is also regarded as a good thing, something to be defended and possibly deepened within the states where it exists and perhaps even to be extended into the international sphere.

This chapter approaches the significance of citizenship in the modern world from a rather different direction, essentially by considering the part it plays at a supra-national, or rather supra-state, level. Here I argue that citizenship can be seen as part of a régime of government which operates both by promoting the rule of territorial states over populations and by deploying a range of devices to regulate the conduct of states and the populations under their control. If there is an important sense in which all states are equally sovereign within this regime, there is another, no less important, sense in which some states are considerably more equal than others (Clark 1989). We shall see that the inequalities involved here, especially those associated with globalization and liberal internationalism, have important implications for the character of citizenship in the world today.

The chapter begins with a brief defence of my use of the word 'government' to refer to aspects of the system of states and especially to the modern partitioning of humanity into citizens of states and a significant minority of migrants, refugees and stateless persons. It then moves on to consider the emergence and subsequent globalization of the system of states, focusing especially on the manner in which, following the dismantling of direct imperial rule in the nineteenth and twentieth centuries, citizenship changed from being the condition of a small minority of the world's population to become the condition of the overwhelming majority. The shift from direct imperial rule to independent statehood provides us with a frame in which the character of modern citizenship can best be understood.

Government

Aristotle's *Politics* uses the term 'government' primarily to denote 'the supreme authority in states' (1988, 1279a, 27), which suggests that government should be seen as emanating from a single centre of control, and modern political analysis has generally followed this usage. Aristotle also writes of the government 'of a wife and children and of a household' (1988, 1278b, 37–8), the government of a slave and a government that one exercises over oneself. In his own discussions of government, Michel Foucault notes that, for all the many differences between them, these otherwise distinct practices all share a concern with 'the way in which the conduct of individuals or of groups might be directed ... To govern, in this sense, is to structure the possible field of action of others' (2001, 341) – or, indeed, of oneself. Thus, while it will often act directly to determine the behaviour of individuals, government also aims to influence their actions indirectly, by acting on the manner in which they regulate their own behaviour and the behaviour of others.

While he promotes this more general understanding of government, Foucault also acknowledges that, from the beginning of the modern period, one form of government has been seen as having a quite distinct status: namely, 'the particular form of governing which can be applied to the state as a whole' (Foucault 2001, 206). He observes, for example, that those who wrote of the art of government in the early modern period 'constantly recall that one speaks also of "governing" a household, souls, children, a province, a convent, a religious order, a family', but he also notes that they treat these 'other kinds of government as internal to the state or society' (Foucault 2001, 205–6), thereby always giving the government of the latter a superior status. This modern understanding of government thus follows the classical view not only in assuming that the government of a state should have 'regard to the common interest' (Aristotle 1988, 1279a, 17) but also in treating the state as 'the highest of all' forms of community (1988, 1252a, 5). Government, in this special sense, is clearly focused on the state as a whole but, Foucault insists, the work of governing the state extends well beyond the institutions of the state itself. It need not be seen as emanating from a single centre of control and it will often be performed by elements of what is now called civil society – by religious organizations, employers, financial institutions, legal and medical professionals and voluntary associations, and also, less directly, by markets and other institutionalized patterns of interaction.

Influential figures in the disciplines of public administration and international relations have used the term 'governance' to describe such forms of governing 'without government', suggesting that the work of governing within states is increasingly being conducted by public–private partnerships and by formal and informal networks involving a variety of state and non-state agencies, while, in the international sphere, states and other actors are regulated by an expanding web of conventions, treaties and international agencies, all of which operate without the backing of an overarching Hobbesian power.[1] For all their differences, these various literatures all suggest that activities within states and in the spaces between them are governed in ways which cannot properly be grasped by the state-centred view of government with which I began this section.

1 There is a substantial literature in both fields. See, for example, Rhodes (1997); Rosenau and Czempiel (1992).

We shall see that this suggestion has important implications for our equally state-centred understanding of citizenship. My own view is that, if government in its most general sense is a matter of structuring the possible fields of action, then the organization of citizenship within the modern system of states can itself be seen as a regime of government, albeit one that operates, like civil society and the market, with no controlling centre. However, it is of no particular importance for my argument here whether we use 'government', 'governance' or some other term to refer to this aspect of the modern system of states. What matters, rather, is that we acknowledge the presence of significant elements of design in the modern partitioning of humanity into citizens of states and a small minority of others. There are, in fact, many such elements of design in the modern system of states and some of them will play an important part in the discussion that follows.

The Modern System of States

Systems of states have appeared in many parts of the world – in the Americas, China, Europe, South Asia, the Malay Archipelago and Western classical antiquity – but, for reasons which need not concern us here, the system dominated by the modern West is the first of these to have become truly global in scope. This system has its origins in seventeenth-century European attempts to contain the political problems arising from the existence of powerful religious differences between Catholics, Lutherans and Calvinists by granting territorial rulers supreme political authority within their domains, leaving it to rulers and their subjects to reach some accommodation in matters of religion. These political arrangements were designed to pacify warring populations, but they also had the effect of transforming political conditions in the Western part of Europe, essentially by assigning populations which had been subject to a variety of overlapping and conflicting sources of authority to sovereign states which were themselves acknowledged as having the primary responsibility for the government of the populations within their territories.[2]

Where the classical view of politics treats the state as 'the highest of all' forms of community (Aristotle 1988, 1252a, 5), the development of the modern system of states reflects the emergence of a more complex form of political reason. The state clearly retains its privileged position with regard to its own population, but there are also important governmental contexts in which the 'international community' – the order represented by the system of states – is now regarded as 'the highest of all'. My argument is that the development of modern citizenship within this order has fundamental consequences for its role in the world today.

We can begin by noting that the Westphalian system of states operates as a regime of population management by assigning responsibility for the government of populations to a plurality of independent sovereign states, and further that, as we have already seen, the government of these states is expected to have 'regard to the common interest' (Aristotle 1988, 1279a, 17) – the common interest, that

2 There is an extensive literature on the emergence of the Westphalian system and its geo-political effects. See, for example, Held (1995); Hirst (1998); Schmitt (1996); Spruyt (1994); Walker (1993).

is, of its own citizens. Citizenship, in this respect, is clearly divisive in two rather different respects, separating the citizens of a state not only from the citizens of other states but also from the non-citizen residents who occupy a lesser status within the state itself (Isin 2002). This chapter focuses on the first of these divisions. In effect, the institution of citizenship requires each state to be particularly responsible for looking after its own citizens – a view which has underpinned the development of welfare states in the prosperous societies of the modern West – and promotes a correspondingly exclusive sense of solidarity among the citizens themselves. Some discussions[3] treat the kind of national sentiment involved here as resulting from a natural tendency to feel more responsible for those who are closer to us: to members, first, of the family or household, then of the local community or region, then of the state or nation, and only then to people in other parts of the world. I prefer the contrary view, which sees such sentiments as products of institutional arrangements, not as their 'natural' (and therefore final) causes: the formation of such national sentiments is itself a consequence of the governmental partitioning of humanity into the populations of discrete and independent states.

On the other hand, the view that each state is primarily responsible for looking after its own suggests also that it does not have the same responsibility for looking after others. Thus, while acknowledging that we may all have responsibilities towards the populations of other states, it treats these as being of secondary importance at best. It suggests to the rest of the world that the people of states such as Afghanistan, Burundi or Bangladesh should be regarded as having primary responsibility for their own condition, and that if their states fail them – especially if they do so in a manner which appears to threaten the interests of other states – then it may be necessary for the international community to step in and sort them out. There is a remarkable denial of history and, indeed, of responsibility at work in this perception, but the point I want to make here is a slightly different one. The assignment of responsibility for the regulation and the welfare of populations to the states to which they belong has clear positive effects, effects whose importance is demonstrated most dramatically in cases where states are unable to live up to this responsibility. But it also has important effects of a very different kind. In particular, it tells the people of each state that, while they might generously accept a few refugees from time to time, the welfare of other populations is not their primary responsibility – that, of course, individual members of these populations have human rights but, as the UN Declaration of Human Rights so eloquently insists, the responsibility for securing those rights ultimately rests with the states to which they belong. This is precisely the brutal and demeaning vision which dominates the treatment of refugees and many other actual or would-be migrants in the world today.

We can note, secondly, that where contract theory tends to present the state as constituted internally, by real or imaginary agreements between its members – as do many of the contributions to this volume – the account of the system of states presented here suggests that the sovereignty of a state is in part a function of its recognition as a state by other members of the system (Weber 1995). Government of the state is not restricted to the activities of the state itself or to developments

3 Miller (2000) is a good example.

within its borders: it also appears in the organization of relations between states. The rights of states to manage their own affairs, for example, have always been heavily qualified (as rights commonly are) by a corresponding set of responsibilities to what is often called the 'international community' – that is, to the overarching system of states to which they belong.

This point gives a very different twist to the Aristotelian view of the citizen as both ruler and ruled. Not only are there important respects in which citizens are not the collective rulers of the state to which they belong – as, in fact, has always been the case – but, to the extent that they do rule, this serves to reinforce their subordination to agencies and forces over which they have little real control.[4] Thus, while all contemporary states, even the most powerful, are to some degree subject to the general supervisory mechanisms of the enlarged system of states – to a variety of international conventions, treaties and a developing framework of international law on the one hand, and the 'civilizing' effects of international trade on the other – a clear majority of the new states which emerged from the twentieth-century end of empire, along with many non-Western states in territories which had never been colonized, also find themselves subject to the supervisory mechanisms, which we consider briefly below, of the more specific international regime of development. Some of these states (with more than a little help from their friends) have played the development game with a notable degree of success, while others have tried to play by radically different rules, usually with unhappy results, but most have fallen somewhere between these extremes.

The normative force of the contractarian account of the state has never been based on a claim to historical realism. Accordingly, we should be careful not to read too much into this discrepancy between contract theory and the actual history of the system of states. Contract theory is concerned less to understand the character of modern states than it is to justify (and in some respects to limit) their claims to supreme authority over their own citizens and territory. It is this normative imperative which produces the view that citizens should engage with their own state as if, whatever its actual history, it had emerged through formal or informal agreements amongst numerous individuals who then became its subjects.[5] The normative implications of the contractarian view thus tend to reinforce the governmental thrust of the modern system of states by promoting the belief among citizens that, in Aristotle's words, the state is 'a body of citizens sufficing for the purposes of life' (1988, 1275b, 21–2). It is this view of the state which underlies the modern understanding of citizenship as a matter of relationships between individuals and the state to which they belong, and between these individuals themselves. It suggests not only that sovereignty is

4 There are many other reasons for this condition too, of course. I have argued elsewhere that the institutions of representative government – which reflect the predominant modern understanding of democracy – are clearly designed to ensure that citizens play a strictly circumscribed role in the government of the state to which they belong (Hindess 2000c).

5 Cf. Kant's insistence, in 'The Metaphysics of Morals', that 'for all practical [that is, moral] purposes' the origin of sovereign power 'is not discoverable by the people who are subject to it ... The subject ought not to indulge in speculations about its origin ... as if its right to be obeyed were open to doubt' (Kant 1970, 143).

essentially a matter of the internal relations between a state and its citizens on the one hand, and of the capacity of a state to defend itself against outsiders on the other, but also that the state, in turn, has a particular responsibility for securing the welfare of its own citizens.

A third implication is that effective government within the member states of the Westphalian system is predicated on political conditions that operate above the level of the individual states themselves. This suggests not only that the order secured within the more successful states depends in part on the order which prevails in the relations between states, but also that much of the disorder within less successful states may also be a product of this latter order. The European system of states and the sovereignty which that system secured for participating states provided conditions which made possible the internal development of citizenship which Marshall (1950) described as involving the emergence, in roughly this order, of three sets of rights: the *civil* rights to liberty and equality before the law; the *political* right to vote and to participate in the political process; and the *social* right to participate fully in a way of life that is shared by the citizens as a whole. Recent commentators have disputed many aspects of Marshall's argument (Bulmer and Rees 1996), but their criticisms have rarely engaged with the strictly intra-state focus of his analysis.

Finally, at least in its early stages, the Westphalian states system was specifically European, covering territories and populations in parts of Europe by means of treaties and understandings between participating states. It imposed few constraints on the conduct of these states towards those who inhabited territories not covered by these agreements, who were seen as possessing no sovereign states of the European kind (Schmitt 1996). Thus while European states were consolidating their rule over their own populations – in part through the development of the civil and political rights of citizenship – some of them were also engaged in imperial adventures elsewhere. This brings us to the globalization of the system of modern states, with its consequences for the subsequent globalization of citizenship, which I consider in the following section.

The Expansion of the States System

The subordination of substantial non-European populations to rule by European states was clearly a central feature of European imperialism, but a second feature was no less important for our purposes: the incorporation of those populations and the territories they inhabited into the European system of states. In a different but related development, the remainder of the non-European world was brought into the system of states indirectly: through the deployment by European states of a standard of civilization in their dealings with independent states elsewhere (Gong 1984), the imposition of elaborate systems of capitulations which required the latter to acknowledge the extra-territorial jurisdiction of Western states (Fidler 2000), and what Gallagher and Robinson (1953) have called 'the imperialism of free trade'.

Direct or indirect imperial domination was the form in which the European system of states first became global in scope, but this process of incorporating non-European populations into the European system of states was followed, more or less rapidly, by a second stage in the globalization of the European states system. The achievement of independence throughout much of the Americas during the nineteenth century, and its achievement or imposition elsewhere during the twentieth, dismantled one aspect of imperial rule while leaving the state and the institutions of citizenship within it as, in Michael Hardt and Antonio Negri's words, 'the poisoned gift of national liberation' (2000, 135). This imperial legacy has consequences for citizenship at a number of different levels.

We can begin by noting that the second, twentieth-century, wave of independence marks the point at which citizenship became an almost universal human condition. However, the citizenship which developed through the transition from imperial rule to independent statehood followed a radically different trajectory than the one traced by Marshall and other sociologists for modern Western states. One consequence is that the condition of citizenship in post-colonial states is seriously constrained by the governmental institutions and practices inherited from the colonial period, most of which were predicated on a view of the subject population as considerably less civilized than their rulers. While we might expect such a view of the bulk of the subject population to be held by the political/administrative class in all modern states, it was more pronounced – or, at least, more freely expressed – in the case of populations subject to direct imperial rule. Colonial rule by Western states involved a clear distinction between citizens and subjects, and a systematic development of what eventually became known, in the case of Britain's African possessions, as indirect rule – a form of government which worked through institutions that relied on what were thought to be indigenous customs and structures of authority.[6]

Precisely because they adapted what were thought to be indigenous practices to the demands of administrative convenience, the detailed character of these ersatz governmental arrangements varied from one colonial administration to another. Their overall effect, however, was to institutionalize a differentiated pattern of relations between the colonial state and sections of the subject population which reinforced, or even created, divisions between them (Appadurai 1993) and promoted forms of localized authoritarian rule – a regime which Mamdani (1996) aptly describes as one of 'decentralized despotism'. While independence has displaced the colonial distinction between citizen and subject, the laws and administrative practices inherited from the period of indirect rule have often continued to limit the civil and political rights of citizenship.

A second consequence of this trajectory relates to the argument of Marshall and many social policy analysts in the West that the role of the state's social policy was to ensure that citizens were not in fact excluded from participation in the life of their society by reason of poverty, ill-health or lack of education. This sociological literature focuses on the prosperous (and predominantly Western) states of the OECD, but it is worth noting here, since its insistence on the role of the state in securing the social rights of citizenship serves to mark another significant difference

6 The most influential British statement of the case for indirect rule is Lugard (1923). However, the practice of working through what were believed to be indigenous institutions was a pervasive feature of Western imperial administration (Malinowski 1929; Mamdani 1996).

between citizenship in the West and citizenship elsewhere. While these social rights are comparatively well established in most Western states – in spite of considerable neo-liberal pressure – they have barely had a chance to develop in the majority of other states. Thirdly, the imperial legacy of communal division suggests that the challenge to citizenship posed by ethnic, linguistic, religious and other group memberships within the state, or cutting across its boundaries, should not be seen simply as a product of late twentieth-century developments. On the contrary, there is an important sense in which this challenge has been a condition of post-colonial states from the beginnings of citizenship itself.

At a rather different level, the growth of political independence in the modern sense both expanded the membership of the system of states and inaugurated a radically new way of bringing non-Western populations under the rule of that system (Seth 2000). These populations thus found themselves governed both by modern states of their own and by the overarching system of states within which their own states had been incorporated. I noted earlier that, as with other regimes of government which possess no controlling centre – the workings of an established market or of civil society, for example – some members of the modern system of states are clearly more equal than others. Like the modern states which have been established in territories that were never directly colonized, the newly independent states are recognized as members of the international system of states, but few have been admitted to its more exclusive inner circles. As a result, they are subject to regulation by international financial agencies which are clearly dominated by Western concerns and, in particular, by an updated version of the European 'standard of civilization', which requires them to demonstrate their fitness to participate in various international arrangements (OECD, GATT and its successor, WTO, providing the most obvious examples) and which dominates the rhetoric of intervention by the 'international community' (Cooper 1991; Kaplan 2000).

I noted earlier that the idea of a 'standard of civilization' played an important part in the conduct of relations between Western states and independent states elsewhere during the imperial period. Like the 'civilizing mission' of Western imperialism, the standard of civilization treated the greater part of humanity as being in considerable need of improvement and, in particular, as unable to properly manage its own affairs. Governmental programmes of improvement or development remain influential in the post-colonial world, but the discourse of improvement has taken a radically different form – in part, no doubt, because its earlier, imperial versions can hardly be voiced in public without offending the leaders and citizens of independent states.[7]

7 What may be said in private is often a different matter. A brief prepared by Australian government departments for a 1997 meeting of Economic Ministers of the Pacific Islands Forum described the leaders of member states in the following terms: 'Used to ambitious but unrealised development plans, they may balk at settling for modest but achievable objectives'; 'have generally shirked hard decisions'; 'he is boastful and vain – having spent heavily on grandiose monuments – can irritate others'; 'Temperamentally volatile, he is still given to Third World posturing against Western colonialism' (Pacific Islands Report website, available at: <http://166.122.164.43/archive/1997/August/08-04-11.html>). Rather than question the content of this brief, Australian media reports focused on the diplomatic blunder involved in allowing its content to be made public.

It would clearly be a mistake to treat this project of improvement as if it were simply imposed on the rest of the world by Western states. It is also pursued – as it was during the colonial period – by influential groups in the ex-imperial domains themselves. Nevertheless, the most powerful forces behind this project of improvement are to be found in the liberal West itself. The old imperial divisions between citizens, colonial subjects and non-citizen others has been displaced by a post-imperial globalization of citizenship, and indirect rule within imperial possessions has been superseded by an even less direct form of decentralized rule – reminiscent in many respects of the older system of capitulations (Fidler 2000) – in which the inhabitants of post-colonial successor states are governed through sovereign states of their own. This is also to say, of course, that they are ruled through states which are themselves governed by the regulatory regimes of the modern system of states, and, in particular, by international financial institutions and that fundamental liberal instrument of civilization, the market. Indeed, it is tempting to suggest that the use of markets to regulate the conduct of states has become increasingly prominent as we move further away from the decolonizations of the mid twentieth century. This reflects the concern of the 'international community' to tighten supervision over what it regards as weak and poorly performing states.

International financial institutions and development agencies are now promoting 'good governance' within states, which is seen as involving the implementation of basic human rights and democracy. Governments of states are expected to be at least minimally responsive to the wishes of their citizens; the citizens in turn are expected to 'own', or at least to go along with, the policies of their government, and the language of 'ownership' now plays an important part in development discourse. Joseph Stiglitz, while still Vice-President of the World Bank, described the Bank's proposed Comprehensive Development Framework as involving:

> a new set of relationships, not only between the Bank and the country, but within the country itself … Central is the notion that the country (*not just the government*) must be in the driver's seat (Stiglitz 1999, 22–3 – emphasis added).[8]

The point, in other words, is to get the citizens themselves to accept responsibility for implementing the conditions imposed by the Bank. The promotion of reforms designed to limit the freedom of action of governments, and therefore the ability of citizens to influence their actions, goes hand-in-hand with the promotion of democracy as a central component of good governance.

Conclusion

I began this chapter by observing that citizenship is generally regarded as a good thing and, rather than challenge this view directly, I have tried to suggest that citizenship should be seen, like other human arrangements, as something that often cuts both ways. Thus, for the inhabitants of any state it is usually preferable to be a citizen of that state – or a wealthy, well-connected foreigner – than it is to occupy a lesser

8 See also Wolfensohn (1999) and the critical discussion in Palast (2003, Chapter 4).

status. In this respect, at least, the possession of citizenship is clearly beneficial – and its beneficial effects are considerably increased if one is fortunate enough to be a citizen of one of the prosperous (and overwhelmingly Western) states of the OECD, most of which have secured some approximation to the civil, political and social rights which Marshall regards as necessary for the full development of citizenship. These rights are poorly developed in many post-colonial successor states, but, even in these cases, it is usually far better to be a citizen than not.

On the other side of the ledger, we have seen that there is an important sense in which citizens are never the only rulers of the state to which they belong, and, further, that their participation in rule serves also to reinforce their subordination to agencies and forces over which they have limited control at best. This last point applies to the citizens of any state, but it can be especially consequential for those who belong to states which are subject to supervision by international financial agencies and the international development regime. That citizens' rule is subject to significant external constraints is not the primary cause for concern here – quite the contrary in fact. What should concern us, rather, is the grossly unequal character of the international order from which these constraints derive.

I noted also that the institutions of citizenship are divisive in two rather different respects. In the first, which has been the focus of my discussion in this chapter, citizenship provides states with a means of distinguishing between those who belong and those who do not, and, more importantly perhaps, with entirely legitimate grounds for excluding, if they so choose, the latter from some or all of the benefits they accord to citizens, including the right to reside in the state's own territory. Since states are expected to look after their own, and most of the world's citizens in fact belong to its less advantaged states, we might say that the international citizenship regime plays a part in protecting the privileges of the wealthy. There are good reasons for resisting attempts – whether by states or by political theorists – to present citizenship as one's primary political identity and the state as one's principal focus of loyalty. Commitments which cut across national boundaries may well threaten the role of citizenship within the larger system of states, and possibly even the design of the system more generally, but their development is surely to be encouraged.

Finally, lest this last point be seen as lending support to the idea of cosmopolitan citizenship, I should perhaps conclude by returning briefly to the second sense in which citizenship can be seen as divisive, namely, in separating the citizens of a polity from those of its inhabitants who are regarded as occupying a lesser status. Cosmopolitan citizenship is clearly intended to undermine the divisiveness which sets the citizens of one state against those of another, and in this respect its universalism is something to be welcomed. Unfortunately, however, its relationship to this second kind of divisiveness is more problematic. The cosmopolitan figures of the European Enlightenment rarely found any difficulty in combining their universalism with the view that much of humanity was not yet – and in some cases might never be – able to properly manage its own affairs. Such elitist universalisms clearly underlay both the 'civilizing missions' of Western imperialism and the 'standard of civilization' which Western states deployed in their relationships with independent states elsewhere, and it is far from clear whether contemporary Western cosmopolitanism has entirely overcome their limitations. Nor, in particular, is it clear that a concern for the welfare of humanity is best pursued through the Western idiom of citizenship.

These remarks can perhaps be construed as an admonition to Indonesian Muslims not to take Western high talk about citizenship too seriously. Instead, they should study the actual state arrangements and power contexts in which both rhetorics and practices of citizenship are embedded, and then consider what countervailing perspectives their own heritage might lead them to suggest by way of qualification and moderation of Western political doctrine.

References

Ahluwalia, P. (2001), *Politics and Post-Colonial Theory: African Inflections* (London: Routledge).

Appadurai, A. (1993), 'Number in the Colonial Imagination', in C.A. Breckenridge and P. van der Veer (eds), *Orientalism and the Postcolonial Predicament. Perspectives on South Asia* (Philadelphia: University of Pennsylvania Press).

Aristotle (1988), *Politics* (Cambridge: Cambridge University Press).

Barnett, M.N. (1997), 'Bringing in the New World Order: Liberalism, Legitimacy and the United Nations', *World Politics* 49: 4, 526–51.

Barry, A., Osborne, T. and Rose, N. (eds) (1996), *Foucault and Political Reason: Liberalism, Neo-liberalism and Rationalities of Government* (Chicago: University of Chicago Press).

Bhabha, H.K. (1994), *The Location of Culture* (London: Routledge).

Bulmer, M. and Rees, A.M. (eds) (1996), *Citizenship Today: The Contemporary Relevance of T.H. Marshall* (London: UCL Press).

Clark, I. (1989), *The Hierarchy of States: Reform and Resistance in the International Order* (Cambridge: Cambridge University Press).

Cooper, R. (1991), *The Post-Modern State and the World Order* (London: Demos).

Dean, M. (1991), *The Constitution of Poverty: Toward a Genealogy of Liberal Governance* (London: Routledge).

Dean, M. (1999), *Governmentality: Power and Rule in Modern Society* (London: Sage).

Dean, M. (2002), 'Powers of Life and Death Beyond Governmentality', *Cultural Values: Journal for Cultural Research* 6: 1–2, 119–38.

Dean, M. and Hindess, B. (eds) (1998), *Governing Australia: Studies in Contemporary Rationalities of Government* (Melbourne: Cambridge University Press).

Dillon, M. (1995), 'Sovereignty and Governmentality', *Alternatives* 20: 2, 323–68.

Donzelot, J. (1979), *The Policing of Families* (New York: Pantheon).

Fidler, D.P. (2000), 'A Kinder, Gentler System of Capitulations? International Law, Structural Adjustment Policies, and the Standard of Liberal, Globalized Civilization', *Texas International Law Journal* 35, 387–413.

Foucault, M. (2001), 'Governmentality', in J.D. Faubion (ed.), *Essential Works of Foucault*, vol. 3 (London: Allen Lane).

Gallagher, J. and Robinson, R. (1953), 'The Imperialism of Free Trade', *The Economic History Review* VI (Second Series): 1, 1–15.

Giddens, A. (1995), *Profiles and Critiques in Social Theory* (London: Macmillan).

Gill, S. (1995), 'Globalization, Market Civilization, and Disciplinary Neoliberalism', *Millennium* 24, 399–423.

Gong, G.W. (1984), *The Standard of Civilization in International Society* (Oxford: Oxford University Press).

Hardt, M. and Negri, A. (2000), *Empire* (Cambridge, Mass: Harvard University Press).

Held, D. (1995), *Democracy and the Global Order: From the Modern State to Cosmopolitan Governance* (Cambridge: Polity).

Hindess, B. (2000a), 'Citizenship in the International Management of Populations', *American Behavioural Scientist* 43: 9, 1486–97.

Hindess, B. (2000b), 'Divide and Govern: Governmental Aspects of the Modern States System', in R. Ericson and N. Stehr (eds), *Governing Modern Societies* (Toronto: University of Toronto Press).

Hindess, B. (2000c), 'Representation Ingrafted upon Democracy', *Democratization* 7: 2, 1–18.

Hindess, B. (2001), 'Not at Home in the Empire', *Social Identities* 7: 3, 363–77.

Hindess, B. (2002), 'Neo-Liberal Citizenship', *Citizenship Studies* 6: 2, 127–43.

Hirst, P. (1998), 'The International Origins of National Sovereignty', in *From Statism to Pluralism* (London: University College London Press).

Isin, E. (2002), *Being Political: Genealogies of Citizenship* (Minneapolis: University of Minnesota Press).

Kant, I. (1970), *Political Writings* (ed. Hans Reiss) (Cambridge: Cambridge University Press).

Kaplan, R.D. (2000), *The Coming Anarchy* (New York: Random House).

Lugard, F.D. (1923), *The Dual Mandate in British Tropical Africa* (Edinburgh: W. Blackwood).

Malinowski, B. (1929), 'Practical Anthropology', *Africa* 2, 22–39.

Mamdani, M. (1996), *Citizen and Subject: Contemporary Africa and the Legacy of Late Colonialism* (Princeton: Princeton University Press).

Marshall, T. (1950), *Citizenship and Social Class* (Cambridge: Cambridge University Press).

Miller, D. (2000), *Citizenship and National Identity* (Oxford: Polity).

Pagden, A. (1998), 'The Genesis of "Governance" and Enlightenment Conceptions of the Cosmopolitan World Order', *International Social Science Journal* 155, 7–15.

Palast, G. (2003), *The Best Democracy Money Can Buy* (New York: Penguin Putnam).

Raeff, M. (1983), *The Well-Ordered Police State: Social and Institutional Change through Law in the Germanies and Russia, 1699–1800* (New Haven and London: Yale University Press).

Rhodes, R.A.W. (1997), *Understanding Governance* (Buckingham: Open University Press).

Rose, N. (1999), *Powers of Freedom: Reframing Political Thought* (Cambridge: Cambridge University Press).

Rose-Ackerman, S. (1999), *Corruption and Government: Causes, Consequences and Reform* (Cambridge and New York: Cambridge University Press).

Rosenau, J.N. and Czempiel, E.-O. (eds) (1992), *Governance without Government: Order and Change in World Politics* (Cambridge: Cambridge University Press).

Schmitt, C. (1996), 'The Land Appropriation of a New World', *Telos* 109, 29–80.

Seth, S. (2000), 'A "Postcolonial World"? Contending Images of World Politics', in G. Fry and J. O'Hagan (eds), *Contending Images of World Politics* (London: Macmillan).

Spruyt, H. (1994), *The Sovereign State and Its Competitors: An Analysis of Systems Change* (Princeton: Princeton University Press).

Stiglitz, J. (1999), *Participation and Development: Perspectives from the Comprehensive Development Paradigm* (Seoul: World Bank).

Walker, R.B.J. (1993), *Inside/Outside: International Relations as Political Theory* (Cambridge: Cambridge University Press).

Walters, W. (2000), 'The Invention of Economic Europe', presented at the International Studies Association Conference, Chicago, 20–24 February.

Weber, C. (1995), *Simulating Sovereignty: Intervention, the State and Symbolic Exchange* (Cambridge: Cambridge University Press).

Wolfensohn, J.D. (1999), *A Proposal for a Comprehensive Development Framework* (Washington: World Bank).

Chapter 15

Religious Pluralism in Indonesia

Azyumardi Azra

> And if your Lord had willed, whoever is in the earth would have believed, all of them, all together. Would you [O Muhammad] then constrain the people, until they are believers (*Qur'an*, 10:99).

> Islamic revelation presents a theology that resonates with the modern pluralistic belief that other faiths are not merely inferior manifestations of religiosity, but variant forms of individual and communal responses to the presence of the transcendence in human life. All persons are created in the divine nature (*fitrat* Allah), with a disposition that leads to the knowledge of God, the Creator, to whom worship is due simply because of the creation (Sachedina 2001, 14).

The term 'pluralism' is one of the most important catchwords in the era of globalization. As Sachedina argues, pluralism in our present world, with its diversity of cultures, belief systems and values, inspires both exhilaration at the endless shadings of human expression and dread of seemingly irreconcilable conflict, even among the followers of religion. The invocation of pluralism has become as much a summons as a celebration; an urgent exhortation to the citizens of the world to come to terms with their increasing diversity (Sachedina 2001, 22). Quite apart from continued political conflicts among nations and countries, the world continues to see seemingly endless conflicts between Christians and Muslims, Hindus and Sikhs, Tamils and Buddhists. Worse still, religious conflicts have taken place among followers of one single religious tradition; between Sunnis and Shias or even among Sunnis within Islam; between Catholics and Protestants; among Hindus, and the like. All of these hard realities have imparted the urgent need for religious pluralism based on the principle of inclusiveness, which would counsel accommodation, not conflict, amongst competing claims to religious truth in religiously and culturally heterogeneous societies.

Furthermore, religious pluralism appeals for an active engagement with the religious other not simply to tolerate but to understand. Toleration does not require an active engagement with the other; it makes no inroads on mutual ignorance. In a world in which religious differences historically have been manipulated to burn bridges between communities, recognition and understanding of religious differences require all believers to enter into knowledgeable dialogue with one another, even in the face of major disagreements. If this occurs, religious pluralism may function as a working paradigm for a democratic, social pluralism in which people of diverse religious backgrounds form a community of global citizens (Sachedina 2001, 35).

Islamic Roots of Pluralism

Historically and sociologically speaking, Islam has long been familiar with religious pluralism at various levels. Indeed, the *Qur'an* itself as a divine revelation has been a source of different interpretations among Muslim scholars, and so made Muslims well acquainted with differences and diversity in the area of religion. Thus well-known interpretations of the *Qur'an* include the exterior (*zahir* or *shari'ah*) and the interior (*batin* or *tasawwuf*), the real and the metaphorical, the certain (*qat'i*) and the uncertain (*zanni*). As Moussalli argues, many sciences and schools of language, tradition (*hadith*), exegesis (*tafsīr*), jurisprudence (*fiqh*), theology (*kalam*), Sufism (*tasawwuf*) and ethics (*akhlaq*) were shaped, developed, legitimized and de-legitimized around the *Qur'an* (Moussalli 2001, 85). While only a limited number of *Qur'anic* verses speak of political disunity, many others speak positively of diversity of tribes, sects, nations and peoples, as well as races and languages. The verses of the *Qur'an* also acknowledge the natural differences in the intellectual and physical capabilities of human beings. They view the different ways of living as a natural and even a divine aspect of creation. The *Qur'an* nowhere calls for a forcible unification of this diversity.

Pluralism among Muslims is, of course, also related to the different historical, social, cultural, political and economic conditions of Muslims. In fact, there are a number of cultural realms among Muslims that reflect the very pluralism of the Muslim world. These cultural realms are: Arab, Persian, Turkic, Sudanic (Black Africa), the Indian sub-continent, Malay-Indonesian, Sino-Islamic and Western hemisphere. Each of the cultural realms, to a certain degree, represents the distinctive cultural expression of its Muslim population. Therefore, it is wrong to assume that Islam is monolithic. In fact, pluralism is a fact of life among Muslims.

Southeast Asian Pluralism

Pluralism and diversity are striking realities in Southeast Asia. As Hefner (2001, 4) argues, few areas of the non-Western world illustrate the legacy and challenge of cultural pluralism in a manner more striking than in the Southeast Asian countries of Malaysia, Singapore and Indonesia. J.S. Furnivall, a British administrator and political writer before the Second World War, introduced the concept of plural societies and identified the countries known today as Indonesia, Malaysia and Singapore as the most striking examples. According to Furnivall, a plural society is a society that comprises 'two or more elements of social orders which live side by side, yet without mingling, in one political unit'. He further maintained that this situation is accompanied by a caste-like division of labour, in which ethno-religious groups play different economic roles. This social segregation in turn gives rise to what Furnivall regarded as these societies' most unsettling political trait: their lack of 'common social will'. Facing this unfortunate situation, Furnivall asserted that unless some kind of formula for pluralist federation could be devised, Southeast Asian pluralism seemed doomed to a nightmarish anarchy (Furnivall 1944, 446, 468–9; Hefner 2001, 4–6).

Furnivall's 'doomed scenario' by and large failed to materialize. In contrast, post-war Southeast Asia saw the establishment of independent Indonesia and the Malaysia Federation in which Singapore was a part. But national independence stimulated the rise of ethno-religious sentiment in the struggle for control and power of the new states. As a result, the region has been marked by ethno-religious conflict and violence. Malaysia was swept by fierce communal violence in the years following the Second World War and again on a much larger scale in 1969. Chinese-dominated Singapore witnessed ethnic riots in 1964, and in 1965 pulled itself out of the two-year-old federation with Malaysia after a dispute over the rights of Malay and Chinese citizens. Indonesia saw outbreaks of communal violence in the late 1950s and 1965; more shocking yet, Indonesia has been shaken by bitter, though intermittent, ethno-religious violence since 1996 – the final years of President Soeharto's rule – up until today.

The Indonesian Islamic Roots of Pluralism

Indonesia is one of the most pluralistic societies in terms of ethnic, linguistic, cultural and religious differences. The Indonesian archipelago – which consists of more than 17,800 islands, isles and islets – and its history make Indonesia an extremely pluralistic society. Reflecting the diverse ethnic groups living in the country, Indonesians speak over 525 languages and dialects.

As far as the religious life is concerned, according to some estimates, the total population of Indonesia is about 206 million people, of which 87.21 per cent are Muslims, 6.04 per cent are Protestants, 3.58 per cent are Catholics, 1.83 per cent are Hindus, and 1.34 per cent are other religions and spiritual groups. The Indonesian government officially recognizes Islam, Protestantism, Catholicism, Hinduism, Buddhism and Confucianism.[1]

Despite its religious diversity, Indonesia has until recently been generally known as a country where a number of great world religions meet and develop in peaceful coexistence. The early history of the spread of Islam and Christianity in the archipelago had been largely peaceful, though bitter contests and struggles took place in certain areas. It was arguably the consolidation of Islam and Christianity in much of the period of the twelfth to seventeenth centuries that produced boundaries among the adherents of these religions (Reid 1993; Azra 2000). Further, some have argued that Indonesian Islam is radically syncretic, reflecting the distance of the archipelago from precisely Mecca and Medina, where Islam was originally revealed and developed. Thus the American anthropologist Clifford Geertz famously wrote

1 The Constitution of Indonesia, Article 29(2), states: 'The state guarantees the right of all citizens to worship according to his or her own religion or belief.' However, a presidential edict by Soekarno in 1965 limited the number of official religions recognized by the government of Indonesia to only six — Islam, Protestantism, Catholicism, Hinduism, Buddhism and Confucianism. For most of the New Order, Confucianism was not recognized in practice. A major gain in religious freedom in Indonesia was the official recognition of Confucianism in a speech by President Susilo Bambang Yudhoyono in February 2006 (Bush 2007).

of the 'religion of Java' (1960) rather than of Islam in Java. Indeed, Geertz proposed that there were three variants of Islam in Java particularly and, by extension, in the archipelago generally; *priyayi* (aristocrat Muslims), *santri* (strict and practising Muslims), and *abangan* (nominal Muslims). According to Geertz, the *priyayi* variant was heavily influenced by Indic-Sanskrit culture, whereas the *abangan* variant was too indigenous, syncretic and even animistic. Therefore, in his judgement, it is only the *santri* variant, with its heavy orientation to Middle Eastern Islam, that is the real Islam; and members of this variant are numerically few amongst the population.

Recent studies have tended to rebut Geertz's interpretation. As has been shown by Azra (2004) for the period of the seventeenth to eighteenth centuries and beyond, and by Laffan (2003), Islam in the archipelago has never been cut off from that in the Middle East. In fact, there is a great deal of intense connections, networks and religio-cultural exchanges among Muslims in the two regions. All these in turn have influenced the course of Islam in the archipelago, including Java. These have been shown by such scholars as Hefner (1985), Woodward (1985), Ricklefs (1998), Riddell (2001) and many others.

Even though Indonesia is increasingly known as the largest Muslim nation in the world, it is not an Islamic state. Politically and ideologically, Indonesia is a state based on *Pancasila* (five principles):

1. Belief in one supreme God;
2. Just and civilized humanism;
3. The unity of Indonesia;
4. Democracy;
5. Social justice.

Proposed initially by Soekarno, the first President of the Republic of Indonesia, *Pancasila* was (and still is) a compromise between secular nationalists who advocated a secular state and Muslim leaders who demanded an 'Islamic state'. After a series of 'Islamizations' of all the five principles – that was also accepted tacitly by non-Muslim groups – Muslim leaders in the end accepted *Pancasila* and regarded it as having no incompatibility with Islamic teaching (Madjid 1994, 57–8).

Muslim acceptance of *Pancasila* is no doubt one of the most important Indonesian Islamic roots of pluralism. For the majority of Indonesian Muslims, *Pancasila* is, in line with a verse of the *Qur'an*, a '*kalimah sawa*', a common platform, among different religious followers. Addressing the Prophet Muhammad, the *Qur'an* has this to say:

> Say: O the people of the Book [*ahl al-Kitab*, that is the Jews and Christians]; come to common terms between us and you; that we worship none but God, that we associate partners with him, that we erect not, from ourselves, lords and patrons, other than God … (Q, 3:64).

Indeed Adam Malik, who was once Vice President during the Soeharto period, maintained that *Pancasila*, in Islamic perspective, is in a similar spirit to the *modus vivendi* that was created by the Prophet Muhammad in Medina after having migrated (*hijra*) from Mecca. The Prophet laid down the *modus vivendi* in a famous document called the 'Constitution of Medina' (*mithaq al-madinah*). The document includes a provision which states that all Medinan factions, including Jews, were one nation (*ummah*) together with Muslims, and that they have the same rights and duties as Muslims. Adam Malik interprets the 'Constitution of Medina' as a formula for a state based on the idea of social and religious pluralism (Madjid 1994, 64). Unfortunately, however, the Soeharto regime used *Pancasila* as a tool for repression, and the forced implementation in 1985 of *Pancasila* as the sole ideological basis of all organizations in the country led to a loss of faith in it as a basis for Indonesian religious pluralism.

Contemporary Religious Conflict in Indonesia

Since much of the second half of the 1990s, Indonesia has been marked by social unrest and violence in various parts of the country. Although much of the violence has been caused by political and economic factors, the rest has been associated with religion, or at least has had strong religious overtones. An example that is often put forward in this context is the religio-communal violence in Ambon and other parts of the Maluku archipelago which involves Muslim groups on the one hand and Christian groups on the other (Azra 2001; 2002). There is also evidence of a religious colouration in the Poso (Central Sulawesi) conflict and in violence that erupted among Muslim and Christian groups not long after the Maluku violence.

Nonetheless, it is important not to conclude that most of the recent conflicts and violence in Indonesia have been religiously motivated. On the contrary, most are rooted in the economic and political problems that have not been solved since the time of Soeharto's New Order. Religious symbols came only later as rallying cries in the confrontation. Granted that communal riots have taken place more often with an increasingly larger scale of people involved since the second half of the 1990s; the eruption of communal violence may be the tip of an iceberg of political and social discontent, not only among the lower classes of the population, but also among the middle classes, based, at least initially, on the economic injustices and deprivations that occur during an apparent 'economic boom'. Later this economic discontent amalgamated with political injustices and deprivation that most Indonesians had suffered since the 1970s, and the unusual succession of the presidency from Soeharto to Habibie, following the monetary, economic and political crises in May 1998, shook not only Indonesian political unity, but also produced further conflict and violence in Indonesian society.

The Ambon communal violence, which erupted in January 1999 and worsened and spread to other parts of the Maluku Province, is perhaps the most often quoted as a clear case of religious conflict in Indonesia in recent years. Communal conflict and violence in Ambon and other places in Maluku, such as Halmahera and Ternate, involve the Muslim community on the one hand and the Protestant community on the other. The large-scale violence between the two religious groups resulted not only in the killing of a large number of people (both Muslims and Christians), but also in the burning of mosques, churches, houses, markets and other public buildings and facilities (Azra 2002, 87–91).

It is no secret of course that Muslims and Christians in Maluku have long been involved in a sort of race to gain the upper hand in religion, economic and politics of the region (Azra 2000). According to more reliable sources, Islam came to Maluku in the fifteenth century, and by the turn of that century, the Ternate Sultanate had been established. The Portuguese, who came to Maluku in 1513 not only to trade, but also to spread Christianity, soon challenged the Sultans of Ternate. However, the Portuguese surrendered in 1575 after a long siege of their fort in Ternate by Sultan Baabullah. Before long, the European forces were again coming to Maluku. This time the Dutch, who initially came in 1599, began to take control of one area after another in Maluku. Later, with their firm grip on control, Dutch missionaries were also in a strong position to spread Christianity in Maluku. After Indonesia gained independence on 17 August 1945, groups of Moluccan Christians, who used to possess political, military and economic privileges during colonial times, proclaimed the independence of the South Moluccan Republic on 25 April 1950. This separatism, despite the fact that it created prolonged political problems for both the Republic of Indonesia and the Netherlands, failed to realize its political ambitions. But deep suspicions remain, particularly among the Muslims about their Christian fellow citizens, and are also apparent in the recent conflict and violence.

Nonetheless, over the last two decades at least, the Ambon or Maluku communal riots have their root causes in the contest for economic resources and the increasingly disproportionate distribution of political power in the local bureaucracy between Muslims (consisting of indigenous Maluku and migrants, better known as the BBM [Buginese, Butonese and Makasarese], all from South Sulawesi) and indigenous Christians. The New Order government of President Soeharto failed to address these latent problems. Instead, the regime tried to conceal the problems, mainly through the all too familiar security approach. In the framework of this approach, no one had been allowed to discuss the problems openly and thus find feasible and viable solutions, since all issues involved here were those of SARA (Suku, Agama, Ras, Antar golongan, or ethnicity, religion, race, inter-group), which were considered by the regime to be very sensitive and divisive.

Furthermore, during the Soeharto era, the demographic composition of the Maluku Province changed rapidly. According to some reports, up until 1970, the indigenous Christians constituted a slim majority of the total population. Since the early 1980s, however, with the improved economy and better means of transportation, the BBM people have come steadily in large numbers and settled in various areas of Maluku, particularly in Ambon. With their arrival, the Muslims in Maluku increasingly outnumbered the Christians. This development not only affected the demographic composition, but also resulted in increasing changes in the fields of economics and politics. Before long, BBM migrants dominated the Maluku economy, as economic opportunities were widely opened for them, since the native Christians were more interested in being civil servants than traders. The resentment of the native Christian population increased since almost all the BBM migrants were Muslims.

Communal relations rapidly worsened when the Muslims became increasingly politically mobile. To take one obvious example, the last two governors of Maluku

Province have been Muslims. This seemingly unstoppable Muslim political mobility challenged the Christians who used to dominate the local bureaucracy, and undoubtedly was an important factor in the rapid growth of ethnic and religious hostilities. All these demographic, economic and political changes strained the already fragile fabric of Maluku society, waiting for the right time to explode.

Therefore, the sudden fall of President Soeharto and the shaky authority of President Habibie soon rekindled the embers of the conflict and tension within the Ambon or Maluku society as a whole. Triggered by a quarrel between a Christian youth and Muslims over a city public bus fare, large-scale riots erupted in Ambon, the very night before the Muslims celebrate *Īd al-Fitr* or *Eid ul Fitr*, the celebration which marks the end of the fasting month of Ramadan. Since that time, intermittent clashes and violence between Christian and Muslim groups have continued, leaving large numbers of people dead and countless homes, markets and other buildings completely destroyed. Clashes and riots, which initially erupted in Ambon, the capital city of Maluku Province, spread to some other parts of the province, giving the strong impression that communal riots are far from being resolved by the central government which already has many problems to deal with.

One of the most important factors responsible for the prolonged communal riots has been the indecisiveness of the police and military. So far, they have failed to put an end to the continuing conflicts. At the same time, there is strong evidence that Indonesian security forces are also entangled in the violence. Some members are taking a position of defending either the Christian or Muslim groups. Worse still, they use their armaments to confront groups of people who do not belong to their religion. This is why the military commander in Jakarta has replaced most of the security forces in Maluku with those recruited from other places in Indonesia. But again, by and large this policy has also failed. The election of Abdurrahman Wahid brought new hopes for a peaceful settlement of the Ambon case. President Wahid, a few days after his instalment, assigned Vice President Megawati Soekarnoputri to resolve the conflict through dialogue and other peaceful means. But the situation in Ambon remained unsettled. Outbursts of violence continued to take place. Vice President Megawati, in turn, proved very indecisive, and failed to implement any policy that could put an end to the conflict. But the situation in Ambon remains unsettled. Outbursts of violence continue to take place.

Conclusion

Looking at the conflict and violence between Muslim and Christian groups in Indonesia, it becomes clear that this conflict is far from typical of Indonesia as a whole. This prolonged conflict has spread at most to Poso in Central Sulawesi, but not to anywhere else in Indonesia. There are of course conflicts and riots in other places in Indonesia, such as in West Kalimantan, Central Kalimantan and Aceh, but these have nothing to do with religion, and mostly to do with economic and political grievances. Therefore, one might conclude that, by and large, religious diversity and peaceful coexistence among the followers of different religions in Indonesia remain intact and that the prospects for religious pluralism in Indonesia are quite bright.

The problems that exist are largely problems of governance, and not problems of constitutional principle.

References

Abu Khalil, Shawqi (1990), *Tasamuh al-Islam wa Ta'asub Khusumih* (Beirut: Manshurat Mu'assasat).

Azra, Azyumardi (2000), 'The Race between Islam and Christianity Theory Revisited: Islamization and Christianization in the Malay-Indonesian Archipelago 1530–1670', *Documentatieblad voor de Geschiedenis van Nederlandse Zending en Overzeese Kerken* 7: 2, 26–37.

Azra, Azyumardi (2001), 'Islam and Christianity in Indonesia: The Roots of Conflict and Hostility', in J.A. Camilleri (ed.), *Religion and Culture in Asia Pacific: Violence or Healing?* (Melbourne: Pax Christi & Vista Publication).

Azra, Azyumardi (2002), 'Communal Riots in Indonesia: The Decline of Indonesian Nationalism and the Rise of Separatism', in Chaider S. Bamualim, Dick Van Der Meij and Karlina Helamnita (eds), *Communal Conflicts in Contemporary Indonesia* (Jakarta: Center for Languages and Cultures, State Islamic University [UIN] and Konrad Adenauer Stiftung).

Azra, Azyumardi (2004), *The Origins of Islamic Reformism in Southeast Asia: Networks of Malay-Indonesian and Middle Eastern 'Ulama'* (Canberra, Honolulu and Leiden: ASAA and Allen and Unwin; University of Hawaii Press; KITLV).

Bush, R. (2007), 'One Step Forward', *Inside Indonesia*, April–June (Asia Foundation), available at: <http://www.insideindonesia.org., accessed 27 September 2007.

Eickelman, D.F. (2002), 'Islam and Ethical Pluralism', in S.H. Hashmi (ed.), *Islamic Political Ethics* (Princeton: Princeton University Press).

Esack, Farid (1996), *Qur'an, Liberation and Pluralism: An Islamic Perspective of Interreligious Solidarity against Oppression* (Oxford: Oneworld Publications).

Furnivall, J.S. (1944) [1939], *Netherlands India: A Study of Plural Economy* (New York: Macmillan).

Geertz, C. (1960), *Religion of Java* (Glencoe: Free Press).

Hashmi, Sohail H. (2002), *Islamic Political Ethics: Civil Society, Pluralism, and Conflict* (Princeton: Princeton University Press).

Hefner, R.W. (1985), *Hindu Javanese, Tengger Tradition and Islam* (Princeton: Princeton University Press).

Hefner, R.W. (1999), 'Religion: Evolving Pluralism', in D.K. Emmerson (ed.), *Indonesia beyond Suharto: Polity, Economy, Society, Transition* (Armonk, NY and London: ME Sharpe).

Hefner, R.W. (ed.) (2001), *The Politics of Multiculturalism: Pluralism and Citizenship in Malaysia, Singapore and Indonesia* (Honolulu: University of Hawaii Press).

Laffan, M.F. (2003), *Islamic Nationhood and Colonial Indonesia: The Umma below the Winds* (London and New York: RoutledgeCurzon).

Madjid, N. (1994), 'Islamic Roots of Modern Pluralism: Indonesian Experience', *Studia Islamika: Indonesian Journal for Islamic Studies* 1: 1.

Moussalli, A. (2001), 'An Islamic Model for Conflict Resolution', in Abdul Aziz Said (ed.), *Peace and Conflict Resolution in Islam: Precepts and Practice* (Lanham, MD: University Press of America).

an-Na'im, Abdullah Ahmad (1990), *Toward an Islamic Reformation: Civil Liberties, Human Rights, and International Law* (Syracuse: Syracuse University Press).

Reid, A. (1993), *Southeast Asia in the Age of Commerce 1450–1680: Volume Two, Expansion and Crisis* (New Haven: Yale University Press).

Ricklefs, M.C. (1998), *The Seen and Unseen Worlds in Java, 1726–1749: History, Literature, and Islam in the Court of Pakubuwana II* (St. Leonards, Australia and Honolulu: ASAA, Allen and Unwin, and University of Hawaii Press).

Riddell, P.G. (2001), *Islam and the Malay-Indonesian World: Transmission and Responses* (London and Singapore: C. Hurst and Horizon Books).

Sachedina, Abdulaziz (2001), *The Islamic Roots of Democratic Pluralism* (Oxford: Oxford University Press).

Woodward, M.R. (1985), 'The Shari'ah and the Secret Doctrine: Muslim Law and Mystical Doctrine in Central Java', PhD dissertation, University of Illinois, Urbana-Champaign.

Chapter 16

Nationalism and Liberalism

John Kane

Introducing this topic in an exchange between Islamic and Western scholars in Indonesia, I must admit to having felt some uncertainty about the relevance of a chapter centred on the political thought of Thomas Hobbes. In stages, however, Islamic scholars enlightened my ignorance of the history of Islamic political philosophy, which, I discovered, had a distinctly Hobbesian cast. A powerful government capable of awing subjects or citizens into peaceful coexistence seemed as logically needful to Islamic thinkers as it had to the great seventeenth-century British philosopher. Moreover, the problem of properly securing people's allegiance to the earthly Leviathan – which, I argue here, was a latent problem for Hobbes that pointed the way to some form of nationalism – seemed not irrelevant to the present condition of Indonesia, with its huge diversity of peoples and languages and its need to accommodate so disparate an array within the confines of a modern nation state. I was encouraged to hope, therefore, that the following reflections on a conundrum at the heart of Western liberal democracy might have some interest and resonance in the Indonesian context.

It has been argued that it was merely fortuitous that liberalism and nationalism arose together in Europe to form a union enabling wealth creation within cohesive national boundaries (Meyer 1998, 63). But the alliance, however practical, presents theoretical problems. The principles of nationalism are not the founding principles of liberalism. Liberalism gives priority to individuals over community. The protection of individual rights, not collective utility or popular will, is its paramount concern. The core liberal idea is that the sole legitimacy of the political state resides in its function as an instrument for the protection of individual rights to life and property. Liberals have therefore been highly suspicious of, and resistant to, all 'collectivist' or 'communitarian' arguments.

It seems anomalous, then, that liberals should have privileged a particular form of community, namely the national one. Liberal states are *nation* states, 'nation' implying something higher than the mere political organization of power for security purposes. A nation is a community (even if only an 'imagined' one – Anderson 1983) that has traditionally demanded something more from its members than obligatory obedience to order-securing rules. Liberal nation states have demanded – and received – love that transcends individualism and encourages sacrifice.

Liberals have, for the most part, accepted nationalism without worrying much about whether it contradicts their own most basic, individualistic assumptions. Even today many accept that liberalism is dependent on the existence of some kind of nationalist sentiment, arguing that the latter ensures the social and cultural integration presumed necessary for the smooth functioning of liberal democracy. Aware that traditional nationalism based on blood and descent has lost the intellectual and moral respectability it once had, modern nationalist liberals seek some benign 'civic' form strong enough to promote a sense of commonality and belonging, but not so strong as to encourage xenophobia (Miller 1995; 1998; Barry 1999).

One of the arguments put forward by David Miller on the need for a nationalist sentiment concerns the sacrifices he believes are required for meeting the demands of social justice. He claims that there is unlikely to be democratic support for the redistribution of resources unless citizens regard themselves as bound to the beneficiaries by strong ties of community, and by a sense of common identity (Miller 1998, 59, 236).[1] In this chapter I want to look at the larger sacrifice required by the need for defence at times of threat, which reveals most starkly the tensions liberalism suffers through its de facto association with the national community.

I will begin with a brief account of liberal individualism and the challenge presented to it by various critiques, particularly those of 'communitarians' in the context of multicultural policy. I will discuss the instinctive liberal distrust of group or community rights that cannot be reduced to individual rights, and note the significant exception made, explicitly or tacitly, for the case of national communities. I will then look at the loss of intellectual and moral respectability suffered by theories of nationalism in recent times, despite the continuing force of nationalism in the world, and ask what it implies for the cogency of liberal theory that it has tied its fortunes to such a questionable phenomenon. Finally, I will attempt to address this question through a return to liberal foundations in the work of Thomas Hobbes, and particularly to his failure to provide theoretically for the effective defence of the commonwealth. I will argue that this defect is correctible by appeal to Hobbes' own account of love and gratitude, which bind individuals to their commonwealth and to each other in a way that pure self-concern cannot. This, then, may indicate theoretical foundations for a form of nationalism on which (a perhaps modified) liberal individualism can be argued to depend.

Liberalism and its Critics

What is an individual? What is a community? What is a nation? None of these questions, however one may take them, admits of a simple or singular answer. Perhaps they do not even make much sense formulated in this manner. The 'is' suggests an existent 'thing' that can be isolated, examined and accurately described. But what is most often at issue for individual, community and nation is the very *mode of existence* to be imputed in each case. It often seems easier to address causal questions about how individuals, communities or nations emerge and act upon the world than to answer questions about what, existentially, they 'are'.

---

1 Many of the arguments put forward by civic nationalists are more concerned with democratic functioning than with liberal values as such (see, for example, Taylor 1996). I am more concerned here with the liberal element in liberal democracy than with its democratic aspects, though of course the conjunction of liberalism with democracy is no less problematic theoretically than that with nationalism.

Further, it is hard to give a definite answer to any of these questions without apparently pre-determining answers to the others. This is not just because in characterizing individuals we must define the nature of their relationship to communities, or because in defining the 'super-community', nation, we are obliged to describe its relationship to the various communities and individuals it enfolds. It is because any description we offer will have ideological import in the sense of expressing a priority of one category over another. That human beings are social creatures is undeniable, but does it follow that human individuals are reducible to the social collectives in and from which they emerge? One might as easily say (as some do) that societies, since they contain nothing but individual human beings, are therefore reducible to the latter. Many of the most fundamental arguments about politics revolve around this question of which category is to be regarded as – logically, ontologically, causally or morally – prior.

In modern political theory, liberalism argued the priority of the individual over communities or collectives. Individuals lived in communities, of course, but liberals took these to be mere voluntary associations that people might enter or leave at will. Any stronger notion implied an unwarranted collective check on that liberty to which individuals had a 'natural' right simply by virtue of being individuals. Since liberty without existence was meaningless, natural rights were held to extend also to an individual's possession of life and the means of subsistence – in other words, to property. The essence of liberal political theory, therefore, was that pre-existent individuals voluntarily formed societies for their mutual advantage, and established governments over those societies to defend their natural rights to liberty and property. The sole justification of government lay in its performance of this latter function. Government was therefore conceived to be a purely instrumental means to individual ends with no particular value in itself – indeed, it was often regarded as a necessary evil, and a potential danger to the very liberty it was instituted to protect.

Left-wing opponents of liberalism insisted instead on the essentially collective nature of human reality. Marxists argued that 'bourgeois individualism' mistook (intentionally even if not consciously) the egoistic individuals of civil society for representatives of a universal class displaying the real nature of humankind. In reality, according to the Marxist view, they formed but a moment in the historical evolution of class relations, necessary for developing the capitalist mode of production but destined to be superseded by, or reunited in, a genuine community during the higher stages of communism (see Barry 1999). Bourgeois individuals were an historical fact, but liberal individualism was merely a self-justifying, ideological fiction. A similar perspective could be detected in the work of various 'postmodern' writers, some of whom viewed the 'self-choosing' liberal individual as the creation of a totalizing political system that purposefully individuated subjects (that is, determined them as individuals) (Foucault 1983; Connolly 1988). Others argued the virtual dissolution of the individual self within a fabric of determinative social relations – the necessarily social individual was reduced to a 'subject position' within various 'language games', 'narratives' or 'discourses'. 'A self', said Lyotard, 'does not amount to much' (1997, 15).

Liberals, of course, vehemently rejected Marxist views (which they saw as ultimately tyrannical over individuals) and were ambivalent about those of the postmoderns (the political implications of whose theories were often unclear – but see Corlett 1989; Young 1989; 1990). They were more agitated, however, by 'communitarian' criticism that arose within their own ranks and that deployed similar critiques. So-called communitarians were usually less intent on destroying liberal values than in applying a corrective by pointing out that 'the social fabric sustains, nourishes, and enables individuality rather than diminishes it' (Etzioni 1996; see also Bellah 1996; Barber 1984). They argued that people were inevitably and beneficially dependent upon one another, unable to achieve or even conceive of individual goods outside of the communities and traditions that both form them and provide the context of their meaningful action (MacIntyre 1984; Walzer 1983). Communities were 'constitutive' of people's very selves (Sandel 1982) and therefore prior to individuality and to individual liberty (Taylor 1977; 1992). Communitarians diagnosed a sense of loss, even of pathology, in societies that promoted the liberal ideal of individual autonomy. They noted a loss of psychic connection to others, a loss of mutuality, and of a type of relationship that transcends the liberal's contractarian notion of mutual exchange for benefit. Such relationships were held to constitute part of one's individual identity, and to make up an essential part of any coherent notion of the good life (Phillips 1993).

The force of the communitarian challenge was felt most strongly by liberals over the issue of 'multiculturalism' (Kane 2002, 98–101). In an era concerned to lay old ghosts of racialism, liberals in multicultural states felt impelled to confront the problem of ethno-cultural groups that, on the one hand, were the objects of unjust discrimination and, on the other, sometimes resisted assimilation to liberal-individual values. The liberal commitment to equality was tested by the first condition, the liberal value of toleration by the second.

The communitarians argued that toleration should be extended from individuals to the particular communities to which they belong and which support them in their being (Raz 1994; Kymlicka 1995). Cultures or communities should be held to have protective rights deserving of respect. Charles Taylor went so far as to recommend 'that we recognize the equal value of different cultures; that we not only let them survive, but acknowledge their worth' (Taylor 1992, 64). But this 'politics of recognition', as it was labelled, seemed to imply that liberal individual rights did not apply universally, a contention that other liberals rejected. Natural rights were so firmly attached to individuals in liberal theory that it was difficult, if not impossible, to conceive of them as attaching to groups of any kind, since group rights might, on occasion, be held legitimately to trump those of individuals. Whatever moral significance might attach to the preservation of cultural identity, it could not give rise to a collective right analogous to the rights that safeguarded an individual's liberty and autonomy (Narveson 1991; Stier 1998). Even Will Kymlicka, one of the principal advocates of multicultural group rights, stressed that these should not permit groups to restrict the autonomy of their members – individual liberty was to remain an inviolable principle.

More interesting from the perspective of this chapter, however, was the intended purpose of the group rights that Kymlicka originally proposed. These were meant to gain some measure of cultural protection for national minorities (for example, indigenous 'first nations' or Quebecois French) from the assimilative pressures of the dominant cultures within a state (Kymlicka 1995). Group rights could therefore be claimed only by sub-national groups and not by ethnic immigrant groups within a multicultural polity. This was a highly significant restriction in the context of liberal theory. It represented a tacit recognition of a longstanding exception to the liberal denial of rights for groups or communities. That exception was precisely the nation to which liberal individuals belonged.

Liberalism and Nationalism

Liberals have typically pursued their individual goals within national political cultures. In accord with liberal theory, the legal and political authority of the state provided a stable environment in which individuals, accorded the status of equal citizenship, could comfortably pursue their private ends (in particular, their economic ends). Yet the liberal state quickly became something more than an institutional device for the protection of natural rights to life and property. It turned into something larger than the collection of individuals who comprised it, something to which those individuals were presumed to belong in a particular way, and to which they owed a special allegiance and special duties, even love. The nation was a community that itself had rights – for example, rights to national self-determination, or non-interference by other nations – rights that could not be reduced to individual rights. It was also a community that could and did demand sacrifices from its members in the confidence that it had a right to do so.

Liberal theory thus privileged one particular form of community. Whenever the connection was explicitly noted, as it was by John Stuart Mill, the essential national principle was simply presumed to prevail. 'Where the sentiment of nationality exists in any force [and however it might have arisen], there is a *prima facie* case for uniting all members of the nationality under the same government, and a government to themselves apart' (Mill 1972, 392).[2] But this was hardly a liberal justification for government, since nationalism in Mill's time presumed a prior and supra-individual identity of which individuals partook. Nineteenth-century thinkers, influenced by writers like Johann Herder (1968), understood nations as distinct cultural-linguistic entities united by blood and by attachment to place. Nations were the products of organic historical growth and therefore 'natural' (the two English words share the same Latin root, *nasci*, to be born). It seemed to an age marked by both the ascendancy of the sovereign state and the romantic elevation of nature, that natural justice required that every true nation be self-determining within its own state.

Yet the liberation of peoples and cultures suffering the oppressive yoke of foreign domination, however laudable, rested on a presumption different from the individualistic premises of liberalism. Indeed, there has never been any principled reason why national states should not be anti-liberal. Worse, from the perspective of classical theory, it was argued that even liberal governments were dependent on a prior national principle. Free institutions, Mill said, were almost impossible in a state

2 This is also Ernest Gellner's (1983, 1) definition: 'Nationalism is primarily a political principle, which holds that the political and the national unit should be congruent.'

containing mixed nationalities that precluded 'fellow-feeling' and sense of common identity (Mill 1972, 392).

This conjunction of liberalism and nationalism should perhaps have become even more embarrassing once the theory of nationalism turned into an intellectual scandal. It had always been a scandal for Marxist thinkers, of course, because the nation proved to be a more powerful cohesive force than international proletarian solidarity. Even avowedly Marxist regimes could not, ultimately, dispense with nationalist sentiment. Stalin mobilized the Soviet masses to defeat the Nazi invasion not by pleading communist ideology or by urging loyalty to the party, but by a frank appeal to love of Mother Russia. Nor did ideology long sustain fraternal solidarity once communism had spread to other parts of the world. The Soviet Union, China, Vietnam and Cambodia all pitted their enmity against each other as much as, if not more than, against the nations of the decadent West. Communism proved to be quite as amenable to, and perhaps as dependent upon, the formation of national varieties as had capitalism before it. Neither bourgeoisie nor workers showed any profound inclination to think or act as a 'world class'.[3]

But in the twentieth century, nationalism became a scandal for liberally minded people as well, people of the kind that had once been fervent supporters of nineteenth-century 'liberal nationalism'. Jingoistic imperialism, fascist outrage, attempted genocide, ethnic cleansing, all seemed to reveal the darkly xenophobic potentiality of the ethno-cultural nation. Nationalism's moral stock fell among liberal intellectuals, who began to look toward transnational forms of governance that might relegate the sovereign nation state to a more subsidiary role. Yet the force of nationalism in the world appeared undiminished even at the start of the twenty-first century. Though some argued that increasing cultural and economic integration signalled the eventual decline of the nation state, politicians continued to play the nationalist card at crucial moments, confident that people would respond with feelings of love, loyalty and sacrifice. Nations continued to engage in bitter struggles to free themselves from domination or fragmentation, or to gain hold of disputed territory, in order to constitute themselves as true nation states (Lind 2002).

It was just this continuing strength of nationalism that was the greatest scandal so far as scholars were concerned, even greater than the loss of moral respectability. For all its undeniable effectuality, nationalism no longer seemed to have any intellectual or theoretical credibility. Political power was allegedly accompanied by 'philosophical poverty' (Anderson 1983, 5). The principal problem was the allegedly 'fictive' nature of the nation, which could always be shown to be a political creation rather than a primordial existent. Though nations were new things in history, they must appear to 'loom out of an immemorial past' (Anderson 1983, 11). The creation of nations involved the creation of myths (or downright falsehoods) about the nation's origins – thus the ironic definition of a nation as 'a society united by a common error about its origin and a common aversion to its neighbours' (Ginsberg 1963, 2). If traditions were required to prove antiquity, then traditions would be invented (Hobsbawm

3 Benedict Anderson's well-known book, *Imagined Communities: Reflections on the Origin and Spread of Nationalism* (1983, 4), declared its aim to be to offer a more satisfactory interpretation of this 'anomaly' than it had hitherto received.

and Ranger 1983). It was for this reason that Hobsbawm claimed that no serious historian of nations and nationalism can also be a committed political nationalist: 'Nationalism requires too much belief in what is patently not so' (1990, 12).

But if nationalism is, in the end, no more than a form of irrationalism, it can hardly provide a basis for serious political theory any more than for serious history. At best it may be the object of political analysis, amenable, like racism perhaps, to socio-psychological explanation. It surely cannot be deployed as a philosophical category with respectably normative force. As in Marx's view of religion, it can perhaps be explained only by being explained away.[4] Bad enough that liberalism should have made itself dependent on any form of community at all, worse to have hitched its fortunes to an imagined community[5] lacking either theoretical or historical justification.

It may be thought that the case would be better for 'civic nations' whose identities are allegedly founded more on loyalty to rational political principles and perhaps a particular political history rather than on pre-existing ethno-cultural commonalities or the heritage of blood. This is certainly the hope of contemporary liberals who argue the compatibility of liberal values with 'thin' conceptions of national identity (Barry 1999). There is reason, however, to doubt the soundness of this hope, given that even civic nations feel the need to invent their own sustaining myths and (as Mill virtually admitted) are themselves generally underpinned by explicit or implicit 'ethnic' criteria (such as 'race' or religion) (Wiebe 1975; Smith 1986; Kane 1997). I take the essence of nationalism to be not rational assent but love, love of something transcending oneself that is yet an important source of one's self-identity – of a country identified as one's own, or of a people who are one's own. Such love easily transforms into hatred of those who would threaten or hurt one's own, and provides the motive for the lover to be prepared to sacrifice him- or herself for the beloved when necessary. It is exactly the political mobilization of such love and hatred for the purposes of warfare that has characterized nationalism in modern times, and given it the appearance, to the eyes of cool liberals, of an irrational and detestable primitivism.

It would be unfortunate, then, if liberalism's historical success was, in fact, dependent upon the preservation of 'primitive' communal passions that had no place within its own theoretical assumptions. If it were so, would this reveal a fatal flaw in theoretical liberalism itself? I want to suggest that liberal individualism in its purest form is indeed flawed, but that its dependence on some form of nationalism may be more than simply expedient. To make this argument, I want to return to liberal

---

4 Religion's real power over people's minds was, according to Marx, the result of the fantastical solace it afforded for present suffering, a solace bought at the price of obscuring the real forces preventing happiness here on earth. Nationalism could be regarded as a political illusion that is the secular extension of the religious illusion Marx sought to dispel, useful for binding people to political structures that, on deeper analysis, are inimical to their true happiness (Cocks 2002, 26–30).

5 Anderson's formulation implies a contrast to 'real' communities in which people deal with each other face to face. This is to suppose that face-to-face human communities are transparently existent and not themselves crucially the products of 'imagination'. The same goes for 'individuals', as the beginning of this chapter indicates.

foundations. The seeds of the problem were, I will claim, already there in the work of the most profound of the theorists who ushered in the modern era, Thomas Hobbes. They can be discerned in his arguments concerning the obligation of subjects to defend their 'commonwealth' against external enemies.

Hobbes was not, of course, a modern liberal (the word was not coined until the nineteenth century), and certainly not a liberal democrat concerned with constitutionalizing the power that human beings had created through their covenanting (that honour went to Locke). But no author pursued so determinedly and with such apparent logical force a path from the motives of solitary, fearful, self-interested individuals to the foundation of a sovereign power to which all were morally obligated. For Hobbes, the limits of an individual's obligation were logically set by the singular motive that impelled them to inaugurate the sovereign power, self-preservation. But this, I claim, was a potentially fatal flaw in his theory that threatened the very existence of his sovereign state. Moreover, I will argue that the answer to Hobbes' dilemma can be found in Hobbes himself, and that it lay in an appeal to another motive – love – that (just as in nationalism) transcended the self while simultaneously confirming it. My intuition is that if Hobbes' trenchant individualism can be shown to be dependent on according priority to some larger collective entity, then all extreme individualisms may prove similarly dependent.

The Hobbesian Dilemma

Hobbes famously argued that commonwealths were inaugurated by the agreement of free and equal individuals wishing to escape from a competitive 'state of nature' that he characterized as 'the war of all against all'. Unable to ensure their individual security in a world where every person, however strong, was equally vulnerable to the might or cunning of others, individuals covenanted together to establish a Leviathan state with the overawing power necessary to provide protection and justice for all. In exchange for this protection, individuals contracted away the natural right they had possessed in the state of nature to pursue their own interests to the maximum extent and by whatever means possible. This transfer of right was, said Hobbes, a voluntary act, 'and of the voluntary acts of every man, the object is some good to himself' (*Leviathan* 1, 14, 66; Hobbes 1996, 88, emphasis in original). In other words, the sole basis for the allegiance that each owed the state was, for Hobbes, nothing more than the individual benefit it bestowed upon him or her.

The commonwealth thus established may be more or less large, but it could not conceivably be universal. Hobbes therefore presumed the existence of a multitude of commonwealths that would remain, in the absence of an overarching power, in the original state of nature with respect to one another. Each commonwealth must therefore be prepared to defend its members from the aggression of others, which meant in practice mobilizing citizens for defence. The question then arose whether individuals could be obligated to risk or sacrifice their lives, given that obligation was founded solely on the sovereign's capacity to ensure individual self-preservation. This was an especially pressing question for Hobbes since he had argued, consistent with his initial premises, that self-preservation was a natural right that could not be covenanted away. He was adamant that 'no man can transfer, or lay down his right to save himself from death, wounds, and imprisonment, (the avoiding whereof is the only end of laying down any right)' (*Leviathan* 1, 14, 29; Hobbes 1996, 93). Even a justly condemned criminal did not forfeit – could not forfeit – his right to resist death, injury or imprisonment at the hands of established authority. Hobbes insisted that, in such individual cases, men by nature chose the lesser evil (danger of death in resisting) rather than the greater one (certain death in not resisting), and that they had always the right to do so.

It may be thought that this reasoning would also establish the collective case for resisting destruction of the commonwealth. At the most, however, it established a right to collective defence and not an obligation for individual citizens to assist in that defence. Indeed it is not clear that Hobbes' individualistic premises supported such a move, though it was one he seemed to make when he explored 'the true liberty of a subject; that is to say, what are the things, which though commanded by the sovereign, he may nevertheless, without injustice, refuse to do' (*Leviathan* 2, 21, 10; Hobbes 1996, 144). Hobbes argued that these things were revealed by a logical test. According to him, the sovereign's commands are in effect our own, since we have authorized the sovereign to make them on our collective behalf. We cannot justly disobey the sovereign's commands if doing so would frustrate the end for which sovereignty was ordained, namely our own security and survival. By the same token, however, we are not obligated to obey any command that requires us to harm ourselves (for example, an order to confess to crimes even if we have indeed committed them), for this would frustrate the end of sovereignty (*Leviathan* 2, 21, 12–15; Hobbes 1996, 144–5).

Despite this, Hobbes argues that we are sometimes obliged to obey when the sovereign commands us to do some dangerous thing, such as fight an enemy. He admits that refusal is not always unjust, even if the sovereign may have the right to punish such refusal by death. Avoiding a battle may be cowardice, he says, but is not injustice. Yet he goes on to argue:

> But he that enrolleth himself as a soldier … taketh away the excuse of a timorous nature; and is obliged, not only to go into battle, but also not to run from it, without his captain's leave. And when the defence of the commonwealth, requireth at once the help of all that are able to bear arms, every one is obliged; because otherwise the institution of the commonwealth, which they have not the purpose, or courage to preserve, was in vain (*Leviathan* 2, 21, 16; Hobbes 1996, 145).

Whatever the case with the enlisted soldier, the latter argument obliging collective exertion in defence of the commonwealth is one, not of logical, but of practical necessity: no common defence, no commonwealth. The logical contradiction is surely to be willing to die for an institution whose only purpose is to ensure one's preservation. It is of course possible to mount a moral argument that people who share the benefits of mutual association are obligated also to share the risks, including the risks of defence. Hobbes no doubt depends implicitly on this argument here, though it does not follow from his original premises. But even if we allow it, we must ask from what particular motive Hobbes expects a fearful individual to act in fulfilment of such a duty. The traditional reply, and the one many would still give today, would be honour – the honour of defending and perhaps sacrificing for one's community, or the fear of being thought dishonourable for failing to do so. But this reply is hardly available to Hobbes, in whose system honour was a degraded commodity.

Honour is said by Hobbes to be no more than the appearance of power, and the reputation that power confers among one's fellows.[6] He writes that it does not alter the case of honour 'whether an action (so it be great and difficult, and consequently a sign of much power), be just or unjust: for honour consisteth only in the opinion of power' (*Leviathan* 1, 10, 48; Hobbes 1996, 62). The Hobbesian irony is that this opinion of differential power is largely illusory in the state of nature, where 'the weakest has strength enough to kill the strongest' and where men are inclined to view their own gifts and ambitions as equal to everyone else's (*Leviathan* 1, 13, 1–2; Hobbes 1996, 82). Moreover, the desire for honour is portrayed by Hobbes as merely a petty form of human pride, which in the guise of glory or reputation is identified as one of the three main causes of destructive quarrel.[7] In the absence of a common power able to overawe all, he says, 'every man looketh that his companion should value him, at the same rate he sets upon himself'. So it happens that men do violence 'for trifles, as a word, a smile, a different opinion, and any other sign of undervalue' (*Leviathan* 1, 13, 5–7; Hobbes 1996, 83–4). One function of the common power set up to keep all in awe is to repress such impulses of honour. Indeed, since honour is identified with power, the unparalleled power of the sovereign virtually extinguishes all honour among individual subjects by humbling them to the same level of comparative powerlessness (*Leviathan* 2, 18, 19; Hobbes 1996, 121–2).

Hobbes' political theory is intended to be strictly 'realistic' about the human condition and therefore disillusioning about human pride and honour. He believes he can reveal the logical necessity for government – and thus the true foundations of political obedience and obligation – by assuming nothing more than self-interested, always-vulnerable individuals whose desire to live well inevitably pits them against every other (and commits them to 'a perpetual and restless desire for power after power, that ceaseth only in death'). The sovereign state that these individuals agree to create for their own protection therefore appears wholly instrumental, a mere prudential means to securing private ends. Hobbes claims that the establishment of a sovereign power introduces law and justice into the world, since he holds that until there exists a power capable of enforcing law and justice, these cannot exist. But sovereign power does not seem to create a political community capable of commanding the true loyalty and devotion of its members. Hobbes seems fatally unable to transcend his own individualistic premises through either logic or an appeal to a sense of honour he has intentionally devalued. In the matter of defence of the commonwealth, such a failure may be disastrous.

There is, however, a possible line of argument to be found in *Leviathan* that might deal with the problem. It derives from Hobbes' account of the emotions evoked in

6 Hobbes takes evidence of superiority in anything – speech, judgement, ability to hurt or help – as signs of power which cause people to honour those that display them and to dishonour those that lack them.

7 The other two are competition (for mastery of resources and people) and 'diffidence' (or fear of one another that forces men to use violence to defend their own).

giving and receiving benefits, in particular his analysis of those circumstances that call forth a response of love. Hobbes argued that, when a person we consider our equal confers upon us greater benefit than we can possibly return, we may pretend to love them but in fact will secretly hate them:

> For benefits oblige; and obligation is thraldom; and unrequitable obligation, perpetual thraldom; which is to one's equal, hateful. But to have received benefits from one, whom we acknowledge for superior, inclines to love; because the obligation is no new depression: and cheerful acceptation, (which men call gratitude), is such an honour done to the obliger, as is generally taken for retribution (*Leviathan* 1, 11, 7; Hobbes 1996, 67).

In other words, great benefits received from a superior do not put us any more deeply in that superior's debt than we were beforehand. Generosity is not therefore cause for resentment but for gratitude, and gratitude is the only recompense that the superior needs or requires.

Looking at this in the larger context of Hobbes' political theory, it is clear that the greatest benefits that a member of a commonwealth ever receives come from the sovereign power. That power provides the security and internal peace that are the necessary conditions for science, industry, arts, letters and society (*Leviathan* 1, 13, 9; Hobbes 1996, 84) – for everything, in other words, that makes life worthwhile, and even for life itself. If gratitude to a superior for benefits received inclines to love, then the sovereign, who is infinitely superior to any individual in power and beneficence, would appear to be worthy of the greatest love imaginable.

Honour finds its proper role here, too. If honour is recognition of superior power, then honour must be due to the sovereign above all else. Significantly, Hobbes connects honour to both love and to fear. 'To show any sign of love, or fear of another is to honour; for both to love, and to fear, is to value.' The subject must surely fear the sovereign's power, value the sovereign's exercise of that power, and love the sovereign for the indispensable benefits that this exercise bestows. Elsewhere, Hobbes connects honour and love to goodness. He writes: 'Honour consisteth in the inward thought and opinion of the power and goodness of another.' The passion that arises from the 'internal honour' of power is fear; the passion that arises from the internal honour of goodness is love (*Leviathan* 2, 31, 8–9; Hobbes 1996, 238–9). Though Hobbes takes a relativistic view of good and evil, he argues that all men agree at least that peace is good, and therefore also the means to it (*Leviathan* 1, 15, 40; Hobbes 1996, 105–6). Since the sovereign is the *only* means and guarantor of peace, the sovereign must also be the supreme source of all earthly goodness, therefore again deserving of supreme love. (It is significant that Hobbes called his Leviathan the 'earthly god', akin to the heavenly God whose presumed goodness and power commands our greatest love and fear.)

If the desire for self-preservation cannot guarantee the willingness of subjects to risk their lives for the commonwealth, the necessary impulse may nevertheless come from a love that is naturally evoked by gratitude. This is a love, moreover, that testifies to and helps sustain our bond of mutual dependence with all our fellows in the commonwealth. In Hobbes' theory, individuals do not covenant with the sovereign but with each other to create the sovereign, which remains therefore *from* them but *above* them all. Since the sovereign power is sustained by the continuing agreement of all, its effectual existence is both a sign and a product of every person's enduring, vital connection to his or her fellows.

It may seem curious that the earthly god we love is our own creation, our individual selves writ large, an entity whose deeds and actions we claim as our own. Yet this identification merely gives our love greater motive force. Indeed it opens the way for a theoretical rather than merely contingent and fortuitous connection of liberalism and nationalism. For nationalism, I have said, is but love of one's nation. And what is that but the love of something identified as a source of great beneficence that is, in some special sense, *our own*? The nation allows us to transcend our banal individuality and to find an identity in something greater than ourselves which is nevertheless of ourselves. It clearly separates 'mine' from 'thine', and in so doing binds us to our fellow nationals. It gives us a motive for love that may be demonstrated, when required, in service and in sacrifice.

Conclusion

If Hobbesian love and gratitude, centred on effective government, do indeed provide a foundation for some form of nationalism, it is clearly not of the ethno-cultural variety. It is perhaps more like the civic nationalism alleged to underpin citizenship in liberal democratic countries. Modern liberal democrats, however, are shy about speaking plainly of 'love', which seems to raise the spectre of the irrational passion they suppose to infuse the more virulent strains of national feeling. Yet one of the central problems for political citizenship since ancient Greek times has been to loosen people's primary bonds to local community, tribe or clan and to re-attach them to a civic polity that offers more and different kinds of rewards. It has never been deemed sufficient to rely solely on the self-interest of the citizen to achieve this, though that was fundamental too. Love of the polity that provided larger life opportunities and experience was encouraged. In Renaissance Italy, civic amour was actually required for the granting of citizenship rights (Riesenberg 1992).

If my argument is correct, then liberal individualism's attachment to nationalism may not be so anomalous after all. In fact, it may rest on a requirement that individuals must love something larger than themselves that is nevertheless of themselves and which thus attaches them to the thing loved and also, practically, to their fellow citizens. This something is the polity that provides the conditions and opportunities that make a liberal life possible. But if that is so, then liberal political theory begins to resemble much older conceptions of political citizenship, though it cannot be identical to them, since ancient patriotism is not the same as modern nationalism, however much these may be confused and conflated.

The relevance of these problems to the Indonesian context with which I began is arguable. Much of my discussion may seem very remote from the streets of Jakarta. However, I suspect that my argument is a good deal more relevant to the problem of how to reconcile a modern state with Indonesian Islam than it first seems. Like almost every country in the modern world, the borders of the state called Indonesia have been arbitrarily determined by history. They enclose a diverse set of peoples whose natural love and interest are attached to particular localities and to specific kith, kin or religion. If the arbitrary state is to be something more than a mere geographical entity, much more than force will be required to bind these diverse peoples together. They must find reasons to love the greater family that Indonesia aspires to be. The artificial forcing of love and identity by emphasizing real or illusory external threats common to all, though a familiar feature of modern nationalism, has been shown to import serious dangers. The state seeking genuine security must embark on a more serious form of nation-building, one that attempts, through good government and an evident will to justice, to provide rewards and engagements that give positive reasons for general allegiance, that give each a part in the common enterprise and each a reason to call the new nation one's own. To this extent, the radical task for Indonesia may be nation-building, and a modern democracy may only work within an overwhelmingly Islamic society if there is clear commonality of loyalty and obligation beyond Islam itself.

References

Anderson, B. (1983), *Imagined Communities: Reflections on the Origin and Spread of Nationalism* (London: Verso).

Barber, B. (1984), *Strong Democracy: Participatory Politics for a New Age* (Berkeley: University of California Press).

Barry, B. (1999), 'Statism and Nationalism: A Cosmopolitan Critique', in L. Brilmayer and I. Shapiro (eds), *Global Justice: NOMOS XLI* (New York: New York University Press).

Bellah, R. (1996), *Habits of the Heart: Individualism and Commitment in American Life*, Revised Edition (Berkeley: University of California Press).

Cocks, J. (2002), *Passion and Paradox: Intellectuals Confront the National Question* (Princeton: Princeton University Press).

Connolly, W. (1988), *Political Theory and Modernity* (Oxford: Basil Blackwell).

Corlett, W. (1989), *Community Without Unity: A Politics of Derridarian Extravagance* (Durham, NC: Duke University Press).

Etzioni, A. (1960), *The New Golden Rule: Morality and Community in a Democratic Society* (New York: Basic Books).

Etzioni, A. (1996), 'A Modern Commmunitarian Proposal', *Political Theory* 24: 2, 155–71.

Foucault, M. (1983), 'Why Study Power?', in H. Dreyfus and P. Rabinow (eds), *Michael Foucault: Beyond Structuralism and Hermeneutics* (Chicago: University of Chicago Press).

Gellner, E. (1983), *Nations and Nationalism* (Oxford: Basil Blackwell).

Ginsberg, M. (1963), *Nationalism: A Reappraisal* (Leeds: Leeds University Press).

Herder, J.G. (1968) [1784–91], *Reflections on the Philosophy of the History of Mankind*, Abridged, and with an introduction by Frank E. Manuel (Chicago: University of Chicago Press).

Hobbes, T. (1996) [1651], *Leviathan* (Oxford: Oxford University Press).

Hobsbawm, E. (1990), *Nations and Nationalism since 1780: Programme, Myth, Reality* (Cambridge: Cambridge University Press).

Hobsbawm, E. and Ranger, T. (eds) (1983), *The Invention of Tradition* (Cambridge: Cambridge University Press).

Kane, J. (1997), 'Racialism, Democracy and National Identity: The Legacies of White Australia', in G. Stokes (ed.), *The Politics of Identity in Australia* (Melbourne: Cambridge University Press).

Kane, J. (2002), 'Democracy and Group Rights', in G. Stokes and A. Carter (eds), *Democratic Theory Today* (Cambridge: Polity Press).

Kymlicka, W. (1995), *Multicultural Citizenship: A Liberal Theory of Minority Rights* (Oxford: Clarendon Press).

Lind, M. (2002), 'National Good', *Prospect*, October issue, available at: <http://www.prospect-magazine.co.uk/highlights/essay_oct/index.html>.

Lyotard, J-F. (1997) [1979], *The Post-Modern Condition: A Report on Knowledge* (trans. G. Bennington) (Minneapolis: University of Minnesota Press).

MacIntyre, A. (1984), *After Virtue*, 2nd Edition (Indiana: University of Notre Dame Press).

Meyer, W.J. (1998), 'The Politics of Differentiated Citizenship', in K. Slawner and M.E. Denham (eds), *Citizenship after Liberalism* (New York: Peter Lang Publishing).

Mill, J.S. (1972) [1859], *Utilitarianism, Liberty, Representative Government* (ed. H.B. Acton) (London: J.M. Dent & Sons).

Miller, D. (1995), *On Nationality* (Oxford: Clarendon Press).

Miller, D. (1998), 'The Left, the Nation-State, and European Citizenship', *Dissent*, Summer, 47–51.

Narveson, J. (1991), *Property Rights: Original Acquisition and Lockean Provisos* (Ontario, Canada: University of Waterloo).

Phillips, D.L. (1993), *Looking Backward: A Critical Appraisal of Communitarian Thought* (Princeton, NJ: Princeton University Press).

Raz, J. (1994), 'Multiculturalism: A Liberal Perspective', *Ethics in the Public Domain: Essays in the Morality of Law and Politics* (Oxford: Clarendon Press).

Riesenberg, P. (1992), *Citizenship in the Western Tradition: Plato to Rousseau* (Chapel Hill: University of North Carolina Press).

Sandel, M. (1982), *Liberalism and the Limits of Justice* (Cambridge: Cambridge University Press).

Smith, A.D. (1986), *The Ethnic Origin of Nation* (Oxford: Blackwell).

Stier, M. (1998), 'How Much of Communitarianism is Left (and Right)?', in P.E. Lawler and D. McConkey (eds), *Community and Political Thought Today* (Westport, CT: Praeger).

Taylor, C. (1977), 'What is Human Agency?', in T. Mischel (ed.), *The Self* (London: Blackwell).

Taylor, C. (1992), *Multiculturalism and the Politics of Recognition* (Princeton: Princeton University Press).

Taylor, C. (1996), 'Why Democracy Needs Patriotism', in J. Cohen (ed.), *For Love of Country: Debating the Limits of Patriotism* (Boston: Beacon Press).

Walzer, M. (1983), *Spheres of Justice* (New York: Basic Books).

Wiebe, R.H. (1975), *The Segmented Society: An Introduction to the Meaning of America* (New York: Oxford University Press).

Young, I.M. (1989), 'Polity and Group Difference: A Critique of the Ideal of Universal Citizenship', *Ethics* 99, 250–74.

Young, I.M. (1990), *Justice and the Politics of Difference* (Princeton, NJ: Princeton University Press).

Chapter 17

Pluralism and Universalism

George Crowder

Can individual liberty conceived as personal autonomy be upheld as a political ideal of universal application? The classic answer in the affirmative is given by John Stuart Mill in *On Liberty*, where he argues for 'individuality', the capacity to make one's own plan of life through a process of critical reflection, as a central component of human well-being and a salient standard for public policy. Personal autonomy in this sense is valuable, for Mill, both as a means to social progress and as an end in itself. Progress follows from the energy and experiments in living generated by strongly self-directing individuals who are prepared to question and depart from prevailing norms and practices. Personal autonomy is also valuable in itself as one of the distinctive marks of humanity: 'it is the privilege and proper condition of a human being, arrived at the maturity of his faculties, to use and interpret experience in his own way' (Mill 1974, 122). Following Mill, many modern liberals, although not all, have made personal autonomy central to their conception of the human good, and have argued that the protection and promotion of autonomy is the overriding purpose of the liberal state (Raz 1986; Kymlicka 1995).

The universality and primacy of personal autonomy has always had its critics, however. Mill's doctrine was disputed in his own day by conservatives like James Fitzjames Stephen, who feared its corrosive effect on the traditions they believed essential to the maintenance of social unity (Stephen 1967). In its current form, the case for personal autonomy is contested from several points of view, including those of communitarianism, feminism and postmodernism (MacIntyre 1981; Sandel 1982; Coole 1993). Perhaps the most frequent objection, and certainly one of the most influential, can be aligned with 'multiculturalism'. This is that the exaltation of personal autonomy by Mill and other liberals represents the outlook of only one kind of culture, namely that of the modern individualist West, among others (Tully 1995; Parekh 2000). While the autonomy of the individual is indeed an appropriate ideal for that kind of culture, other ways of life are based on different conceptions of the good, emphasizing values such as social solidarity, and respect for authority, tradition and religion that are no less legitimate. Consequently, it is argued, personal autonomy is not a genuinely universal good but rather the political expression merely of one particular culture among others. To advance autonomy as a universal goal is imperialistically to impose it on ways of life where it has no place, or not such a prominent place. Even within liberalism, the primacy of personal liberty is disputed in similar terms. For some liberals, personal autonomy, although admirable in context, is too culture-bound and consequently sectarian a value to be presented as the basis of a liberal political settlement that would be acceptable to non-liberal minorities (Larmore 1996; Galston 2002).

In this chapter, I challenge the multiculturalist attack on personal autonomy as a universal ideal. This attack is often based on forms of cultural relativism. In opposition to relativism, I propose value pluralism – a view associated in particular with Isaiah Berlin – as a more satisfactory ethical starting point; one that balances recognition of legitimate cultural diversity with the possibility of intercultural criticism. However, Berlinian pluralism, too, has been used recently as a platform for the multiculturalist attack on personal autonomy in the work of John Gray, Bhikhu Parekh and William Galston. I argue that this tendency rests on a misunderstanding. Properly understood, Berlinian pluralism is primarily about the plurality of goods, not cultures. It does imply a case for cultural diversity, but only within the limits set by norms promoting a diversity of goods, including a commitment to personal autonomy. Far from undermining personal autonomy as a universal value, Berlinian value pluralism generates a distinctive argument in its favour. I end by briefly considering the relevance of value pluralism to an Islamic society such as Indonesia.

Cultural Relativism

The multiculturalist attack on personal autonomy is often based on strong forms of cultural relativism. Cultural relativism is the view that there are no moral principles or values that apply universally, only particular moral judgements made from within the standpoint of the moral code of a specific culture. To judge a culture from the 'outside' is to apply to that culture standards that are alien and inapplicable to it. In short, cultural relativism holds that cultures are indefeasible moral authorities. If a practice has cultural backing, then it is necessarily valid according to the relevant cultural terms. Conversely, if a practice or a value is rejected by a given culture, then for that culture it can have no validity. On this view, Millian personal autonomy is often presented by multiculturalists as merely a value privileged by modern Western individualist cultures, one that has no validity for those cultures that endorse different values (for example, Parekh 1994).

This relativist approach receives a good deal of support from contemporary moral and political theory. Many communitarians, for example, lean in this direction when they emphasize the extent to which individual persons are 'embedded' or 'situated' in, or constituted by, the cultural matrix in which they are brought up. A person wholly constituted by the traditions and norms of her community cannot do other than express those norms in making moral judgements. For communitarians, it would seem that our judgements must always reflect the standards of our own societies. Michael Walzer, for example, seems to adopt a cultural relativist position in his *Spheres of Justice* (1983), when he defines 'justice' as whatever is given by the 'shared understandings' of a particular community. Much contemporary multiculturalism looks like a direct extension of this kind of thinking (see, for example, Young 1990; Tully 1995; Parekh 2000).

The standard objections to this kind of strong relativism are very familiar – although evidently not familiar enough given the resilience of the relativist view.

First, the evidence usually presented in favour of cultural relativism, namely that there are in fact many different cultural codes, is logically inadequate. From the fact of disagreement, it does not follow that all parties to the disagreement are equally correct. People who think that the earth is flat disagree with those who think that it is round, but that does not mean that both views are valid. Similarly, just because different beliefs are held in different cultures, it does not follow that such beliefs must be accepted as correct (Rachels 1986, 18–20).

Secondly, if cultural relativism were true, then we would have to accept as morally valid many practices which seem, for many reasons, worthy of criticism. The standard list includes the following: honour killings, forced marriages, female circumcision, withholding of medical attention from children, ritual scarring, general subordination of women, and so forth (Parekh 2000, 264–5). All of these practices are culturally endorsed, and therefore morally valid on the relativist view. One may add to the list many broader categories of behaviour or policy: imperialism, racism, homophobia, fascism, Nazism. Note that the point about objectionable practices applies not only to the criticism of other cultures, but also to the criticism of one's own (Rachels 1986, 21). According to cultural relativism, cultural endorsement is the moral bottom line, so any practice that can be said to be endorsed by one's own culture is just as sacrosanct as the practices of other cultures. Further, there is no logical connection between cultural relativism and toleration, as is often supposed. On the contrary, cultural relativism undermines any broad case for toleration, since toleration, like any other good on this view, can be defended only so far as it is endorsed by a particular culture. Intolerant, imperialist cultures cannot be gainsaid (Barry 2001, 253–4).

It is sometimes said that cultural relativism merely invites us to step outside our own cultural point of view in order to try to appreciate the perhaps unfamiliar perspectives of others. This is admirable so far, but strong cultural relativism goes much further, and indeed makes such cross-cultural understanding impossible. To appreciate other cultural outlooks, one might think, is to understand that their practices, which at first seem strange to us, are actually in place for a reason. But strong cultural relativism asserts that a sufficient reason for any practice is simply that the practice is backed by the culture. Since a 'culture' is simply the sum of such practices, this is no justification at all, but rather equivalent to saying 'we do this here because we do this here' (Barry 2001, 253).

Indeed, not only does cultural relativism add nothing to our understanding of cultures, if true it would make any such understanding impossible. On the relativist view, our values are entirely those of our own culture. The values of other cultures would be entirely alien to us, to such an extent that it is doubtful that we would recognize them as 'values', comparable with our own, at all (Berlin 1990, 80–82). This problem is compounded by forms of relativism that apply not only to values but to rationality or understanding as well, namely 'cognitive' relativism. If, on inquiry, a culture-based practice seems to rest on mistaken beliefs or faulty reasoning, the multiculturalist reply is sometimes that different rationalities or standards of truth are at work, and that one must not impose one's own, necessarily culture-relative, standard of truth. But this view is incoherent. If cultural outlooks were so completely incommensurable, then we would have no conception of other cultures even counting as 'cultures' comparable with our own, and so would not even be able to formulate the notion of 'cultural' difference (Benhabib 2002, 30–31). Moreover, cognitive relativism, if true, would of course apply to its own claims, leading to the paradoxical conclusion that relativism is both true and untrue, even from its own point of view.

The central thrust of cultural relativism is its characteristic claim that cultures cannot be questioned morally – that to say that a practice is culturally endorsed is necessarily to accept the practice as valid. Instead, we should be seeking a middle ground in which universality and diversity are combined, making possible both respect for cultures and criticism of cultures.

Value Pluralism

I propose Isaiah Berlin's conception of value pluralism as a candidate for this middle ground. This is the notion that although there may be some universal goods, these and other human values are irreducibly plural, often conflicting and sometimes incommensurable. Berlin contrasts pluralism with the monist view that all ethical questions have a single correct answer and that all these answers dovetail within a single, coherent moral system (Berlin 1997, 6–16; 2000a, 11–14; 2002, 212–17). Such a system will be dominated by one value, or a small set of values, which overrides or serves as a common currency for all others. For Berlin, monism is potentially authoritarian, since it seems to point to a single vision of the good, and therefore of the good political society, as universally valid and justifiably enforceable, even at great cost. If a single value overrides or commensurates all others, then that value by definition justifies the sacrifice of all others.[1] Monism, according to Berlin, does not do justice to the depth and persistence of conflict in human moral experience. Rather, the world that we encounter in ordinary experience is a world of moral conflict, disagreement and dilemma (Berlin 2002, 213–14). In such a world there is no possibility, even in principle, that all goods can be realized simultaneously, or that there is only one rational way of ranking them. If goods are incommensurable, then each is its own measure and, depending on the circumstances, there will be many reasonable ways of ranking them. Consequently, there is no possibility in a pluralist world of a 'final solution' to all moral and political problems, no possibility of moral or political perfection (Berlin 2002, 212).[2]

---

1 Not all monists are authoritarians, however. Berlin's view is not that monism is linked to tyranny by necessity, but that monism can lead to authoritarianism along a slippery slope of psychological association. His position here parallels his famous account of the way positive conceptions of liberty, although not necessarily anti-individualist, are vulnerable to becoming twisted in that direction 'not always by logically reputable steps' (Berlin 2002, 179).

2 Berlin's account of the truth of value pluralism, which rests on our 'ordinary experience' of moral conflict (Berlin 2002, 213), is not conclusive. Monists could reply that our perception of these conflicts is superficial and compatible with there being an underlying monist order we have not yet understood. On the case for value pluralism in general, see

But pluralism might seem to undermine not only utopianism and totalitarianism, but also any reasoned moral or political position. Some pluralists interpret the incommensurability of values to mean that incommensurable values are wholly incomparable with one another, and that choices among them must be ultimately non-rational, or not guided by any reason that is decisive over others (Raz 1986; Riley 2000; 2001; 2002). Berlin sometimes appears to endorse this interpretation, for example in his essay on Machiavelli where he writes that, 'entire systems of value may come into collision without possibility of rational arbitration' (Berlin 1997, 320). However, the strong interpretation of incommensurability is neither Berlin's only view nor his best. He repudiates it explicitly in a later article, where he insists that reasoned choice among incommensurable goods is possible, if not in the abstract then at least in (some) particular cases (Berlin and Williams 1994).

Although incommensurability may place problems in the way of reasoned decision-making, it does not rule out reasoned choice within a particular context. Choosing among incommensurables is always hard in two senses: first, such choices always involve loss, because gains in terms of one value can never wholly compensate for sacrifices in terms of an incommensurable value; secondly, because choices among incommensurables cannot be guided or justified by any monist standard, such as utilitarianism. However, decisive reasons to choose in one direction rather than another may be generated by context. As Berlin puts it: 'the concrete situation is almost everything' (Berlin 1990, 15).

What kind of context will guide such choices, and how exactly will they do this? Berlin says little on this subject, but he does sometimes refer to following 'the general pattern of life in which we believe' (Berlin 2002, 47), and to judgements 'dictated by the forms of life of the society to which one belongs' (Berlin 1990, 18). What these passages suggest is that conflicts among incommensurables in particular cases always arise in a context that includes certain background commitments, and that we may be able to appeal to such background commitments in order to resolve such conflicts rationally. Of course, what our background commitments are will often be uncertain, and one set of commitments will often conflict with others.

The idea that reasoned moral decision-making is possible without commensuration departs from the standard positions offered by utilitarians and Kant, but is scarcely unique or original to Berlin. The classic statement of this view is Aristotle's account of *phronēsis*, or practical reasoning.[3] On this view, human morality is too complex to be reduced to rules. Rather, one should imitate the person of practical wisdom who decides how the competing considerations should be balanced in a given situation, through accumulation of experience in dealing with cognate situations.

Nussbaum (1986; 1992b); Raz (1986); Stocker (1990); Lukes (1991); Nagel (1991); Kekes (1993); Hurka (1996); Chang (1997); MacKenzie (1999).

3 The following account of Aristotelian practical reasoning and its links with value pluralism draws on the work of Nussbaum (1986; 1990; 1992a; 1992b; 2000), and Richardson (1997). Nussbaum's pluralist reading of Aristotle is disputed by Larmore (1996, 163–7).

Pluralism and Relativism

How is Berlinian pluralism different from cultural relativism? It might seem at this point that there is very little difference. Pluralists acknowledge at least some universal values, but where these are incommensurable, they are left with the problem of how to choose rationally among such values when they clash. Although reasoned choice among incommensurables is not ruled out, this possibility seems limited so far to the context of personal and social background commitments. If so, reasoned choice under pluralism seems to be relative to 'the general pattern of life in which we believe' or 'the forms of life of the society to which we belong', a position scarcely distinguishable from cultural relativism.

It is worth reconstructing Berlin's response to this problem, especially in those texts where he traces the beginnings of an explicitly pluralist outlook to Vico and Herder. Berlin is interested in these thinkers as representatives of an eighteenth-century 'Counter-Enlightenment' which provided a salutary antidote to the most powerful strain of monism in modern times, namely the scientism of the French Enlightenment. The dominant view among the French *philosophes* was that the methods of the natural sciences, which had been so successful in explaining the workings of the physical world, would do the same for the social world. Vico and Herder were among the first to rebel against this scientistic approach to knowledge, arguing that genuine understanding of human conduct is not possible through external observation and measurement alone. Unlike other phenomena, human activity is purposive and can be grasped only by adopting, if only in imagination, the inside view of the human actors themselves: the practice of *Einfühlen*, or 'feeling oneself into' the worldview of people in other times and places (Berlin 2000b, 14, 18–19, 197, 212–13).

This stress on the inside view is the key to Berlin's distinction between pluralism and relativism, but it seems initially to compound the difficulty (Momigliano 1976). Vico, for example, is presented as primarily a historicist thinker who rejects any notion of a permanent human nature or natural law, and who argues that each stage in the evolution of a culture or civilization has its own distinctive character and outlook. That outlook includes its own set of values, and these are the only appropriate measures of its achievement. Thus Berlin writes that for Vico human values 'belong to, and are effective and intelligible at, only their specific stage in human history' (Berlin 2000b, 61). Again, 'each phase is incommensurable with the others, since each lives by its own light and can be understood only on its own terms' (Berlin 1990, 75). Comments such as these look like strong statements of a relativist acceptance of the moral authority of cultures. The appearance of relativism is even stronger in Berlin's interpretation of Herder, for whom cultures or 'nations' rather than civilizations or historical phases are 'incommensurable'. Each culture possesses its own unique 'centre of gravity', which is 'intelligible each in its own terms (the only terms there are)' (Berlin 2000b, 211, 219, 235). Each way of life realizes 'an ideal of indefeasible validity' such that 'we are forbidden to make judgements of comparative values, for that is measuring the incommensurable' (Berlin 2000b, 233–4). If this view is indeed Herder's, how can he be other than a cultural relativist?

Yet Berlin insists that Vico and Herder are not relativists, for a reason that again appeals to the notion of the inside view. If cultural relativism were true, Berlin argues, then people would see things only from the point of view of their own culture. They would be 'insulated', occupying 'windowless boxes' whose dimensions would constitute their entire world (Berlin 1990, 85). But the world is not like this because, as Vico and Herder show, the inside view of a given culture is, at least in part, accessible to other human beings in other times and places by means of *Einfühlen* (Berlin 1990, 82). What makes this imaginative sympathy possible is that, contrary to relativism (at least in its stronger forms), there is sufficient universality of human experience to make other cultures comprehensible to us, and through that comprehension to allow us to appreciate their values as genuine values that we might imaginably live by ourselves. Thus our evident capacity to understand and empathize with the values of other cultures and historical periods presupposes certain 'limits of humanity', a common 'human horizon' or shared field of moral experience (Berlin 1990, 80; 1997, 10). Our ability to understand other cultures implies a set of universal values.

It might be objected that to understand the values of other cultures is not necessarily to share them (Kateb 1999, 1030; Lessnoff 1999, 220). Just because I understand another culture's valuing of human sacrifice does not mean that I agree with it and thereby share a common commitment to human sacrifice. But the objection trades on an ambiguity in the term 'value' which is to some extent present in Berlin's own usage. If 'value' in this example means the specific practice or norm of human sacrifice, then of course my understanding the practice does not commit me to endorsing it for myself. However, if my understanding is a genuine, internal understanding in Berlin's sense, then I necessarily appreciate the deeper purposes or goals which the practice serves – the 'values' which stand behind the practice or which the practice expresses. It is these deeper values that I can then see myself as sharing, even if I strongly reject the particular way they are expressed in the practice confronting me. Even though I am repelled by human sacrifice, I can understand that the practice is intended, however wrong-headedly, to express a reverence for regeneration, fertility and ultimately life itself (Westermarck 1960, 188–9). It is these underlying values that I can identify with and that imply a common moral horizon.

The important point that emerges from Berlin's discussion is that while relativism divides moral experience into discrete, non-communicating compartments or perspectives, value pluralism implies the existence of a significant moral horizon shared by all human beings. It is this that enables pluralism, unlike relativism, to strike a balance between respect for cultural difference and recognition that some cultural practices deserve criticism. On the one hand, the human horizon explains, as strong relativism cannot, why 'members of one culture can understand and enter the minds of, and sympathise with, those of another' (Berlin 1990, 84). On the other hand, the common horizon also provides a basis for cross-cultural criticism, since fundamental human goods may be denied or inadequately realized by a particular culture or ideology. So, for example, the human sacrifice practised by the Aztecs might be rejected on the ground that although ostensibly serving the valid goal of regeneration, its claim to do so rests on grossly mistaken beliefs concerning natural causality. The underlying values are identifiably human and genuine, but the institution is misguided even when judged by those same basic terms.

It should be admitted, however, that the human horizon implied by pluralism is unlikely by itself to invalidate many cultural practices. Certainly, it is not substantial enough to indicate any value as specific as personal autonomy as a requirement for the good human society. Berlin's own account of the human horizon is ultra-thin. The idea, as we have seen, is that of the common 'limits of humanity' or 'human horizon' beyond which behaviour is no longer recognizably human and understanding is impossible (Berlin 1990, 11, 80). Someone who sees no difference between kicking a pebble and killing his family is beyond the human pale, because his values or purposes are literally incomprehensible (Berlin 1978, 166). But the actions of the Nazis, although morally detestable to most people, are not incomprehensible in this way; Berlin is quite explicit about this (Berlin 2000a, 12–13; Jahanbegloo 1993, 38). Rather, those actions are performed in the service of values that we can recognize as human – such as group belonging and self-esteem. Consequently, the practices themselves, although we revile them, must be acknowledged as, lamentably, human. On this view, therefore, not even Nazi society is excluded by Berlin's common moral horizon. The common horizon excludes only what is not recognizably human, and consequently permits almost anything. It certainly permits societies which endorse violent death, hunger and slavery, at any rate for some.

Could Berlinian pluralists respond by making their account of moral universality 'thicker' or more demanding, so that it would be satisfied by fewer non-liberal societies? A model for this move might be provided by the 'human capabilities' approach of Martha Nussbaum and Amartya Sen, according to which a good life for a human being requires the possession of real capacities to exercise certain essential 'human functions', the list of these being fairly detailed and extensive (Nussbaum 1990; 1992a; 1992b; 2000; Nussbaum and Sen 1993). It could then be argued that such capacities are best realized under a liberal form of politics. The general difficulty with this strategy is the obvious tension between identifying goods at a sufficient level of specificity to single out liberalism as a necessary political context, and on the other hand ensuring that the goods are described in sufficiently general terms to count as genuinely universal, in the sense of essential or desirable for any good life. While such an approach should not be ruled out prematurely, it is probably best to remain sceptical of it (Crowder 2007b, 218–20).

The importance of the pluralist commitment to the notion of universal values is not so much that we can read off specific ethical and political commitments from the universals themselves. Rather, the significance of the universals is threefold. First, the human horizon rules out the strongest forms of relativism. If there are universal values, even if these are highly generic, then it cannot be true that cultures are wholly incommensurable. Within the common horizon, cultures must overlap, sharing at least some of the human values. If cultures are not wholly incommensurable, then they are not morally sovereign. Rather, they can, at least in principle, be subjected to criticism on the basis of the universal values or of other cross-cultural principles, if any such can be found.

Secondly, if cultures are not wholly incommensurable, it follows that pluralism is primarily about the plurality not of cultures but of goods (and sub-goods). No doubt the plurality of goods will also lead to considerable cultural variation, since distinct packages of goods will be pursued in divergent ways by different groups of people. But legitimate cultural variation will be parasitic on the plurality of goods, which is more radical. If this were not true, and pluralism involved an acceptance of cultural pluralism on a level with the plurality of goods, then there would be nothing to separate pluralism from cultural relativism. But pluralism is distinguishable from relativism, and it is so in part because it refers primarily to the plurality of goods, not cultures. I shall draw out the implications of this shortly.

Thirdly, even if the universals are too thin or generic to provide, by themselves, much critical leverage against cultures, they suggest an important point of critical principle. This is that, under pluralism, appeal to personal or social context is not the only criterion for choosing rationally among conflicting incommensurable values. Rather, when incommensurables conflict, good reasons to choose among them may be generated by principles derived from value pluralism itself. The idea of pluralism itself implies a number of general rules for deciding value conflicts along lines that cross the boundaries between cultures. The universals provide some of these, but I shall argue that there are others, indeed much more decisive.

Pluralism and Multiculturalism

So far I have argued that the multiculturalist attack on the universality of personal autonomy is often based on strong cultural relativism; that strong cultural relativism suffers from several serious defects, in particular its uncritical endorsement of any and all cultural practices; and that a superior alternative to relativism, which achieves a more satisfactory balance between legitimate diversity and critical judgement, can be found in Berlinian pluralism. Does this mean that the coast is now clear for personal autonomy to be reasserted as a universal ideal? Not yet. First, I have to confront claims that such a conclusion is denied by value pluralism no less than by cultural relativism.

The question of the political implications of pluralism is highly controversial. Roughly speaking, there are two main schools of thought: a liberal school which follows Berlin in seeing pluralism as somehow linked to liberal political values and forms, and a non-liberal school which denies any such link.[4] The most prominent representative of the non-liberal camp is John Gray (1993; 1995a; 1995b; 2000). For Gray, the basic message of pluralism is that there are many incommensurably different values and virtues, and that these, combined in various ways, yield many distinctly legitimate forms of life, or cultures. Liberalism, which privileges goods such as toleration and personal autonomy, is only one such legitimate form of life. Other cultural forms, which emphasize different combinations of goods, are no less

4 Defined in these terms, the liberal pluralist school includes Hausheer (1983); Crowder (2002a; 2002b; 2004; 2007a; 2007b); Dzur (1998); Blokland (1999); Lukes (1991; 2003, chapters 6–8); Galston (2002); Riley (2000; 2001; 2002). The chief exponents of explicitly anti-liberal pluralism are Gray (1993; 1995a; 1995b; 1998; 2000), and Kekes (1993; 1997; 1998). In addition, some writers have argued that liberalism should be defended but not on the basis of value pluralism: E. Mack (1993); Crowder (1994) (an argument now superseded by the later pieces listed above); Larmore (1996, chapter 6); Newey (1998); Dworkin (2001); Gaus (2003). For related discussions, see A. Mack (1999).

legitimate. Therefore, liberalism has no justified claim to universal superiority. The only reasonable form of liberalism, from a pluralist point of view, is 'agonistic', that is, accepting of its own merely local rather than universal validity. On Gray's reading, pluralism implies a strong form of multiculturalism in which liberalism features as only one valid form of life among others. Consequently, personal autonomy is, on this view, only one good among others, properly privileged only where a liberal individualist culture is in the ascendant.

Even interpretations of pluralism more favourable to liberalism are not necessarily committed to the privileging of personal autonomy. In this category is William Galston (2002), who gives Berlinian pluralism an explicitly liberal reading, but who rejects personal autonomy as the central value of a liberal pluralism. Like Gray, Galston sees pluralism as implying a commitment to cultural diversity. Unlike Gray, Galston argues that this diversity is best accommodated by liberal universalism. Liberalism is not neutral among conceptions of the good, as claimed by some liberal theorists such as Rawls (1971; 1993) and Dworkin (1977; 1985); the liberal state unavoidably rests on and promotes a distinctively liberal conception of the good. However, the liberal conception of the human good is uniquely 'capacious', that is, accommodating of different ways of life. At any rate, this is true so far as liberalism is conceived along 'Reformation' lines as based on maximum toleration of different ways of living, including non-liberal ones. Toleration-based liberalism can accommodate even non-liberal forms of life as long as these are themselves tolerant of their own members' 'right of exit' from the group. But liberal conceptions of the good cease to be adequately capacious when they take an 'Enlightenment' form, in which their goal is the promotion of a substantive form of life based on personal autonomy. Enlightenment liberalism, Galston argues, is too 'sectarian', because it excludes too many conceptions of the good under which personal autonomy is not regarded as a desirable ideal. For Galston, pluralism implies the universal validity of liberalism as the most capacious political container for legitimate cultural diversity, but this must be 'Reformation' or toleration-based liberalism, not the autonomy-based liberalism of Mill.

Both Gray's non-liberal pluralism and Galston's Reformation liberal pluralism, although different in important respects, suffer from the same general problem. They identify pluralism too closely with cultural pluralism, thereby eroding the distinction between pluralism and cultural relativism. Both Gray and Galston correctly associate pluralism with the endorsement of diversity. But they are too quick to move from the idea of a diversity of goods to that of a diversity of cultures. Thus Gray concludes in favour of a cultural diversity of which liberalism is only a part, while for Galston liberalism is universalized, but only as an instrument for cultural diversity. In neither view is there sufficient critical attention to the content of the cultures in question, with the result that in each case pluralism is presented as implying much the same uncritical endorsement of cultures as cultural relativism.

How can pluralists criticize cultures? Appeals to human well-being have already been mentioned and their limitations noted. A more promising candidate, I suggest, is a 'diversity' criterion, but one that refers primarily to a diversity not of cultures but of goods or values. The general idea is captured by Bernard Williams:

> … if there are many and competing values, then the greater the extent to which a society tends to be single-valued, the more genuine values it neglects or suppresses. To this extent, more, must mean better (Williams 1978, xvii).

Pluralism implies not simply respect for cultural diversity, but the promotion of cultural patterns that are themselves internally diverse. That imperative cuts across respect for cultures, which may themselves promote the plurality and diversity of human goods to varying degrees.

The imperative behind this can be labelled 'taking incommensurable values seriously'. If pluralism is true, then there are many legitimate human goods, each with its own distinctive value.[5] To acknowledge the truth of pluralism is therefore to honour those goods, that is, to endorse them prima facie. This does not mean that pluralists must endorse all such goods equally in every particular case, since clearly there is insufficient 'social space' to do this within the life either of an individual or even of a society (Rawls 1993, 57). But pluralists should affirm all such goods as possessing real value, even if they must choose against them in concrete instances. If a good is genuine, then we should promote it where we can, and where we cannot we must choose against it with regret and for a reason. In general, we should prefer those options which tend to promote more distinctive values rather than fewer. We should, that is, generally favour a general policy of value diversity. At the level of social policy, this means that pluralists should prefer cultures with a greater degree of internal diversity or complexity to those that tend to be more simple or single-valued. Certainly pluralists will also favour a diversity of cultures, but they will rate a diversity of internally diverse cultures more highly than a diversity of monochrome cultures (Crowder 2007a).

This is a broadly liberal position. An 'internally diverse' culture is one which leaves room for its members to interpret its fundamental precepts and values in different ways, and so to follow divergent paths, pursuing many different goods, within the overall cultural framework. Liberal cultures, with their stress on individual liberty and, subject to the legitimate demands of individual liberty, on toleration for multiple ways of life, answer to that description. But where does personal autonomy come in? Might it be true that pluralism implies support for a diversity of liberal cultures, but also be true – as Galston would argue – that these should be based on toleration or negative liberty rather than personal autonomy?

Pluralism and Personal Autonomy

A distinctively pluralist case for personal autonomy can be constructed as follows. Pluralism imposes hard choices on us. To cope well with those choices we need

5 By 'value' here, I mean an objective contribution to human well-being, not just something valued de facto by particular persons or societies, Berlin's usual view of universal value: Berlin (2002, 45); Jahanbegloo (1993, 37). I depart from Berlin on this matter because his account makes all values a function of empirical preference, thereby commensurating them in a way inconsistent with the fundamental message of value pluralism: see Crowder (2002a, 73–4, note 1).

to develop certain dispositions of character, or virtues. Those virtues overlap the character traits distinctively promoted by liberal forms of politics, in particular a capacity for personal autonomy. In short, liberal cultures promote the personal autonomy required for coping successfully with the exigencies of choosing among conflicting incommensurables. Because hard choices are unavoidable under pluralism, so too is personal autonomy if we are to choose well.

This argument depends on a significant assumption. Liberal virtues like personal autonomy are necessary to cope well with choices under pluralism if to 'cope well' with such choices means to choose for a good reason. It is only if we are first committed to rational choice under pluralism that we will need the virtues requisite to practical reasoning, including the capacity for critical reflection inherent in individual autonomy. But why should we be committed to reason here? Why not say that from a pluralist point of view rational choice is itself merely one value among others, and that one may equally cope with pluralist choice by plumping arbitrarily among the alternatives? A reply is suggested by Nussbaum, who argues that practical reasoning is 'architectonic' among the basic human functions she identifies, in the sense that it is necessary to 'organise and arrange all of the others, giving them in the process a characteristically human shape' (Nussbaum 1990, 226). Similarly, under pluralism practical reason is needed to organize choices among incommensurable goods. In the absence of practical reasoning, our choices would be arbitrary, incoherent and perhaps self-defeating. Unless we think critically about how the ends we endorse fit together, we are in danger of creating lives that, as John Kekes puts it, 'are too scattered … In such lives there are many values, but between their favourable evaluation and realization come the distractions of other values whose realization also recedes for the same reason' (Kekes 1993, 97–8). Lives such as these are undesirable from a pluralist point of view because they fail to do justice to, or to take seriously, the goods they purport to value. I shall return to this notion of taking goods seriously in a moment.

So, to cope well with the hard choices that pluralism imposes upon us is to choose for a reason. Further, to choose well in this context requires that we develop certain dispositions of character, or virtues. I propose four candidates for 'the pluralist virtues'. The first is generosity or open-mindedness, which is closely connected to the idea of taking plural values seriously. If a good is genuine, then we must promote it where we can, and where we cannot we must choose against it with regret and for a reason. The implication is that we should approach pluralist choices with a certain attitude, namely one of respect for the full range of human goods and lives, including those we cannot accommodate within our own decisions. This amounts to a high degree of generosity or open-mindedness when dealing with the values and cultures of others (Walzer 1995). For the same reason, pluralists should approach their choices with what Berlin calls 'a sense of reality', a feeling for the real costs of moral and political decisions, conditioned in particular by the implications of incommensurability (Berlin 1978, 111, 207). This is the second pluralist virtue, 'realism'. Thirdly, pluralists' rejection of neat abstract rules and insistence on the particularity of moral solutions should make them attentive to the relevant details of the choice situation, including the claims and circumstances of those people affected by the choice (Nussbaum 1992b, 101). Fourthly, in the absence of decisive monist rules, pluralists need to be flexible in tailoring their judgement closely to the situation to which they attend.

The final step in my argument is the claim that the pluralist virtues are also characteristically liberal virtues. Generosity towards the range of human goods and lives is a recognizable trait of liberalism at its best (Galston 2002, 61–2). One sees it, for example, in Mill's valuing of individuality and social diversity (Mill 1974, chapter 3; Berlin 2002, 218–51). Pluralist flexibility also overlaps the liberal commitment to personal autonomy, the most distinctive of liberal virtues, at any rate on the Enlightenment view. To judge rationally in the light of value pluralism is to judge for one's own reasons in a strong sense, that is, autonomously. In part, this is because conflicts among incommensurable goods cannot be decided for good reason merely by the mechanical application of a standard monist rule. If utilitarianism, for example, depends on only one possible ranking of incommensurables, then utilitarian calculation can be no more than one consideration among others in pluralist judgement. The rational pluralist judge cannot rely on utilitarianism or any other ready-made monist procedure to resolve deep moral conflicts, but must go behind such perspectives to weigh the values they embody for themselves.

Nor, contrary to the conservative view of Kekes (1993; 1997; 1998), can pluralists answer such questions merely by appealing to the authority of local tradition. Traditionalism is really another name for cultural relativism, which I criticized and distinguished from Berlinian pluralism earlier. A further reason for pluralists to question the authority of tradition focuses on the fact of widespread disagreement about human beings concerning the content of the good life or human well-being. This is, of course, especially evident in modern societies, but on the pluralist view the problem is rooted in the moral experience of humanity at large. For pluralists, reasonable disagreement concerning the good life is a permanent possibility in all human societies because of the deep structure of human value. Traditional and other conceptions of the good life are essentially generalized rankings of incommensurable values. The wide range of genuine human goods implies a wide range of legitimate permutations of those goods, that is, of reasonable rankings. Many such rankings will be equally reasonable, and concerning these there is consequently room for people to disagree on reasonable grounds. Pluralists cannot resolve the deepest value conflicts simply by citing a local or personal conception of the good, because under pluralism these are subject to reasonable disagreement.

Further, reasonable disagreement about the good is experienced not only among cultural groups or belief systems, but also within them. Indeed, individuals can experience the centrifugal pull of incommensurable goods not only interpersonally but also within themselves. Berlin's own inner conflicts, surely among the deepest sources of his pluralism, are a case in point (Ignatieff 1998, 246–7, 250–51, 287). Here, too, there is a link between pluralism and personal autonomy. For where the nature of the good life is subject to reasonable disagreement, conceptions of the good cannot be permanent bases for decision, but must be subject to revision themselves. That kind of decision is possible only through the exercise of personal autonomy.

Conclusion

If my argument is correct, it provides a strong reply to the multiculturalist case against personal autonomy as a universal standard. In addition, Berlinian pluralism provides a more promising ethical platform for multiculturalism itself, which balances appreciation of cultures through the inside view with the possibility of cross-cultural criticism suggested by the human horizon. However, versions of pluralism have been advanced by thinkers such as John Gray and William Galston as a basis for attacking the universality of personal autonomy. I have argued that this approach is based on a flawed understanding of pluralism as primarily cultural pluralism, a view which tends to assimilate pluralism to relativism. Pluralism, properly understood, emphasizes the plurality of human goods more than cultures. It implies a general imperative to promote a diverse range of goods, an imperative which cuts across, and serves as a critical standard for, the performance of particular cultures. Pluralism implies a case not merely for a multiplicity of cultures, but for a multiplicity of internally diverse cultures, that is, for a broadly liberal approach to multiculturalism.

Berlinian pluralism, far from undermining the case for personal autonomy as a universal ideal, implies a distinctive case in favour of that ideal. Pluralism imposes on us choices that are demanding to a degree such that they can be made rationally only by autonomous agents. If pluralism is true, then the best lives, those informed by reasoned choices among the available options, will be characterized by personal autonomy. This is a universal case for personal autonomy since pluralism, if true, is part of the moral experience of all human beings. Consequently, its implications for good moral choice apply not merely to self-conscious pluralists, or to any particular form of society rather than any other, but to moral life in all human societies.

My argument has implications for an Islamic society such as Indonesia. Both the ideal of personal autonomy, or reasoned critical reflection on the claims of culture, and the idea of pluralism can be found in Islam (Sen 2001, chapter 10; 2006; Crowder 2002a, 184, note 4). Even where the promotion of individual autonomy constitutes a departure from cultural norms, this need not amount to the destruction of a culture since not all such change is cultural destruction (Kymlicka 1989, 196–7; 1995, chapter 8; Barry 2001, 256–7). I have argued, however, that personal autonomy should be regarded as a universal ideal in the sense that it is part of the best kind of human life.

Finally, I do not claim that lives in which personal autonomy plays little or no part are wholly without value. Such lives may exhibit many other goods that are valuable from a pluralist point of view, and must therefore be judged to be good in some degree. Indeed, such lives may well be better than autonomous lives in certain respects. But if my argument is correct, lives such as these cannot be among the best possible overall, since they lack the key capacity for good decision-making in the face of inevitable value conflict.

It remains a further question, however, how exactly that conclusion bears on the proper role of the state. Should the state actively promote autonomous forms of life, as on the view of 'perfectionist' liberal theorists such as Joseph Raz (1986)? If so, how far should it go in that direction, and what kind of policies should it employ? Again, I cannot pursue this issue here beyond noting my belief that pluralism does indeed imply a case for a specifically perfectionist form of liberalism under which the promotion of personal autonomy is a legitimate goal of public policy. This conclusion follows, given the plausible claim that the conditions for personal autonomy, both cultural and economic, are unlikely to be sustained, at least for many people, in the absence of some significant degree of deliberate state intervention (see Crowder 2002a, chapter 9). Here my approach has definite implications for pluralist management by the state of Islamic notions of ethical finality.

Nor does my conclusion in favour of autonomy contradict my pluralist starting point because I do not propose personal autonomy as absolutely overriding. I do advance personal autonomy as a general ideal both for the lives of individuals and for the political or public sphere. If pluralism is true, and my argument about its implications for reasoned choice is correct, then the universal value of personal autonomy stands as a general principle, both in the public and private realms.[6] However, I do not rule out the possibility that there may be some circumstances, in both spheres, where autonomy should yield to other goods. For example, conditions of public emergency may justify the overriding of citizens' autonomy in favour of common security, or it may be that autonomy should sometimes be subordinated to particular professional, family or religious imperatives. Where the exact lines should be drawn in such cases may, of course, be contestable, but such a doctrine can be applied to the complex institutions and divisions of jurisdiction found in an Islamic society.

References

Barry, B. (2001), *Culture and Equality* (Cambridge: Polity).

Benhabib, S. (2002), *The Claims of Culture: Equality and Diversity in the Global Era* (Princeton, NJ: Princeton University Press).

Berlin, I. (1978), *Russian Thinkers* (ed. H. Hardy) (London: Hogarth).

Berlin, I. (1990), *The Crooked Timber of Humanity: Chapters in the History of Ideas* (ed. H. Hardy) (London: John Murray).

Berlin, I. (1997), *The Proper Study of Mankind: An Anthology of Essays* (eds H. Hardy and R. Hausheer) (London: Chatto & Windus).

Berlin, I. (2000a), *The Power of Ideas* (ed. H. Hardy) (London: Chatto & Windus).

Berlin, I. (2000b), *Three Critics of the Enlightenment: Vico, Hamann, Herder* (ed. H. Hardy) (Princeton and Oxford: Princeton University Press).

Berlin, I. (2002), *Liberty* (ed. H. Hardy) (Oxford: Oxford University Press).

Berlin, I. and Williams, B. (1994), 'Pluralism and Liberalism: A Reply', *Political Studies* 42, 306–9.

Blokland, H. (1999), 'Berlin on Pluralism and Liberalism: A Defence', *European Legacy* 4, 1–23.

Chang, R. (1997), 'Introduction', in R. Chang (ed.), *Incommensurability, Incomparability, and Practical Reason* (Cambridge, Mass: Harvard University Press).

---

6 See Galston's idea of treating especially important values under pluralism as rebuttable 'ethical presumptions' (2002, 69–78).

Coole, D. (1993), 'Constructing and Deconstructing Liberty', *Political Studies* 41, 83–95.

Crowder, G. (1994), 'Pluralism and Liberalism', *Political Studies* 42, 293–305.

Crowder, G. (2002a), *Liberalism and Value Pluralism* (London and New York: Continuum).

Crowder, G. (2002b), 'Two Value-pluralist Arguments for Liberalism', *Australian Journal of Political Science* 37, 457–73.

Crowder, G. (2004), *Isaiah Berlin: Liberty and Pluralism* (Cambridge: Polity).

Crowder, G. (2007a), 'Two Concepts of Liberal Pluralism', *Political Theory* 35, 121–46.

Crowder, G. (2007b), 'Value Pluralism and Liberalism: Berlin and Beyond', in G. Crowder and H. Hardy (eds), *The One and the Many: Reading Isaiah Berlin* (Amherst: Prometheus).

Donnelly, J. (1984), 'Cultural Relativism and Universal Human Rights', *Human Rights Quarterly* 6.

Dworkin, R. (1977), *Taking Rights Seriously* (London: Duckworth).

Dworkin, R. (1985), *A Matter of Principle* (Cambridge, Mass: Harvard University Press).

Dworkin, R. (2001), 'Do Liberal Values Conflict?', in R. Dworkin, M. Lilla and R. Silvers (eds), *The Legacy of Isaiah Berlin* (New York: New York Review of Books).

Dzur, A. (1998), 'Value Pluralism Versus Political Liberalism?', *Social Theory and Practice* 24, 375–92.

Galipeau, C. (1994), *Isaiah Berlin's Liberalism* (Oxford: Clarendon Press).

Galston, W. (2002), *Liberal Pluralism: The Implications of Value Pluralism for Political Theory and Practice* (Cambridge: Cambridge University Press).

Gaus, G. (2003), *Contemporary Theories of Liberalism: Public Reason as a Post-Enlightenment Project* (London: Sage).

Godwin, W. (1976) [1798], *Enquiry Concerning Political Justice, and Its Influence on Modern Morals and Happiness* (ed. I. Kramnick), (Harmondsworth: Penguin).

Gray, J. (1993), *Post-Liberalism: Studies in Political Thought* (New York and London: Routledge).

Gray, J. (1995a), *Berlin* (London: Fontana).

Gray, J. (1995b), *Enlightenment's Wake: Politics and Culture at the Close of the Modern Age* (London and New York: Routledge).

Gray, J. (1998), 'Where Pluralists and Liberals Part Company', *International Journal of Philosophical Studies* 6, 17–36.

Gray, J. (2000), *Two Faces of Liberalism* (Cambridge: Polity).

Hausheer, R. (1983), 'Berlin and the Emergence of Liberal Pluralism', in P. Manent, R. Hausheer, W. Karpinski and W. Kaiser (eds), *European Liberty* (The Hague: Martinus Nijhoff).

Hurka, T. (1996), 'Monism, Pluralism, and Rational Regret', *Ethics* 106, 555–75.

Ignatieff, M. (1998), *Isaiah Berlin: A Life* (London: Chatto and Windus).

Jahanbegloo, R. (1993), *Conversations with Isaiah Berlin* (London: Phoenix).

Kateb, G. (1999), 'Can Cultures be Judged? Two Defenses of Cultural Pluralism in Isaiah Berlin's Work', *Social Research* 66: 4, 1009–38.

Kekes, J. (1993), *The Morality of Pluralism* (Princeton: Princeton University Press).
Kekes, J. (1997), *Against Liberalism* (Ithaca: Cornell University Press).
Kekes, J. (1998), *A Case for Conservatism* (Ithaca: Cornell University Press).
Kukathas, C. (2003), *The Liberal Archipelago* (Oxford: Oxford University Press).
Kymlicka, W. (1989), *Liberalism, Community and Culture* (Oxford: Oxford University Press).
Kymlicka, W. (1995), *Multicultural Citizenship* (Oxford: Clarendon Press).
Larmore, C. (1996), *The Morals of Modernity* (Cambridge: Cambridge University Press).
Lessnoff, M. (1999), *Political Philosophers of the Twentieth Century* (Oxford: Blackwell).
Lukes, S. (1991), 'Making Sense of Moral Conflict', in Nancy L. Rosenblum (ed.), *Liberalism and the Moral Life* (Cambridge: Harvard University Press).
Lukes, S. (2003), *Liberals and Cannibals: The Implications of Diversity* (London: Verso).
Macedo, S. (1990), *Liberal Virtues: Citizenship, Virtue, and Community in Liberal Constitutionalism* (Oxford: Clarendon Press).
MacIntyre, A. (1981), *After Virtue* (London: Duckworth).
Mack, A. (ed.) (1999), 'Liberty and Pluralism Issue', *Social Research* 66.
Mack, E. (1993), 'Isaiah Berlin and the Quest for Liberal Pluralism', *Public Affairs Quarterly* 7, 215–30.
MacKenzie, I. (1999), 'Berlin's Defence of Value-Pluralism: Clarifications and Criticisms', *Contemporary Politics* 5, 325–37.
Mill, J.S. (1974) [1859], *On Liberty* (ed. G. Himmelfarb) (Harmondsworth: Penguin).
Momigliano, A. (1976), 'On the Pioneer Trail', *New York Review of Books*, 11 November.
Nagel, T. (1991), 'The Fragmentation of Value', in T. Nagel (ed.), *Moral Values* (Cambridge: Canto).
Newey, G. (1998), 'Value-Pluralism in Contemporary Liberalism', *Dialogue* 37, 493–522.
Nussbaum, M. (1986), *The Fragility of Goodness: Luck and Ethics in Greek Tragedy and Philosophy* (Cambridge: Cambridge University Press).
Nussbaum, M. (1990), 'Aristotelian Social Democracy', in R.B. Douglass, G. Mara and H.S. Richardson (eds), *Liberalism and the Good* (New York and London: Routledge).
Nussbaum, M. (1992a), 'Human Functioning and Social Justice: In Defense of Aristotelian Essentialism', *Political Theory* 20, 202–46.
Nussbaum, M. (1992b), *Love's Knowledge: Essays on Philosophy and Literature* (Oxford: Oxford University Press).
Nussbaum, M. (2000), *Women and Human Development: The Capabilities Approach* (Cambridge: Cambridge University Press).
Nussbaum, M. and Sen, A. (eds) (1993), *The Quality of Life* (Oxford: Clarendon).
Parekh, B. (1994), 'Superior People: The Narrowness of Liberalism from Mill to Rawls', *Times Literary Supplement*, 25 February.

Parekh, B. (2000), *Rethinking Multiculturalism: Cultural Diversity and Political Theory* (Cambridge, Mass: Harvard University Press).

Rachels, J. (1986), *The Elements of Moral Philosophy*, 2nd Edition (New York: McGraw-Hill).

Rawls, J. (1971), *A Theory of Justice* (Oxford: Oxford University Press).

Rawls, J. (1993), *Political Liberalism* (New York: Columbia University Press).

Raz, J. (1986), *The Morality of Freedom* (Oxford: Clarendon Press).

Richardson, H.S. (1997), *Practical Reasoning About Final Ends* (Cambridge: Cambridge University Press).

Riley, J. (2000), 'Crooked Timber and Liberal Culture', in M. Baghramian and A. Ingram (eds), *Pluralism: The Philosophy and Politics of Diversity* (London and New York: Routledge).

Riley, J. (2001), 'Interpreting Berlin's Liberalism', *American Political Science Review* 95, 283–95.

Riley, J. (2002), 'Defending Cultural Pluralism', *Political Theory* 30, 68–96.

Sandall, R. (2001), *The Culture Cult: Designer Tribalism and Other Essays* (Boulder, CO: Westview).

Sandel, M. (1982), *Liberalism and the Limits of Justice* (Cambridge: Cambridge University Press).

Sandel, M. (1984), 'Introduction', in M. Sandel (ed.), *Liberalism and its Critics* (Oxford: Blackwell).

Sartre, J.-P. (1948), *Existentialism and Humanism* (trans. P. Mairet) (London: Methuen).

Sen, A. (2001), *Development as Freedom* (New York: Knopf).

Sen, A. (2006), *Identity and Violence: The Illusion of Destiny* (New York: Norton).

Stephen, J.F. (1967) [1873], *Liberty, Equality, Fraternity*, (ed. R.J. White) (Cambridge: Cambridge University Press).

Stocker, M. (1990), *Plural and Conflicting Values* (Oxford: Clarendon Press).

Tully, J. (1995), *Strange Multiplicity: Constitutionalism in an Age of Diversity* (Cambridge: Cambridge University Press).

Walzer, M. (1983), *Spheres of Justice* (New York: Basic Books).

Walzer, M. (1995), 'Are There Limits to Liberalism?', *New York Review of Books*, 19 October.

Westermarck, E. (1960), *Ethical Relativity* (Paterson, NJ: Littlefield, Adams).

Williams, B. (1978), 'Introduction', in I. Berlin, *Concepts and Categories: Philosophical Essays* (London: Hogarth).

Young, I.M. (1990), *Justice and the Politics of Difference* (Princeton: Princeton University Press).

Chapter 18

Human Rights and Duties in Islam

N.A. Fadhil Lubis

In this chapter, I deal with the basic doctrines of Islam concerning rights and duties, especially in the fields of law and jurisprudence, and elaborate those basic principles that are supportive of the modern concept of human rights, even though the Islamic and Western civilizations may have followed different historical paths in developing these concepts. Given the complexity of the topic, my discussion cannot do justice to the full range of Islamic opinion or to the diverse approaches adopted by different schools of Islamic law. Instead, my aim is to lay out some fundamentals so that the reader can see how it would be possible to find precedents for a contemporary doctrine of rights in the Islamic tradition. It will then not seem far fetched to suggest that Indonesian Islam can embrace a contemporary doctrine of human rights by further developing elements in the Islamic tradition.

The Primacy of Duties in Islam

The term *Islam* is derived from the Arabic root *s l-m*, which means submission or peace. Muslims are those who surrender to God's will or law and as a result, Muslims believe, are at peace with themselves and with God. To embrace Islam is to become a member of a worldwide community of believers (*ummah*). Thus, believers have both an individual and corporate religious identity and responsibility or duty to obey and implement God's will in their personal and social life. In Islam, sovereignty belongs to God, and in Islamic history the caliph/sultan ruled over the Islamic community in accordance with *shari'ah* based on the *Qur'an* and the *Sunnah* (the traditions of the Prophet Muhammad). Muslims, as subjects of the ruler, had duties defined by Islamic concepts rather than rights acquired as members of a political community (Turgay 2003, 292). For medieval Islamic philosophers, legal rules and political ethics were about the duties a human being owed to his/her family, tribe, king and God, by virtue of his/her role and function in the universal order.

Legal Capacity

This approach to duties requires a developed doctrine of legal capacity in order to determine who may or may not have duties. The concept of responsibility in Islamic law is subsumed under that of legal capacity (*ahliyyah*), within which are distinguished the *ahliyyah al-wujuh* (capacity of obligation) and the *ahliyyah al-ada'* (capacity of execution). The former is the capacity to acquire rights and duties, and the latter is the capacity to contract, to dispose, and therefore also validly to fulfil one's obligations; it can be either full or restricted, and is harmonized with the former by considering the 'qualification' (*hukm*), the essential character of the obligation. The highest degree of legal capacity is that of the free Muslim who is sane (*'aqil*) and of age (*baligh*); he is fully responsible (*mukallaf*). Majority is determined more by physical and rational indications, or, failing this, by reaching the age, in most schools of law, of 15 lunar years. The *mukallaf* has the capacity to contract and to dispose (*tasarruf*), he is bound to fulfil the religious duties, and he is fully subject to criminal law, being capable of deliberate intent (*'amd*). Higher demands are made of those who hold public offices and of the witnesses, who must also be 'of good character'. In order to be a *mukallaf*, one has to be *ahliyyah*, meaning the ability or fitness to acquire rights and exercise them and to accept duties and perform them. This indicates two types of capacity: the first is based on the acceptance or acquisition of rights (*ahliyyah al-wujub*) and the other on the performance of duties (*ahliyyah al-ada'*). Capacity for acquisition enables a person to acquire both rights and obligations, while capacity for execution gives him/her the ability to exercise such rights and perform his/her duties.

Muslim jurists use the word *manat* in relation to legal capacity. The *manat* is the basis for the existence of the capacity for acquisition, which is the attribute of being a human. There is agreement among jurists that this form of capacity is possessed by each human being irrespective of his being a *mukallaf*. Capacity for execution, on the other hand, is defined as the 'capability of a human being to issue statements and perform acts to which the lawgiver has assigned certain legal effects'. The *manat* or basis of the capacity for execution is *'aqil* (intellectual capacity) and *baligh* (physical maturity). Muslim jurists divide legal capacity into three types: complete (*kamilah*), deficient (*naqisah*) and imperfect (*qasirah*). Complete capacity for acquisition is found in a human being after his birth. This makes him eligible for the acquisition of all kinds of rights and obligations. Complete capacity for execution is established for a human being when s/he attains full mental development, and acquires the ability to discriminate. Deficient capacity is assigned in cases where the *manat* or basis of legal capacity is not fully developed. Imperfect capacity is assigned in cases where the bases of capacity, being human and possession of discretion, are present, but an external attribute has been introduced that does not permit the recognition of the legal validity of certain acts. Capacity for acquisition may be perfect or imperfect. Imperfect capacity is attributed, in most schools of law, to women. A woman is said, in those schools of law, to possess imperfect legal capacity to perform certain tasks. Those who hold this view deny her the right to be the head of state, the right to be a *qadi* (judge), and the right to testify in *hudud*[1] cases and *qisas*[2] provisions.

Legal obligation (*taklif*) in Islamic legal thought is also based on other criteria. One of them is the principle of the voidability of *taklif ma la yutāq* (obligation which is impossible to fulfil), which is theological in origin, and does not encourage the literal

---

1 The term is used to describe the fixed punishment for certain crimes considered to be 'claims of God': drinking alcohol; theft; highway robbery; illegal sexual intercourse; accusation of *zina'* (extramarital sex).

2 *Qisas* is an Islamic term meaning retaliation.

meaning of *taklif* to be expected. The discussion of the legal obligation proceeds to an analysis of *qudrah* (capability) and *masyaqqah* (hardship). A capability is an essential element in the concept of legal obligation, so that it is the *shart* (condition) or *sabab* (cause) of *taklif.* Hence, any obligation which is not within the *qudrah* of the *mukallaf* (legal subject), is not valid.

Obligation

In Islamic jurisprudence, law has three elements, which interact with each other to give rise to liability and to the obligations to obey the law. The three elements of the *hukm* or a rule of law in the Islamic legal system are: the lawgiver (*hākim*), the act to which the *hukm* is related (*mahkum fih*, also referred to as *mahkum bih*), and the subject who performs the act (*mahkum 'alayh*), that is, the person who is under an obligation to obey the law.

God is the prime source (*shari'*) of all laws in Islamic legal theory, although the *Qur'an* itself also allows the *Sunnah* as a source of laws. This basic norm or rule does two things. First, it provides a standard or criterion with which we can judge whether or not a law is valid. Second, it creates for each Muslim an obligation or duty to obey the law. A subject of an Islamic state does not have to look for some external rule of morality or justice for his/her duty to obey the law. This basic rule determines the character of Islam and gives direction to all interpretation and *ijtihad* (independent reasoning). It is Allah's laws alone that are acceptable to the Muslims. No temporal authority can command a Muslim's obedience, unless the authority is based on the commands of Allah. There is a covenant between a Muslim and his Creator within a Muslim community and this covenant is the basis upon which Muslims, acting upon the commands of Allah, agree to cooperate with each other and to live together in the form of an organized Muslim society (Nyazee 2000, 79).

Revelation and Reason

Does Islamic law recognize certain natural rights or does it consider rights to be granted by *shari'ah* alone? This is a disputed question. If, however, rights are given by the *shari'ah* alone, then they can only be taken away by it. Moreover, any rights granted by the *shari'ah* will exist whether or not they are stated in the constitution of a Muslim state. The courts will have to enforce these rights under all circumstances, and no human authority can justify their suspension. Of course, the state may enact a recommendatory regulation as to the form right and duties must take. However, this regulation should not be in contradiction with *shari'ah* values, and it should support and implement further *shari'ah* injunctions.

Rights

The notion of rights emerged in Islam more slowly than in the West. The corresponding Arabic word to 'right' is *haqq*, but this word is as vague as its English equivalent. The diverse meanings and uses of *haqq* in the *Qur'an*, the *Sunnah* and Arabic literature have also prompted eminent scholars to inquire into its true meaning. The word *haqq* is commonly used in different meanings such as *thabata* and *wajada*, that whose existence one could not possibly deny, *wujub* (incumbent and mandatory), *sahih* (authentic), *sidq* (truth), and *yaqeen or yaqîn* (certainty). However, its important meanings which are relevant to legal discussions, are ownership and possession (*milkiyyah*), due (*naseeb*), just allocation (*hissah*) and a share (*saham*). Similarly, Arabs also used *haqq* for right as a correlative of duty, litigation and lawsuit (*khusumah*). In the *Qur'an*, the word *haqq* and its off-shoots occur 287 times, and it is used in about 18 different meanings.

It is less clear that Islam understands rights as the foundation of law. The early Muslim jurists speak about benefits and interests. For them, interest is the nucleus of the rights, whether rights of God or rights of men. Moreover, all jurists agree that the distinction between the rights of God and the rights of men is that, in the case of the rights of men, the right bearer has the power to extinguish, waive and enforce or transfer his right. Such power is not vested in anyone concerning rights of God. Hence, it may be concluded that Muslim jurists recognize benefit and interest as the foundation of all legal rules, but do not deny the autonomy of the individual will concerning their private rights.

On the other hand, Islamic jurisprudence probably implies a form of natural law. The classical locus for the Islamic idea of good and evil is the *Qur'an* which commands believers to enjoin the good (*ma'ruf*) and forbid the evil (*munkar'*). The logical status of these imperatives remains unclear, however. Consistent with this, the early Muslim jurists were divided as to whether human reason alone could discover and discern *hasan* (good) and *qabih* (bad or evil), but there was a recognition, as Hart puts it, that there are certain principles of human conduct, awaiting discovery by human reason, with which man-made law must conform if it is to be valid (Hart 1961, 182).[3]

What rights do individuals have in Islam? When considering the Islamic view of rights, the writings of Mawdudi (1903–79), an Islamic thinker of considerable fame and influence, are of particular value. Mawdudi enumerates no fewer than 13 rights which citizens have a right to exercise against the government. They include the right to life, dignity, privacy, property, due process, equality before the law, freedom of belief, freedom of assembly and freedom from religious persecution. Moreover, most of the rights which he elaborates can be referenced to fairly unequivocal *Qur'anic* verses.

A generally accepted classification and sub-classification of rights are those proposed by the Hanafi school, which classifies rights as: (a) pure rights of God which are subdivided into eight varieties; (b) rights of man; (c) rights of God and rights of man in which the latter are dominant. God's right (*haqq Allah*) refers to an act of devotion or something that is for the interest of the community at large. The right of God consists of value without which the achievement of civil society is

3 Significantly, the development of natural law theory in the West through the writings of Thomas Aquinas was indebted to the works of Ibn Sina (980–1037) and Ibn Rushd (1126–98).

unfeasible. It is called *haqq Allah* because the violation of such right endangers both the offender and the society. Respect for such a right is the duty of every individual as well as the state, and its violation is the cause of liability in this world and blame in the hereafter. The state is under obligation to constantly watch, observe and implement the rights of God.

The *'ulamā'* or *ulema* have subdivided the rights of God into eight categories, which are as follows:

1. Rights that involve pure rituals and acts of devotion (*'ibadah al-khālisah*) such as prayers, fasting and pilgrimage to Mecca;
2. Rights that comprise both devotion and an element of financial liability (*'ibadah fiha ma'na al-ma'unah*) such as *zakat al-fitr* (alms at the end of fasting month);
3. Rights that consist of financial liability and a sense of devotion (*'ibadah*), for instance, tithe (*'ushr*) is imposed on the produce of fertile land after harvesting for the benefit of the poor and needy;
4. Rights that indicate bare-duty and tax. These rights are illustrated by the land tax (*kharaj*) that is imposed on conquered territories and is payable by the new subjects or those who acquire such land subsequently;
5. Rights that consist of pure punishments (*'uqubat al-kamilah*), for instance, *hudud* (fixed punishment for certain crimes regulated by revelation);
6. Rights that comprise minor punishments (*'uqubat al-naqisah*), for instance, when a murderer is a close relative of the victim, s/he is excluded from the estate of the victim as (additional) punishment;
7. Rights that consist of matters intermediate between devotion and punishment (*al-da'irah bayn al-'ibadah wa al-'uqubah*), for example, expiation (*kaffarah*) of breaking a fast;
8. Independent right (*al-haqq al-qaim bi nafsih*), for example, the right of the poor and needy in one-fifth of the spoils of war and mineral products.

Muslim jurists have defined 'right of man' by reference to human interests and, according to 'Izz 'Abd al-Salam, it consists of the attraction of benefit and the prevention of evil. Hence the right of man is the act of an individual performed for his own interest, or an act the performance of which is beneficial to another party (for example, the right bearer). This will include acts that are emphatically demanded or forbidden, and those that are recommended, reprehensible or optional. The rights of man are illustrated by his transactions with others; thus they include contractual rights, political rights, social rights and property rights. They also include those rights that are conferred by the law, such as the blood money for the relatives of the victim, the right of pre-emption and the right to maintenance between close relatives. Each right has a corresponding duty. A right is secured when the subject who owes the duty brings about the required act, that is, performs the duty owed by him. In cases when the collective right of society and the private right of an individual or a class of individuals merge in the same act, but the collective interest is apparently more important, it is called the prevalent right of God (Badran 1995, 398). The prevalent right of God is illustrated by the prohibition of suicide, wasting of property, and the like. In cases such as these, the *shari'ah* gives priority to the interest of society. In cases when an act violates both the right of God and the right of man, but the consequences of the violation are more detrimental to the victim or his relatives, priority is given to the right of man. In other words, where the purpose of a right is the protection of collective good and personal right of an individual, but the latter is more important than the former, the right of man prevails (Abu Zahrah 1937; Hasan 2004, 302–5).

Under ordinary circumstances, rules involving the rights of God or the rights of man may deal with the interests of all subjects irrespective of their legal capacity. But when a wrong is committed, or it is a matter of personal liability, the writings of Muslim jurists suggest that both under *haqq Allah* and *haqq al-'abd*, contractual promises and penalties for the wrong committed are imposed on legally competent persons only.

Muslim jurists have discussed the distinction between the right of God and the right of men in almost every issue of evidence and procedure. They often validate or invalidate certain proceedings based on this distinction of rights. In *hudud* cases, for example, the legal rules are applied rigidly so much so that the jurists make every effort not to convict the accused except where his guilt is proved beyond the shadow of doubt. In *huquq al-'ibad*, however, there is flexibility in the application of law by prescribing probable standards of proof. It is apparent that the object of such flexibility is that the right of man should be respected utmost and that its violation must not be taken lightly (Zaydan 1967, 155–237). Further, the rights of God are inalienable and beyond the powers of the state or individual to waive, while many of the rights of man are open to waiver. The inalienable rights of the human being are:

1. Rights that do not exist at the time of waiver. Such rights are the rights to maintenance of a wife, the right to pre-emption before a property is negotiated for sale, and the option of viewing;
2. Rights that are essential to one's status and personality. For instance, the right of parents to guardianship is an attribute of parents that cannot be taken away in normal circumstances;
3. The waiver of a right destroys the legal relationship of its bearer with the object of the said right. Thus, a person making a gift could not waive his right to cancel the gift in future, for otherwise it would alter his legal relationship with the object of the gift as its owner;
4. The waiver of a given right harms others. Thus a parent cannot give up his/her parental rights, for the main objective of such rights is the protection of their child, which takes priority over the waiving right of the parents concerning custody. In circumstances other than the above, the rights of man are alienable and may be transferred to another party.

In the *fiqh* tradition, the category of the right of the individual Muslim was mainly used to distinguish cases in which legal actions against the wrongdoer were left to the discretion of the injured party or parties from other cases belonging to the category of the right of God, in which prosecution was mandatory and was to be undertaken by the government. The rights of God are differentiated into eight categories. Interests of higher values, such as devotional or those for the public good, are considered the rights of Allah and individual benefits are considered the rights of the human being.

The writings on the caliphate by jurists such as 'Ali ibn Hazm (d. 1064) mainly concentrated on the qualifications and traits of the caliph. Rights were classified mainly into those of the *imam* and those of the *ummah*, with hardly any room for rights of the individual. Even Ibn Taymiyyah, who subtitles one of his major works *On the Rights of the Ruler and the Subjects* (*fi huquq al-ra'i wa al-ra'iyah*), speaks only of civil individual rights over one's life and possessions and does not mention public or political rights of any sort. In addition to the rights of God and the rights of man, another important classification of rights was introduced by al-Mawardi and al-Farra' and included a new class of state rights. State right (*haqq al-sultanah*) may be referred to as a right enacted by the state based on some evidence of *shari'ah* (which may be some form of *haqq Allah* and *haqq al-'abd*) and/or based on a public interest which the state sees necessary to uphold. The state, in other words, may enact new rights and obligations based on those issues which are mentioned by *shari'ah*, but they are not demanded emphatically nor are they protected by express duties and punishments. This new terminology is used for crimes against the state solely or in combination with the right of man, which are protected by an enacted penal code of the state (*ta'zirat*). Rules regarding offences against a human person not amounting to murder or manslaughter are one of the fields covered by state rights. These types of rights are supplementary to those mentioned under the rights of God and the rights of man. They are operative either after prosecution fails to establish the violation of *haqq Allah* or *haqq al-'abd*, or where the offence is not provided with prescribed forms of punishment.

In Islamic jurisprudence, terms such as right, duty and liberty or power and disability are understood with reference to the actions of agents. In the case of a mandatory act, the agent is under compulsion to perform it. Since in Islam the duty to Allah is different from duty to the state, an act could be the duty to Allah and simultaneously be a right against the state. In such cases, it is not the prerogative of the state to prevent the exercise of such right or refuse to recognize it. Both prevention and refusal are unlawful and void. Thus any right that is a duty to Allah or to the state or both is a mandatory right that one can insist on: otherwise it is a duty. But if the act is not duty to either of them, and it involves some sort of option and choice on the part of the right holder, then it is a right in its ordinary sense. If a right in the ordinary sense is protected by the duty of others, it is title. Otherwise, it is liberty protected by immunity, claims, and other means to facilitate it. This means that the right-bearer can insist on it by demanding means for attaining the said right (the state would be under duty to provide such means), or if he attempts to do something about it, he would have immunity from any criminal or civil proceedings.

The Purposes of *Shari'ah*

There is also arguably a natural law element implied by the purposes or objectives of Islamic law (*maqasid al-shari'ah*). On the whole, Islamic legal thought has been preoccupied with concerns about conformity to the letter of the divine text, and the legal science of *usul al-fiqh* has played a crucial role in the advancement of this cause. The literalist orientation of the juristic thought was generally more pronounced on the part of the traditionalists than of the rationalists. The traditionalists tended to view *shari'ah* as a set of rules, commands and prohibitions that were addressed to the competent *mukallaf* (individual subject), where all that the latter was expected to do was to conform. The precedents of the leading companions of the Prophet (*sahabahs*) indicate, on the other hand, that they saw *shari'ah* not only as a set of rules, but also as a system of values, where the specific rules were the tangible manifestations of those overriding values. The textualist tradition of the early three centuries, however, did not take much interest in this deeper observation, and it was not until the time of al-Ghazzali (d. 505 AH) and then al-Shatibi (d. 790 AH) that significant development took place in the formulation of a theory of the objectives of *shari'ah*.

The *Qur'an* emphasizes in numerous places and in a variety of contexts the purpose, rationale and benefits of its laws, to the extent that the texts stipulating these laws are characteristically goal-oriented. *Shari'ah* generally is predicated on benefits to the individual and the community, and its laws are designed so as to protect these benefits and to facilitate the improvement and perfection of the conditions of human life on earth. This feature of the *Qur'an* is common to its laws relating to both *'ibada* (ritual worship) and *mu'amalah* (civil transactions). Thus, when the text expounds on the ritual of *wudu'*, or ablution for prayer, it adds: 'God does not wish to inflict hardship on you but to make you clean and to complete His favor to you' (Q, 5:7). With regard to the prayer itself, it declares, 'Truly, *salat* restrains promiscuity and evil' (Q, 29:45). With reference to the law of *qisas* (just retaliation), the text similarly adds: 'and in the law of *qisas* there is life for you' (Q, 2:179). And finally, with regard to *zakāt* (alms), the rationale is given: 'in order that wealth may not circulate only amongst the rich' (Q, 59:7).

This can also be seen in the *Qur'an's* characterization of itself as 'a healing to the (spiritual) ailment of the hearts' and 'a Guidance and Mercy' for the believers and mankind (Q, 10:57). The objective of *rahmah* (mercy or compassion) mentioned in these two verses is further substantiated by other provisions in the *Qur'an* and *Sunnah* that seek to eliminate prejudice, alleviate hardship and establish justice. The laws of the *Qur'an* and *Sunnah* also seek to promote cooperation and support within the family and the society at large. The objective of *rahmah*, therefore, is most clearly manifested in the realization of *maslaha* in everyday communal life. The *'ulamā'* or *ulema* have, thus, generally considered *rahmah* to be the all-pervasive objective of *shari'ah*, and have, to all intents and purposes, used it synonymously with *maslaha*.

'Adl or *qist* (justice) is indeed a manifestation of God's mercy, but may also be seen as a principal objective of *shari'ah* in its own right. Certainly the *Qur'an* sees it as such when it states: 'We sent our Messengers and revealed through them the Book and the Balance so that justice may be established amongst mankind' (Q, 57:25). Justice as a value or primary objective is mentioned in the *Qur'an* 53 times in all. *'Adl* – literally meaning to place things in their right and proper place – as a fundamental objective of the *shari'ah*, is to seek to establish an equilibrium between

rights and obligations, so as to eliminate all excesses and disparities, in all spheres of life.

The basic outlook of *shari'ah* advocated by the theory of *al-maqasid* was never completely denied by any of the leading schools of law, although some were more open to the theory and science of *al-maqasid* than others. Indeed, except for the Zahiris, who maintained that the *maqasid* can only be known when they are identified by clear text, the majority of the *'ulamā'* or *ulema* did not even confine *al-maqasid* to the clear text. They understood *shari'ah* to be rational and goal-oriented such that rules that went against the purpose and visions of *shari'ah* were generally unacceptable.

It was not until the early fourth century of the Islamic calendar that the term *maqasid* was used in the juristic writings of Al-Tirmidhi (898). Recurring references to this then appeared in the works of Imam al-Haramayn al-Juwayni (d. 478 AH), who was probably the first to classify the *maqasid* of *shari'ah* into three main categories, and he was followed by many medieval Muslim scholars who have classified the entire range of *maqasid* into three descending categories of importance: *daruriyyāt* (the essential), *hajjiyyāt* (the needs) and *tahsiniyyāt* (the desirables or the embellishments). The essential things that *shari'ah* protects are five, namely life-soul, faith, intellect, lineage and basic property. These are seen as absolute requirements to the survival and spiritual well-being of individuals, to the extent that their destruction or collapse would precipitate chaos and the demise of normal order in society. *Shari'ah* on the whole seeks primarily to protect and promote these essential values, and validates all measures necessary for their preservation and advancement.

Al-Juwayni's ideas were then further developed by his pupil, Abu Hamid al-Ghazali (1111) who wrote at length on the doctrines of *maslaha* (public interest) and *ta'lil* (ratiocination) in his works *Shifa' al-Ghalil* and *Al-Mustasfa min 'Ilm al-Usul.* Al-Ghazali was generally critical of the doctrine of public interest as a source or proof, but validated it where it promoted the *maqasid* of *shari'ah.* As for the *maqasid* themselves, al-Ghazali wrote categorically that *shari'ah* pursued five basic objectives – life, faith, intellect, lineage and property – and that these were to be protected as absolute priorities (Kamali 1998, 401).

The *maqasid* are always used as a reference point for the general principles of the law, although there are rules that help to determining priorities. The three most important of these rules are as follows. Rule 1: the stronger interest shall prevail, that is reflected in the order in which the *maqasid* are listed by the jurists (faith, life, family, intellect and wealth). Rule 2: the public interest is prior to the private. The different categories of the purposes can be understood in terms of public and private interests. Whenever a public interest is in conflict with a private interest, the public interest will prevail. Rule 3: the definitive interest prevails over the probable.

Clearly other examples of this kind can be found. Accepting that the implications of Islamic legal doctrine need some drawing out, there is an abundance of evidence that a form of natural law including a theory of rights was operative in parts of the tradition.

An Evaluation

To say that precedents for a doctrine of human rights exist in the Islamic tradition is not to pretend that rights were adequately articulated in that tradition, or that individual issues were handled in a completely satisfactory way. As often in Islamic history, there are tensions between the norms derived from the Prophet and the tortuous history of actual developments. It is also fair to comment that the existence of outstanding individual figures does not entirely compensate for the lack of generally accepted patterns of practice which fully implement the norms of the Prophet. Thus Muslims very early accepted a discriminatory approach to rights in the case of Muslims who were non-Arabs or not a full member by descent from the Arab tribe. In other examples, it has simply to be admitted that Muslim doctrine and practice were not consistent with the teachings of the *Qur'an* and *Sunnah*.

Nonetheless, there is a humanist side to Islamic jurisprudence, and most jurists agree that laws are laid down in the interest of human beings, although they are divided over whether the human being is free to determine his own interests. The same spirit is operative in many of the lists of Islamic human rights that have been made public in recent years, although many inconsistencies, obfuscations and equivocations are to be found, especially in the areas of freedom of thought, treatment of non-Muslims and women's rights. For example, whereas the English version of article XX (a) of the Universal Islamic Declaration of Human Rights lays down that the husband owes his wife means of support 'in the event of divorce', the Arabic version of the same article uses the phrase 'if he divorces her'. What the English version passes over in silence is, of course, the troublesome problem of the unconditional right to divorce, which most classical *fiqh* opinions have given to men. In addition, the Arabic version invokes the notion of the authority which men have over women, something which the English version omits altogether.

Conclusion

Despite these reservations, the heritage of *shari'ah* and *fiqh* offer rich and varied terrain in which human rights can be grounded. Granted that there are omissions, and shortcomings which our modern ethical sensibilities cannot accept, one should not judge *shari'ah* or *fiqh* harshly. In my view, resources can be found within the Islamic tradition to underpin an Indonesian Islamic political and legal thought which is consistent with modernity, even though the articulation of such political thought will depend in detail on our willingness to learn from and critically assimilate political concepts first articulated in the West. Although the term 'human rights' has only recently come into common use in the Islamic world, concepts analogous to human rights are not entirely without precedent in the rich heritage of Islamic philosophy and theology. Moreover, it can be argued that a form of natural law is implicit in many important Islamic concepts and in the balance which Islam seeks to strike between individualism and community. At the very least, such considerations need to be taken into account as we Indonesian Muslims seek to articulate a theory and practice of human rights relevant to the challenges we currently face.

References

Abu Zahrah, M. (1937), *Al-'Uqubah* (Cairo: Damascus Press).
Al-Ghazali, Abu Hamid (1322 AH), *Al-Mustasfa fi Usul al-Fiqh* (Cairo: al-Matba'ah al-Amiriyah al-Bulaq).
Badran, Margot (1995), *Feminists, Islam, and Nation: Gender and the Making of Modern Egypt (*Princeton, NJ: Princeton University Press).
Guillaume, A. (1970), *The Life of Muhammad: A Translation of Ibn Ishaq's Sirat Rasul Allah* (Oxford: Oxford University Press).
Hart, H.L.A. (1961), *The Concept of Law* (Oxford: Clarendon Press).
Hasan, A.G. (2004), *The Rights and Duties of Women in Islam* (Brunei: Darussalam Publishers).
Haykal, Muhammad Husayn (1976), *The Life of Muhammaed* (trans. Isma'il Ragi al Faruqi) (New Delhi: Crescent Publishing).
Kamali, Muhammad Hashim (1998), *Principles of Islamic Jurisprudence*, 2nd Revised Edition (Kuala Lumpur: Ilmiah Publishers).
Mayer, Ann Elizabeth (1995), 'Human Rights', in John L. Esposito (ed.), *The Oxford Encylopedia of the Modern Islamic World*, vol. 2 (Oxford: Oxford University Press).
Mohammad, Mohammad Tahir Haji (2003), *Rights and Duties in Shari'ah and Common Law* (Kuala Lumpur: Ilmiah Publishers).
Nyazee, Imran Ahsan Khan (1994), *Theories of Islamic Law: The Methodology of Ijtihad* (Kuala Lumpur: The Other Press).
Nyazee, Imran Ahsan Khan (2000), *Islamic Jurisprudence: Usul al-Fiqh* (Kuala Lumpur: The Other Press).
Pipes, Daniel (1985), 'Mawlas: Freed Slaves and Converts in Early Islam', in John R. Willis (ed.), *Slaves and Slavery in Muslim Africa*, vol. 1 (London: Routledge).
Safi, Omid (ed.) (2003), *Progressive Muslims on Justice, Gender, and Pluralism* (Oxford: OneWorld).
Salim, Paul (ed.) (1997), *Conflict Resolution in the Arab World: Selected Essays* (Beirut: American University of Beirut).
Turgay, A. (2003), *Developing a Dialogue with Islamic Communities in South and Southeast Asia* (Ottawa: DFAIT).
Zaydan, J. (1967), *Abbasah* (Kuala Lumpur: Pustaka Antaras).
Zaydan, 'Abd al-Karim' (1984), *Nizam al-Qada fi al-Shari'ah al-Islamiyah* (Baghdad: Mathba'ah al-'Ani).

Chapter 19

Human Rights and Pluralism

Joseph Camilleri

Any discussion of rights and governance in a plural world must first come face to face with the multifaceted and mutually reinforcing upheavals that have buffeted the international system this past century: the phenomenon of 'total war' as reflected in two world wars and the possibility of nuclear war, the profound and seemingly unbridgeable gap between rich and poor, and the increasingly dangerous disruption of planetary ecosystems. To this must be added the organized mass slaughter of innocents, which is at the centre of much contemporary experience – one need only mention the German Holocaust, Hiroshima and Nagasaki, the Cambodian 'killing fields', the ethnic cleansing practices that followed the break-up of the former Yugoslavia, and the Rwandan genocide. These indelible stains on the collective human conscience have inevitably given added poignancy to the human predicament, and paradoxically enough engendered a steadily expanding consciousness of a shared human destiny.

Since the end of the Second World War, we have seen the slow but steady rise of 'world opinion', and increasing attention focused on gross human rights violations, war crimes, crimes against humanity, and more generally the abuse of power. The communications revolution, itself the product of the globalization of market forces, has provided the material basis for a vastly expanded arena of ethical discourse that cuts across national, cultural and religious boundaries. As a consequence, we are seeing, at least embryonically, the growth of new forms of discourse and action that do not replace but complement those of the past. National debate continues to serve as an important form of social participation, but increasingly it interacts with new forms of cultural and political expression and activity, which centre as much on local, regional, transnational and global as on national space (Urry 1999, 266).

Ethical discourse does not, of course, offer instant answers to hard and contentious questions: How are we to interpret the changing face of terrorism and its social and political roots? How appropriate is the 'war on terror' as a response to the problem? What constitutes effective and acceptable approaches to the administration of criminal justice on a global scale? When is 'humanitarian intervention' legitimate? How stable or defensible is the present balance between nuclear haves and nuclear have-nots? How can the Arab–Israeli conflict be resolved? Do unilateralist 'coalitions of the willing' have a place in the management of international crises? What is the future of regional and global institutions? In one way or another, each of these questions points to the need for dialogue centred on the rediscovery, renegotiation and reinvigoration of the twin notions of human rights and humane governance.

The analysis proposed here rests on two assumptions: first, that since the late 1980s human rights have moved much closer to the centre stage of international affairs; and secondly, that this trend is unlikely to be reversed in the foreseeable future. Events in Burma, Cambodia, Rwanda, Indonesia/East Timor, the former Yugoslavia, Afghanistan and Iraq, to name only the most dramatic examples, and the international response to these events make it clear that human rights have become an integral part of the economic, social and political agenda, whether conceived in national, regional or global terms. The contention of this chapter is not that the tensions surrounding the theory and practice of rights have been resolved – or that they can ever be fully resolved – but that dialogue offers the only creative response to these tensions.[1] Our concern here is not therefore to reformulate the competing claims of universalism and cultural relativism, much less to adjudicate in favour of one or other claim.[2] The aim is rather to explore the meaning, usefulness and modalities of dialogue as a response to cultural pluralism.

The Idea of 'Rights' and Cultural Pluralism

We begin the analysis by briefly revisiting the Western conception of human rights. Daniel Skubik describes the Western, and more specifically Anglo-American, tradition in terms of the following key attributes: (1) individuality – each human being is considered to be a separate, distinct whole; (2) moral agency – each person is a free, autonomous agency; (3) moral equality – each individual is deemed inherently equal; (4) rationality – each individual has access to reason; (5) individual integrity – each person has an inherent dignity concomitant with his or her individuality (Skubik 1992, 31). These attributes help to explain the Western preoccupation with negative rights understood as freedom from undue interference or repression by political authority. The stress on negative rights and individual choice is in sharp contrast to the idea of positive rights (understood as freedom to) which emphasizes the needs of others and supports principles of justice.

Though the Western conception has its origins in the Judeo-Christian notion that all men are equal in the sight of God, its modern expression is inextricably linked to the growth of capitalism and to the rise of the merchant and manufacturing classes that gradually displaced the power of monarchs and feudal lords. Over time, it became an integral part of the culture of modernity with its emphasis on rationality, efficiency, predictability, scientific advance and productivity. Partly as a consequence of its global economic, political and military dominance, the West has come to believe in the universality of its dominant discourse and to measure progress in the light of its own achievements.

Western modernity has, in practice if not in theory, tended to rupture the traditional attachments to local community and to create instead mobile and atomized populations whose claim to humanity rests more and more on the

1 This chapter draws substantially on, but also develops, the analysis offered in *Regionalism in the New Asia-Pacific Order* (Camilleri 2003, 280–95).

2 The issues are well rehearsed by Jack Donnelly (1989), Allison Dundes Renteln (1990) and Michael Freeman (2002).

assertion of individual rights vis-à-vis an impersonal, distant and bureaucratized governmental apparatus. An important part of the explanation for this trend is to be found in Western epistemology, and in particular its bias for analytical thinking, the net effect of which has been to interpret and segment society in zero-sum or adversarial terms, and to view one of the primary functions of conflict as identifying winners and losers. Galtung's characterization of 'Western social cosmology' as a complex process of fragmentation and marginalization, though oversimplified, is nonetheless illuminating. It rightly points to the separation of one individual from another, material from non-material needs, and the private from the public sphere. While civil and political freedoms are considered the norm in the public sphere, they can coexist, both normatively and practically, with the widespread incidence of poverty and inequality in the private sphere (Galtung 1990).

To draw attention to these shortcomings is not to ignore the very substantial contribution of the Western liberal tradition, but rather to indicate that it does not represent the last word in human rights discourse. Vincent rightly reminds us that 'three worlds of democracy' have found philosophical and political expression in the West: one modelled on civil and political rights (Locke); the second on social and economic rights (Marx); and the third on collective rights (Rousseau) (Vincent 1986, 51–2). It is fair to say that, of these three, the Lockean view has thus far been the dominant one. The same three tendencies are also to be found in the non-Western world, but here the mix has assumed a different and more subtle complexion.

The contemporary international human rights regime has, of course, been guided largely by the West, which helps to explain the dominance of the liberal democratic tradition. Many of the international human rights instruments were shaped at a time when the vast majority of Asian and African societies had scarcely asserted their right to self-determination. Even in the aftermath of political independence, most Third World countries, though formally participating in human rights forums and institutions, could exercise only limited leverage over a process that was still driven largely by Western perceptions and priorities. The 'Asian versus Western values' debate of the late 1980s and 1990s may therefore be interpreted as a reaction to this phenomenon (Camilleri 2000, 389–91). Though their motives varied widely, East Asian elites, encouraged by their economic success, found it useful to challenge the assumption of a universal human rights consensus (Lee 1994; Mahbubani 1995; Koh 1996). Whether they judged the prevailing Western discourse as prejudicial to their political and economic interests, or whether they hoped to use cultural and civilizational arguments to advance alternative conceptions of regional integration, is open to debate. Whatever the motive, the net effect was to call into question the hegemonic control of human rights discourse (Camilleri 2003, 273–80).

The ensuing acrimony, for example, between the United States and China or between the European Union and ASEAN, seemed at first sight to give added weight to the notion of an impending 'clash of civilizations'.[3] Both sides of the divide were no doubt hoping to extract political advantage from the notion of a deep and

3 The term was first coined by Bernard Lewis (1990) and subsequently adopted by Samuel Huntington (1993) as the central ordering concept in his analysis of the contemporary international system.

perhaps unbridgeable civilizational gap between cultures. The view that the world's major religious and ethical traditions were heading for a civilizational clash based on diametrically opposed conceptions of rights and responsibilities, though seldom explicitly made, became a clearly discernible undertone of much public comment. Such a view is simply not sustainable.

To substantiate this claim, we have reviewed elsewhere the social cosmology of four of Asia's most influential religious and ethical systems: Hinduism, Buddhism, Confucianism and Islam (Camilleri 2003, 280–95). The normative structure of any culture is, of course, a complex phenomenon which cannot be reduced to a religious or ethical tradition, however dominant it may be. On the other hand, for most of the societies under consideration, the religious and ethical worldview is so closely interconnected with other social and cultural variables as to offer useful insights into the dynamics of social and political discourse. The survey, it should be stressed, did not set out to establish some fictitious identity between Asian and Western cultural traditions, but rather sought to sift the evidence pointing to either differences or commonalities.

Each of the great traditions represents, admittedly with considerable variation, a subtle cosmology that combines the individual and the whole. Notwithstanding the importance which the caste system has acquired over the centuries, the Hindu tradition not only tolerates periodic challenges to the hierarchical order, but gives expression to a complex cosmology in which each group respects 'the rights and dignity of the others' (Thompson 1980). The central concept of duty or *dharma* itself points to an ideal of society that provides for 'the righting of injustices, the restoring of balance which men in their ignorance or out of selfish passions had disturbed' (Chatterjee 1983, 19). Buddhism, which emerged as a corrective to Hinduism in the fifth century BC, takes the notion of the renunciation of self to its ultimate conclusion. Human beings are seen as transient or impermanent. On the other hand, the life of the individual is recognized as a unique experience, a unique combination of past and present relationships and experiences. The life of the person is inseparable from the totality of life, hence the centrality of the twin notions of non-injury (*ahimsa*) and compassion in the treatment of sentient beings (Mabbett 1998, 21). Confucianism, for its part, offers an ethical code rather than a supernatural or metaphysical cosmology. But within the complex Confucian and neo-Confucian interpretations of social relationships, we find a profound attachment to personhood, hence the importance of manners, customs and traditions which define obligations, but at the same time reflect and nurture the 'humaneness' and 'humanity' of Confucian ethics (de Bary 1998).

Islam

Islam merits somewhat closer attention here because of the centrality it has assumed in contemporary geopolitics, but also because it is central to the concerns of the workshop to which this chapter contributes. Though Islam is often associated with the societies of North Africa and the Middle East, its demographic centre of gravity lies in South and Southeast Asia, with its adherents accounting for the majority of the population in Pakistan, Bangladesh, Malaysia, Brunei and Indonesia, and for significant minorities in India and the Philippines. In its geographical but also cultural and political manifestations, Islam is itself a highly pluralistic community. One need only consider the composition of the Organization of the Islamic Conference, in which some 57 Muslim governments represent a rich spectrum of political systems and ideologies, 'including monarchies and republics, conservatives and revolutionaries, practitioners of capitalism and disciples of various kinds of socialism, friends and enemies of the United States, and exponents of a whole spectrum of shades of neutrality' (Lewis 1998, 24). There is clearly much more to Islam than the stereotypical image of religious fundamentalism and political extremism conjured up by much media reporting in the West.

There is nevertheless among Muslims of widely diverse religious and political persuasions a sense of unity derived from the precept of 'primordial divine unicity' (*tawhid*) and reflected in the 'communitarian construction of the flock of the faithful' (*umma*) (Sheikh 2003, 21). Viewed within the context of this cosmopolitan unity, the Islamic faith ascribes considerable importance to the closely related concepts of rights and duties. Islamic scriptures, beliefs and traditions do not accord with the Western secular philosophy of the rights of citizens, but a spate of pronouncements and declarations by religious and political leaders suggest that the connections are both numerous and illuminating (Fitzgerald 1993, 19–21). The 1980 Colloquium of Kuwait, jointly sponsored by the International Commission of Jurists, the Union of Arab Advocates and the University of Kuwait, reached the following conclusions:

1. The *Qur'an* and the *Sunnah* present a total way of life which assures both men and women their freedom and their rights;
2. Minorities in Islamic countries have the right to practise their faith, to engage in work of their choice and to avail themselves of public resources;
3. Islam gives learning and science an honoured place in the community, and recognizes freedom of opinion and expression;
4. Islamic law is based on the principle of social equality;
5. In the area of penal law, Islamic principles have regard to individual security (for example, prohibition of torture and false arrest) and the well-being of society.

The Colloquium conceded that Islamic practice did not always match Islamic law, and insisted on the need for a periodic review of *shari'ah* (that is, codification of Islamic law) to deal with the unforeseen circumstances of modern life (Mawdudi 1982, 22–5; Traer 1991, 111–12).

In August 1990, the Nineteenth Islamic Conference of Foreign Ministers issued a more conservative but comprehensive statement, the Cairo Declaration on Human Rights in Islam. It affirmed the principle of human equality, without distinction of race, colour, language, religion, sex, political affiliation or social situation, and declared human beings to be born free, with no one having the right to enslave, humiliate, oppress or exploit them. Numerous other Islamic scholars, jurists and religious leaders have since returned to the same theme, arguing for the compatibility of human rights and Islamic faith, and setting out the basic principles in Islam which define and legitimate these rights (Traer 1991, 113–14).

For Islam, human rights, it should be said, are not merely or even primarily the rights of individuals, but the rights of the community. In the Islamic conception, freedom is affirmed as the necessary foundation for the establishment of a stable community, in which people cooperate for the sake of the common good. Conversely, the function of the stable community and of the resultant political system is to utilize resources so as to satisfy human needs and promote human creativity. The four types of freedom identified by Islam (personal freedom, freedom of expression, freedom of religious beliefs and freedom of private ownership) form part of an 'egalitarian, community-oriented approach to freedom', which distances itself from individualistic liberalism in order to stress participation in cultural creation (Said and Nasser 1980, 75–6).

One other feature of the Islamic understanding of governance is worth highlighting. Whereas the modern Western conception of democracy is often associated with the notion of popular sovereignty, in Islamic theory, as indeed in medieval Christendom, rulers are but God's representatives on earth; their rule ultimately rests on divine authority. The Islamic state becomes a vehicle for God's will, which among other things requires it to prevent all forms of exploitation and injustice, and to nurture instead qualities of purity, beauty, goodness, virtue, success and prosperity (Mawdudi 1982, 9–11). Not surprisingly, in the Islamic tradition it is the duties of rulers rather than the rights of subjects which find stronger expression.

As already intimated, Islamic thought and practice constitute an intricate tapestry of different cultural and theological strands, which in part explains the ambiguous and at times elusive relationship of Islam to governance and rights. The acute tension between traditionalists and modernizers is but one manifestation of this diversity. The idea of the Islamic state is itself open to numerous and at times conflicting interpretations. For some, the Islamic state is the set of institutional and legal arrangements which express and entrench Islamic principles, including notions of justice, equality and the dignity of the human person. For others, the Islamic state is an antidote to the social ills of modernity, offering a path to the restoration of divine will. For others still, it is a response to long years of Western political and cultural domination and to widespread disillusionment with Western lifestyles and the Western model of development (Mayer 1988, 99–100). A vast debate is currently underway within the Muslim world as to the appropriate relationship of religious faith to legal and political practice.

Commonality, Difference and Complementarity

The preceding sketch hardly does justice to the complex relationship between rights and cultural and religious plurality – the sketch we have offered hardly exhausts the cultural or religious diversity to be found globally, regionally or even nationally, nor does the broad brush we have used permit an adequate characterization of any one of the major ethical traditions. Enough has been said, however, to indicate that plurality entails the subtle coexistence of both difference and commonality, which in turn raises the interesting but often neglected possibility of complementarity.

In any case, the conjunction of reciprocal influences across cultures and civilizations is anything but static. The multiplicity of influences, both indigenous and external, which are helping to shape the political culture of any society, are furiously interacting with each other and are, in the process, contributing to the slow but steady transformation of norms and expectations. The emphasis of much conventional analysis on 'the primordial, essentialist, and immutable nature of religion or religiously based social identities, ideational communities, civilizations or culture areas' is at best questionable (Thomas 2000, 13). As Pollis makes clear, 'norms and values are in continual contention and flux in both the West and elsewhere' (Pollis 2000, 24). Which strains are dominant within a given religious tradition at a given moment is likely to be determined by the interaction of multiple social and political forces at that historical juncture. Cultural values and beliefs are the subject of periodic reinterpretation, which cannot but affect inter-religious and inter-cultural communication.

Given these important caveats, what useful generalizations might we make when considering the nature of religious pluralism? First, as numerous writers have observed, the major non-Western religious and ethical traditions, notably Hinduism, Buddhism, Confucianism and Islam, share with Western liberalism, and the Judeo-Christian tradition from which it springs, a sense of the dignity of human life, a commitment to human fulfilment, and a concern for standards of 'rightness' in human conduct (Muzaffar 1999, 25–31; Pollis 2000, 23). A striking commonality, derived from these bedrock principles, is a shared commitment to humane and legitimate governance, although the criteria of legitimacy may vary considerably from one tradition to another. There is, one may reasonably conclude, sufficient common ground between these religious and ethical worldviews to make possible an ongoing conversation about human ethics in general, and political ethics in particular (Friedman 1999, 32–55).

On the other hand, there is no denying that each civilizational current and cultural formation has its own distinctive features. There are at any given historical moment significant differences in metaphysical conceptions, symbolic frameworks and ethical codes. It must not be assumed, however, that differences are necessarily inimical to fruitful normative discourse either within or between the major civilizational strands. One of the key contentions of this chapter is that the dialogical process may benefit as much from difference as from commonality. Differences certainly lead to sharp disagreement and even violent conflict, but they also offer an avenue for the exploration of much needed complementarities.

It is at least arguable that the non-Western traditions we have reviewed, not least Islam, can richly contribute to the universality and comprehensiveness of the evolving global governance and human rights regimes. Five dimensions may be said to characterize their collective contribution. First, they provide a richer and more varied conception of political space, by establishing a closer connection between human rights and human needs, notably those of the disadvantaged (hence the emphasis on social and economic rights). Secondly, they offer a more holistic understanding of the human condition by establishing a closer connection between rights and obligations and between the individual and the community (hence the dual emphasis on rights and responsibilities). Thirdly, they help to situate citizenship within a larger social context, opening up new possibilities whereby the individual can think and act not as a disaggregated atom but as a member of several overlapping collectivities. There is much to be said for a deeper understanding than is evident in the Western liberal tradition of the rights of indigenous peoples, of minorities, but also of the collective rights of peoples to a healthy environment, to security, to a share of the common heritage of humanity (Camilleri 1994).

The other two dimensions flow from the preceding three but have an importance of their own. The first involves a rejection of Western hegemony, that is, a rejection of the view that the West enjoys a monopoly on the definition of human needs and human rights. Western liberal formulations (and the idea of progress on which they rest) are not seen as applying universally across time and space. Human rights standards may be universal in scope at a given moment, but how these standards are understood and applied is likely to change over time. This brings us to the last aspect of the non-Western contribution to human rights discourse, namely the emphasis on consensual decision-making. If participation is one of the criteria of legitimate governance of a nation's affairs, then presumably the same criterion applies when the arena shifts from national to international governance, be it regional or global. In other words, an international system of law and rights is more likely to command universal respect to the extent that it proceeds by way of negotiation, involves all parties concerned and incorporates the insights of their respective traditions.

Civilization Dialogue: Functions and Modalities

The immense challenges posed by economic and technological globalization suggest that, over the next several decades, a dialogue of global proportions will need to emerge – global in the sense that it cultivates the sharing of insights across the major fault lines in the geopolitical and geocultural landscape, not least the fault line separating Islam and the West. Numerous steps have already been taken in this direction, including the establishment of several research and educational centres of 'civilization dialogue' in different parts of the world, the expanding body of scholarly literature exploring the deeper meaning, modalities and practical possibilities of such a dialogue, and the steps taken by the United Nations, the Asia–Europe Meeting (ASEM) and other international organizations to give added legitimacy and potency to the idea.[4] In the course of the twentieth century, and especially over the last 50 years, inter-faith dialogue, not least in Australia, has gained increasingly wider currency and legitimacy (Pratt 1994, 8–11; Baldock 1994, 21–2; Phillips 2003).[5]

Here, it may be useful to dwell, however briefly, on the nature and meaning of inter-civilizational dialogue, so succinctly and sensitively expressed by Mohammad Khatami (1999):

---

4 The UN General Assembly (see resolutions 53/22 of 4 November 1998, 54/113 of 10 December 1999 and 55/23 of 13 November 2000) declared 2001 the 'Year of Dialogue among Civilizations'.

5 Of particular interest in the Asia-Pacific context of Muslim–Christian dialogue was the First Asian Gathering of Muslim Ulama and Christian Bishops in Asia, held in Manila, 18–20 August 2003 (see *Info on Human Development* 2003).

> … 'dialogue' pertains neither to skeptics, nor does it belong to those who believe the truth to lie solely within their own claws and under their own domination. Rather, understanding reveals its beautiful, albeit veiled countenance, only to the wayfarers of the path whose followers travel hand in hand, and in step with each other.

The phrase 'dialogue among civilizations and cultures', which should in fact be interpreted as the process of 'speaking and listening among civilizations and cultures', is based upon such an account of truth (Khatami 1999).

In a similar vein, Hans Koechler has described civilization dialogue as the process where 'the "other" serves as the "corrective" of one's own understanding of the world and one's system of values, and not as the adversary against whom to aggressively assert one's identity and ensure one's very survival' (Koechler 2002). Dialogue is envisaged here as a communicative process, in which the 'seer', that which is seen, and the very act of seeing are reinterpreted in ways that are tailored to the needs of the unipolar moment, taking advantage of, but also critically responding to, the material unification of a shrinking yet fragmenting world.

What, then, are the principal aims of the dialogical project? First, and most obviously, it has to break through the material and psychological walls that have been painstakingly built to protect institutional interests and the politics of fear. Secondly, such dialogue must deepen not only the appreciation of diverse civilizational achievements and perspectives, but also the awareness that such diversity is 'the collective heritage of humankind'.[6] To misunderstand, belittle or exclude any of the major civilizational strands is to impoverish the collective inheritance and to diminish each of its heirs. Thirdly, dialogue needs to encourage and draw sustenance from an emerging conception of citizenship that understands the value of both commonality and difference, and enables them to co-exist, illuminate and reinforce each other.

None of this is to suggest that the theory and practice of dialogue and the wider normative framework of governance are likely to evolve without pain or confusion. The modalities of dialogue will be developed in multiple ways that reflect the specificities of time, space and cultural and political setting. Two important dimensions of the dialogical process are worth stressing. First, citizens and the various communities to which they belong must come to terms with the difficult task of reconciliation. The history of each civilization is steeped in the experience of suffering at the hands of others. Many societies and communities have endured – some continue to endure – the violence and humiliation to which others have subjected them. Yet, many of these same communities and societies have themselves been the perpetrators of violence. Reconciliation will require citizens and communities to share their stories, to listen to one another's experience of pain, to acknowledge past wrongs, and to accept responsibility for righting the wrongs of the past.

To the extent that dialogue facilitates reconciliation, it becomes a force for healing. This primary function is, however, closely connected with and supportive of a second function. Insightfully applied, dialogue can nurture a powerful ethic for reappraising the adequacy of existing forms of human organization and for

6 See UN General Assembly Resolution 56/6, 21 November 2001, *Global Agenda for Dialogue among Civilizations.*

reinvigorating the advocacy of new ones. The implications for states and international organizations, be they regional (for example, European Union, ASEAN) or global (for example, UN Security Council, IMF, WTO, WHO) are far-reaching. These institutions have a tendency to appropriate normative and ethical ideas and symbols in the pursuit of vested interests. Official rhetoric is often used to find favour with powerful constituencies, be they domestic or international. The dialogical project, by definition, subjects the collective fatalism or determinism of powerful structures to probing scrutiny, and allows the diverse civilizational currents to feed the utopian imagination.[7]

The preceding analysis offers no more than a possible trajectory of civilizational dialogue. Such a possibility may or may not materialize, depending on several interdependent variables, two of which merit particular attention: the extent to which the national state will allow the voices of civil society sufficient political space to express themselves; and conversely, the extent to which the discursive practices of civil society will be able to draw on the deepest civilizational insights to influence the political processes of states, but also the international rule of law and the constantly expanding network of regional and global institutions.

In Australia, the pronouncements and actions of national government have not in recent years been especially kind to the culture or politics of dialogue. In foreign and defence policy, as in immigration, refugee and multicultural policy, the accent has been on finding comfort and sustenance in the white Anglo-Australian heritage and the global preponderance of American power. Yet Australia remains well placed to engage in civilization dialogue, for in its midst are represented many of the world's religious and cultural traditions. History and geography have endowed the country with a unique opportunity to weave together the wisdom of diverse civilizational strands – evident in Australia's cultural and religious diversity, in the encounter between indigenous and non-indigenous Australia, and in its proximity to the extraordinarily rich cultural and religious mosaic that is Asia Pacific. Whether in the years ahead Australia's schools and universities, its media, and its religious and political institutions will find ways of making the dialogue of civilizations an integral part of everyday life remains an open question.

References

Baldock, J. (1994), 'Responses to Religious Pluralism in Australia', *Australian Religion Studies Review* 7: 1, 21–31.

Camilleri, Joseph A. (1994), 'Human Rights, Cultural Diversity and Conflict Resolution: The Asia-Pacific Context', *Pacifica Review: Peace, Security and Global Change* 6: 2, 17–41.

Camilleri, Joseph A. (2000), *States, Markets and Civil Society in Asia Pacific*, *The Political Economy of Asia Pacific*, vol. 1 (Cheltenham, UK: Edward Elgar).

7 This dimension is a frequently recurring theme in the work of the Office for Human Development of the Federation of Asian Bishops' Conferences (Wilfred 2002).

Camilleri, Joseph A. (2003), *Regionalism in the New Asia-Pacific Order, The Political Economy of Asia Pacific*, vol. 2 (Cheltenham, UK: Edward Elgar).

Chatterjee, A. (1983), *Srikrsna Caitanya: A Historical Study on Gaudiya Vaisnavism* (New Delhi: Associated Publishing Company).

de Bary, W.T (1998), *Asian Values and Human Rights: A Confucian Communitarian Perspective* (Cambridge: Harvard University Press).

Donnelly, Jack (1989), *Universal Human Rights in Theory and Practice* (Ithaca, NY: Cornell University Press).

Fitzgerald, L.P. (1993), *The Justice God Wants: Islam and Human Rights* (Melbourne: Collins Dove).

Freeman, Michael (2002), *Human Rights: An Interdisciplinary Approach* (Cambridge: Polity).

Friedman, Edward (1999), 'Asia as a Fount of Universal Human Rights', in Peter Van Ness (ed.), *Debating Human Rights: Critical Essays on the United States and Asia* (London: Routledge).

Galtung, Johan (1990), 'International Development in Human Perspective', in John W. Burton (ed.), *Conflict: Human Needs Theory* (London: Macmillan).

Huntington, S.P. (1993), 'The Clash of Civilizations?', *Foreign Affairs* 72: 3, Summer 1993, 22–49.

Info on Human Development (2003), 29, 9–12.

Khatami, Mohammad (1999), 'Address at Florence University', available at: <http://www.persia.org/khatami/s_floruni.html> accessed 23 January 2004.

Koechler, Hans (2002), 'After September 11, 2001: Clash of Civilizations or Dialogue?', Lecture delivered to the Asian Center, University of the Philippines, Manila, 14 March.

Koh, K.L. (ed.) (1996), *Selected ASEAN Documents on the Environment* (Singapore: Asia-Pacific Centre for Environmental Law, National University of Singapore).

Koh, Tommy (1995), 'The 10 Values Undergird East Asian Strength and Success', *The International Herald Tribune*, 11–12 December, 6.

Lee, Kuan Yew (1994), 'The East Asian Way', in N. Gardels (ed.), *At Century's End: Great Minds Reflect on Our Times* (California: ALTI Publishing).

Lewis, Bernard (1990), 'The Roots of Muslim Rage', *The Atlantic Monthly* 266, 60.

Lewis, Bernard (1998), *The Multiple Identities of the Middle East* (London: Weidenfeld and Nicolson).

Mabbett, I. (1998), 'The Khmers', *Sojourn* 30: 1, 1–37.

Mahbubani, Kishore (1995), 'The Pacific Way', *Foreign Affairs* 74: 1, 10–14.

Mawdudi, Abdul A'la (1982), *Human Rights in Islam* (London: Islamic Foundation).

Mayer, Elizabeth (1988), 'The Dilemmas of Islamic Identity', in Leroy S. Rouner (ed.), *Human Rights and the World's Religions* (Notre Dame, IND: University of Notre Dame Press).

Muzaffar, C. (1999), *Debating Human Rights* (New York: Routledge).

Phillips, Scott (2003), 'Inter-Faith Dialogue, Inter-Cultural Dialogue: A Basis for Developing Global Security', unpublished paper.

Pollis, Adamantia (2000), 'A New Universalism', in Adamantia Pollis and Peter Schwab (eds), *Human Rights: New Perspectives, New Realities* (Boulder, CO: Lynne Rienner).

Pratt, D. (1994), 'Christian–Muslim Encounter: From Diatribe to Dialogue', *Australian Religion Studies Review* 7: 1, 8–15.

Renteln, Allison Dundes (1990), *International Human Rights: Universalism vs Relativism* (Newbury Park, CA: Sage Publications).

Said, Abdul Aziz and Nasser, Jamil (1980), 'The Use and Abuse of Democracy in Islam', in J.L. Nelson and V.M. Green (eds), *International Human Rights: Contemporary Issues* (Standfordville, NY: Human Rights Publishing Group).

Sheikh, Naveed S. (2003), *The New Politics of Islam: Pan-Islamic Foreign Policy in a World of States* (London: RoutledgeCurzon).

Skubik, Daniel W. (1992), 'Two Perspectives on Human Rights and the Rule of Law: Chinese East and Anglo-American West', *World Review* 3: 2.

Thomas, Scott (2000), 'Religion and International Conflict', in K.R. Dark (ed.), *Religion and International Relations* (Basingstoke, UK: Palgrave Macmillan).

Thompson, K.W. (ed.) (1980), *The Moral Imperatives of Human Rights: A World Survey* (Washington, DC: University Press of America).

Traer, Robert (1991), *Faith in Human Rights: Support in Religious Traditions for a Global Struggle* (Washington, DC: Georgetown University Press).

Urry, John (1999), 'Globalization and Citizenship', *Journal of World-Systems Research* 5: 2, 263–73.

Vincent, R.J. (1986), *Human Rights and International Relations* (Cambridge: Cambridge University Press).

Wilfred, Felix (2002), 'Religions Face to Face with Globalization', *Info on Human Development* 28, 2–10, 11–12.

Zakaria, Fareed (1994), 'Culture is Destiny: A Conversation with Lee Kuan Yew', *Foreign Affairs* 73: 2, 109–26.

Chapter 20

Civil Society and Tolerance in Indonesia

Saiful Mujani

Introduction

A functioning democracy requires a particular culture, the acceptance by the citizenry and political elites of principles underlying freedom of speech, assembly, religion and the like (Lipset 1994, 3). These freedoms will be possible if citizens tolerate different beliefs held or interests pursued by other citizens. In a democracy, each citizen is normatively supposed to have equal opportunity to achieve his or her goals regardless of cultural, social, political or economic background and interests. These differences can become problematic in the absence of tolerance (Dahl 1971, 108).

In Muslim society, tolerance can refer to attitudes and behaviour of Muslims toward non-Muslims, or vice versa. Historically, tolerance more specifically has referred to the relationship between Muslims and adherents of other Semitic religions, Judaism and Christianity. The relationship between Muslims, Christians and Jews is complex and has fluctuated over the centuries. Bernard Lewis (1985) has written that the sources of intolerance among Muslims toward non-Muslims such as Christians and Jews are not clear. They are partly religious doctrines and partly historical and socio-political experience. The doctrinal sources can be found in the *Qur'an*, for example, a verse which says: '0 you who believe, do not take the Jews and Christians as friends ... they are friends of one another, and whoever among you takes them as friends will become one of them' (Q, 5:51).

Lewis (1985, 14) argues that this doctrinal source should be understood historically. It reflects conflict and tension between Muslims and non-Muslims (Jews and Christians) in the early period of Islam. The emphasis on a historically specific context is persuasive as there are other doctrines which suggest tolerance toward non- Muslims. The *Qur'an*, for example, says:

> Those who believe,[1] and those who profess Judaism, and the Christians and the Sabians, those who believe in God and in the Last Day and act righteously, shall have their reward with their Lord; there shall be no fear in them, neither shall they grieve (Q, 2:62).

This verse and many others indicate that Islam is inclusive toward Jews and Christians, and may become a doctrinal source for religious tolerance. Salvation does not exclusively belong to Islam. In a specific historical context, this tolerant doctrine of Islam may prevail, while in another historical context, intolerant doctrine

1 That is, Muslims.

may be dominant. Lewis locates the problem in the long history of Islam and its encounters with other religions:

> In most tests of tolerance, Islam, both in theory and in practice, compares unfavorably with Western democracies as they have developed during the last two or three centuries, but very favorably with most other Christian and post-Christian societies and regimes. There is nothing in Islamic history to compare with the emancipation, acceptance, and integration of other believers and non-believers in the West; but equally, there is nothing in Islamic history to compare with the Spanish expulsion of Jews and Muslims, the Inquisition, … the wars of religion, not to speak of more recent crimes of commission and acquiescence. There were occasional persecutions, but they were rare, and usually of brief duration, related to local and specific circumstances. … In modern times, Islamic tolerance has been somewhat diminished. After the second Turkish siege of Vienna in 1683, Islam was a retreating, not an advancing force in the world, and Muslims began to feel threatened by the rise and expression of the great Christian empires of Eastern and Western Europe. … In the present mood, a triumph of militant Islam would be unlikely to bring a return to traditional Islamic tolerance – and even that would no longer be acceptable to minority elements schooled on modern ideas of human, civil, and political rights (Lewis 2002, 114, 131).

Muslim tolerance or intolerance is historical. However, once history has constructed a collective memory, and that memory has been reinforced by bitter experiences, religious intolerance is likely to persist. There follows the perception that religion is by nature intolerant, which leads to religious conflict (cf. Huntington 1997). Huntington believes that both Islam and Christianity are intolerant religions. He states:

> The twentieth-century conflict between liberal democracy and Marxist-Leninism is only a fleeting and superficial historical phenomenon compared to the continuing and deeply conflictual relation between Islam and Christianity. … The causes of this ongoing pattern of conflict lie not in transitory phenomena such as twelfth-century Christian passion or twentieth-century Muslim fundamentalism. They flow from the nature of the two religions and the civilizations based on them. Conflict was, on the one hand, a product of difference, particularly the Muslim concept of Islam as a way of life transcending and uniting religion and politics versus the Western Christian concept of the separate realms of God and Caesar … [Islam and Christianity are] both universalistic, claiming to be the one true faith to which all humans can adhere. Both are missionary religions believing that their adherents have an obligation to convert nonbelievers to that one true faith. From its origin Islam expanded by conquest and when the opportunity existed Christianity did also … So long as Islam remains Islam (which it will) and the West remains West (which is more dubious), this fundamental conflict between two great civilizations and ways of life will continue to define their relations in the future even as it has defined them for the past fourteen centuries (Huntington 1997, 210).

Lewis's proposition about Islamic intolerance is more conditional, more historical and more restricted to proponents of Islamic fundamentalism, while Huntington's is more general, or more essentialistic, in the sense that Islam and Christianity are by nature intolerant religions. Like an Islamist, Huntington believes that Islam by nature is a total way of life, which recognizes no truth and salvation in other religions.

Missionary activity is a religious duty. He believes that Christianity has the same nature. When these two missionary and exclusive religions meet, religious conflict and war are unavoidable.

How relevant is Huntington's proposition for Indonesian Muslims? His conclusion about the intolerant nature of Islam is not restricted to a variant of Islam, but to Islam as a whole. Huntington also explicitly views Islam as a total way of life, and therefore all components of Islam are strongly inter-correlated. This argument implies that the ritual component, which is fundamental to any religion, strongly correlates with other dimensions of Islam such as 'Islamic political orientation' and with 'Islamic civic engagement'. If Huntington is correct, these components of Islam are correlated strongly with intolerance toward Christians.

Tolerance

Before exploring these relationships, I will describe the characteristics of tolerance among Indonesian Muslims. Tolerance in Indonesia takes two forms: a specific religion-based socio-political tolerance; and political tolerance in general.

'Tolerance' in this work is defined as 'willingness to "put up with" those things one rejects or opposes' (Sullivan, Pierson and Marcus 1982, 2). There are two different strategies as to how political tolerance is measured. Stouffer's *Communism, Conformity, and Civil Liberty* (1955), for example, treats communism as the target of political tolerance, the extent to which Americans tolerated communist political activity.

More recent studies of political tolerance do not treat a specific group such as communists as the target of tolerance, but rather any group that a person selects as the least liked group (Sullivan, Pierson and Marcus 1982, 60–61). This is 'a content-controlled measure' strategy rather than a specific group target strategy to measure political tolerance. These two strategies are applied here. Stouffer's strategy is applied with Christians as the target of tolerance, and Sullivan, Pierson and Marcus's with the least liked group as the target. In addition, I also include a more general measure of tolerance, tolerance to have members of particular groups as neighbours. It is measured by a single variable: how many societal groups does a respondent reject as neighbours? This information may uncover the most basic pattern of tolerance in a society.[2]

Figure 20.1 displays percentages of groups in the society that people object to having as their neighbours. An overwhelming majority (84 per cent) object to having a communist as their neighbour. In addition, there are smaller proportions who reported that they objected to having Christian or Catholic (16 per cent), Islamist Muslim (14 per cent), Chinese (13 per cent), or Hindu or Buddhist (12 per cent) as their neighbour.

In terms of the percentage of respondents who do not object to having members of other religious groups as neighbours, the intolerant among Indonesian Muslims

---

2 This work relies on data from two national surveys conducted by the PPIM in 2001 and 2002. Regarding the method of the surveys, see the appendix.

is relatively small. This proportion is quite similar to that of many other nations. It is better than Turkey, India, Georgia and Japan, but similar to many consolidated democracies, such as the US, the UK and West Germany (Table 20.1). On the basis of this comparison, one cannot persuasively argue that Indonesian Muslims are intolerant toward other religious groups.

Among Indonesians, there is much less intolerance toward Christians than toward communists. Nonetheless, conflict between Muslims and Christians, including church burnings and bombings, is frequent. These incidents probably reflect tension and intolerance between the two groups, along the lines of Huntington's analysis. To explore this issue, a set of questions was asked both in the 2001 and 2002 surveys.

Respondents were asked: if they would tolerate a Christian as a teacher in a public school; if they objected to a church in a predominantly Muslim community; to Christian religious services in a predominantly Muslim community; and to a Christian becoming president of the country. Figure 20.2 displays the percentage of tolerance among Indonesian Muslims towards Christians gauged by the four items. Only about two out of ten Muslims reported that they do not object to having a Christian as president of the country.

More tolerance is expressed on the issue of religious services or of building churches by and for Christians. About three out of ten Muslims tolerate the religious services. In addition, about four out of ten Muslims did not object to a Christian teacher in a public school. Judged by these four items, a majority of Indonesian Muslims are not tolerant toward Christians. At the descriptive level, at least, Huntington's picture seems accurate.

Although intolerance toward Christians is large, it is smaller than intolerance toward communists. As described earlier, an overwhelming majority of the respondents even object to having a communist as their neighbour. This large

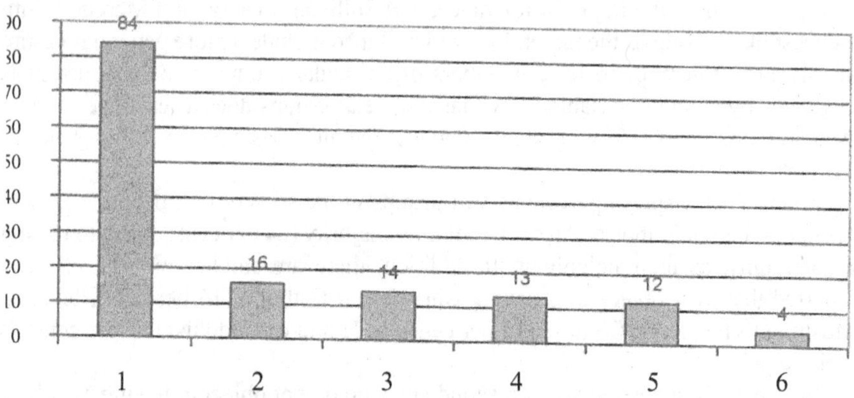

Figure 20.1 Respondents who object to having various groups as neighbours (2002) (%)

Note: 1 = communists; 2 = Christians; 3 = Islamist Muslims; 4 = Chinese; 5 = Hindu/Buddhist; 6 = other

Table 20.1 Intolerance: object to having neighbours of different religious groups in a number of nations

Religion, Nations	% (N)	Religion, Nations	% (N)
Islam		*Orthodox Christianity*	
Indonesia 2002	16.0 (2268)	Georgia	28.3 (2593)
Azerbaijan	18.4 (2002)	Ukraine	17.5 (2811)
Bangladesh 1997	12.7 (1525)	Russia	12.4 (4001)
Bosnia-Herzegovina	27.6 (1200)	*Confucianism*	
Nigeria	21.7 (3769)	Mainland China	12.1 (1000)
Turkey	51.1 (2856)	Taiwan	17.4 (1437)
Catholicism		South Korea	23.1 (2221)
Argentina	6.7 (2081)	Japan	28.8 (1011)
Brazil	13.2 (1149)	*Protestantism*	
Italy	14.3 (2018)	Sweden	15.0 (2056)
Poland	25.9 (1145)	The Netherlands	14.1 (1017)
Spain	11.7 (5358)	United Kingdom	16.4 (1484)
The Philippines	29.1 (1200)	USA	13.3 (3381)
Venezuela	26.0 (1200	West Germany	16.3 (3118)
Hindu			
India	30.4 (4540)		

Source: Except for Indonesia, all nations are from the World Value Survey (WVS) conducted in the 1980s and 1990s. Some nations represent pooled survey data of WVS.

Note: The target group of tolerance for Indonesia is Protestant or Catholic; for all other nations in the WVS the target group is Muslim, except for Turkey, Bangladesh, Azerbaijan, Nigeria and Bosnia-Herzegovina, which are respectively Jew, Hindu, Christian and Orthodox.

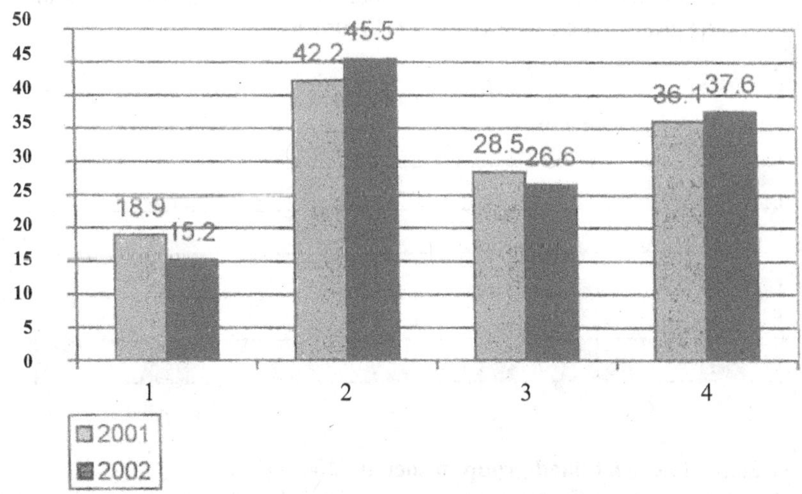

Figure 20.2 Socio-political tolerance of Muslims toward Christians/Catholics (%)
Note: 1 = become president; 2 = become a teacher in public school; 3 = hold religious services; 4 = build a church.

proportion of intolerance toward communists reflects majority opinion among Muslims even when a different strategy is followed.

To follow Sullivan, Pierson and Marcus's content-controlled measure strategy of gauging political tolerance, respondents were asked to select a group that they liked the least, either from a list or from groups in society they designated. Respondents could reply that they do not have any group that they like the least. Target groups on the list were Protestants, Catholics, Hindus, Buddhists, Chinese, Jews, communists, Darul Islam (a pro-Islamic state group) and Lasykar Jihad (Holy War Militia). Those who selected a target group were asked: if they agree or disagree that the group be outlawed; if the group be allowed to have public meetings or demonstrations in their area; and if a member of that group be allowed to run for public office.

Figure 20.3 reveals the percentages. About 85 per cent of the people reported that there is a group that they like least. About six out of ten Indonesians selected communists as the least liked group, and only one out of ten selected Catholics or Protestants. About one out of ten also selected Jews as the least liked group. More Muslims dislike communists rather than religious groups, even though conflicts between Muslims and Christians are frequent. However, conflict between communists and anti-communists in history has been much more extensive, as will be discussed subsequently.

Figure 20.3 portrays tolerance and intolerance not only toward communists but also toward other groups in society that the respondents liked the least.[3] As previously noted, anti-communism as an attitude is not necessarily intolerance: it becomes intolerance when followed by unwillingness to tolerate any political action by a communist. An overwhelming majority of Indonesian Muslims, according to the 2002 survey data, are not tolerant towards these groups. About 83 per cent agree that the least liked group should be outlawed by the government. About the same proportion (86 per cent) would not allow the group to have a public meeting or demonstration in their area. Most people (about 80 per cent) would also not allow a member of the group to be a public official (Figure 20.4).

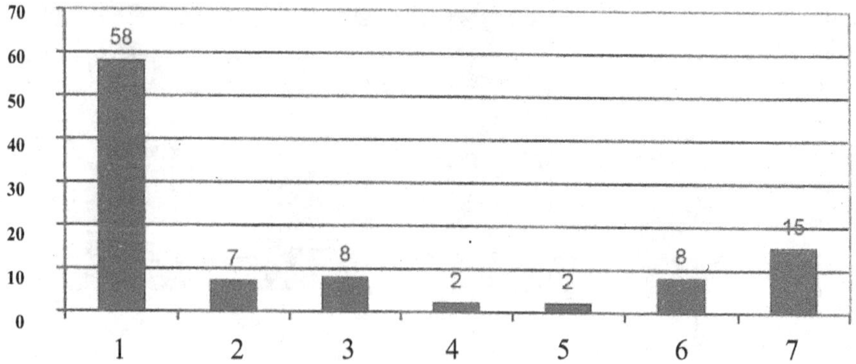

Figure 20.3 The least liked group in society (2002) (%)
Note: 1 = communists; 2 = Christians/Catholics; 3 = Jews; 4 = Islamist groups; 5 = Chinese; 6 = other groups; 7 = none.

3 Other alternative answers are 'uncertain' and 'don't know'.

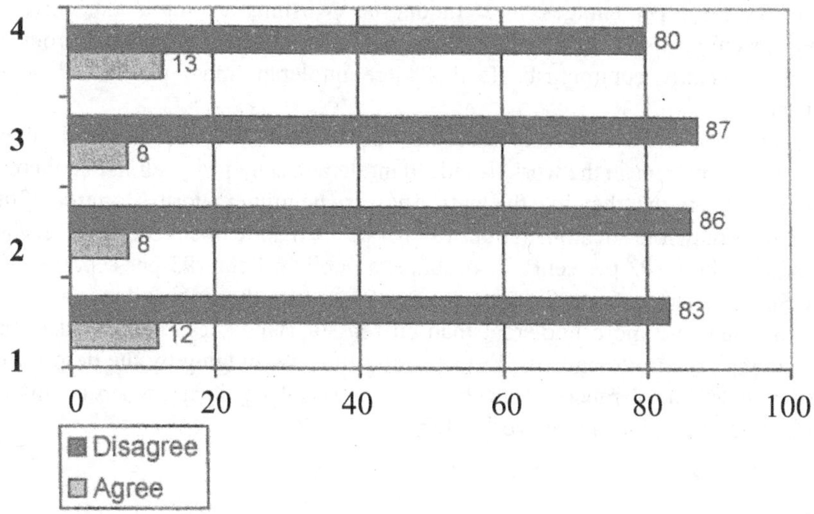

Figure 20.4 Some indicators of political tolerance toward the least liked groups (%)

Note: 1 = allowed by the government; 2 = allowed to have public meetings; 3 = allowed to have demonstrations; 4 = allowed to be a public official.

Table 20.2 Some indicators of tolerance toward the least liked group in several nations

Tolerant attitudes / Religion and nation	Tolerance toward Christians 2001	Tolerance toward Christians 2002	Tolerance toward the least liked group 2002
A. Islam			
Mandatory ritual	-.069**	-.031	-.093**
Suggested ritual	-	-.074**	-
Nahdliyin ritual	-	-	.018
Muhammadiyah identity	-	.077**	-
Islamic civic engagement	-	-.051	.089**
Islamism	-.320**	-.281**	-
B. Non-religion			
Secular civic engagement	.053*	.094**	-
Democratic values	.055*	**.009	-.189**
SES and demography			
Education	.040	.017	-.114**
Rural residence	-.051*	-.066*	-.010
Age	-	.065*	-
Gender: male	-	.087**	-.049
Adjusted R^2	.136	.130	.097
N	1417	1320	1447

Source: PPIM Surveys and World Value Survey

Judging by these percentages, most Indonesian Muslims are intolerant, not only toward specific groups such as Christians, but also toward a least liked group in general, especially communists. Is this large intolerant mass public unique to Indonesia?

Using similar measures of tolerance, the World Value Survey reveals that the mass public in most nations in the world is indeed intolerant. A majority admit that there is a group in society that they like the least. An overwhelming majority disagree: if the least liked group holds demonstrations (87 per cent); if a member becomes a teacher at a public school (93 per cent); or becomes a public official (93 per cent) (World Value Survey). These proportions are slightly larger than those for Indonesia.

Indonesians are more intolerant than citizens of Bangladesh and Sweden, but less intolerant than Azerbaijanis, Filipinos and Indians. Judging by the descriptive statistics, political tolerance among Indonesians is not significant when compared with many other nations in the world (Table 20.2).

Islam

To what extent is Islam responsible for creating intolerant citizens? The answer to this question depends on how Islam is understood. In this work, Islam, as a religion, is understood from a number of dimensions: faith, rituals, social group and political orientations.

Faith

Faith, or *iman,* is about belief in God. This is not a simple 'yes' or 'no' proposition. A person may sometimes believe in God, and sometimes not. For many, perhaps most, individuals, belief is not a constant condition. Therefore, I measure belief in God by the extent to which a person believes in God: always, often, sometimes or never.

In the surveys, almost all Indonesian Muslims reported that they absolutely believe, or never doubt, in God (97.2 per cent). Those who sometimes doubt are about 2 per cent. Only about 1 per cent reported that they frequently doubt or never believe in God. Judging from this, almost all Indonesian Muslims are believers. Because of its low variation, this is not a good measure of Islam for analytical purposes at the individual level. It may be useful as an aggregate measure of faith for a cross-nation analysis.[4]

4 In a pre-test of the 2001 survey, a substantial number of items of faith, constructed according to the pillar of faith (*rukun iman*), were included. I found almost homogenous answers to the items. More than 95 per cent of the respondents reported that they believe in God, the prophecy of Muhammad and other messengers of God, in the *Qur'an* as the word of God, in angels, and in the final judgement. Because of this low variation, these items were dropped. In the 2002 survey, one item of faith, that is, belief in God, is included, to provide a minimal and basic indicator of Indonesian Muslim religiosity.

Mandatory Rituals

In addition to faith in God, Muslims are required to perform a number of rituals. Two of these rituals are the daily five prayers (*salat lima waktu*) and fasting in the month of Ramadan. The five prayers are arranged by time: *salat al-fajr* (early morning), *salat ad-duhr* (noon), *salat al-'asr* (mid-afternoon), *salat al-maghrib* (sunset) and *salat al-isha'* (evening).[5] These practices are highly regulated. The intensity of performing them constitutes a prime definition of Muslim piety.

About 88 per cent of the Muslim respondents reported that they perform the daily five prayers very or quite frequently, and 94 per cent reported that they perform the Ramadan fasting very or quite often.[6] Judging from these percentages, Indonesian Muslims are almost homogenously religious.

Suggested Rituals

In addition to the mandatory rituals, Muslims may perform other ritual activities. These activities are only suggested or highly suggested (*sunnah*). In this study, these activities are called suggested rituals. They comprise reciting the *Qur'an*, collective prayers (*salat berjamaan*), suggested prayers (*salat sunnah*), prayer prior to starting daily work (*berdoa sebelum bekerja*), suggested fasting (*puasa sunnah*), religious classes (*pengajian*) and giving to charity (*sedekah*).

As expected, Muslim religiosity is not homogenous in the suggested rituals. The proportion of Indonesian Muslims who perform the suggested rituals varies markedly: about 59 per cent recite the *Qur'an* very or quite frequently, about 83 per cent pray outside the daily five prayers before they work very or quite frequently, about 59 per cent pray together with others or engage in collective prayer very or quite frequently, about 47 per cent perform the suggested prayers very or quite frequently, about 33 per cent perform the suggested fasting very or quite frequently, and about 61 per cent go to religious classes very or quite frequently. Giving to charity, a voluntary gift of goods or money to the needy in the name of God, is also a suggested practice (Figure 20.5).

Nahdliyin Rituals

Particular Muslim communities, especially Nahdlatul Ulama (NU) members, do other suggested rituals such as asking for prayers from a religious authority (*kiai*) in order to achieve individual goals.[7] About 38 per cent reported that they go to a *kiai* to ask for his blessing for a particular purpose very or quite often (Figure 20.5).

The *kiai* is a popular religious authority in the Indonesian Muslim community. A *kiai* is not only a religious scholar, but also an informal Muslim community leader,

5 A good description of these prayers is Denny (1994).

6 These proportions are the average from both surveys.

7 Regarding *kiai*, see, for example, Dhofier (1982); regarding Tarekat and Nahdliyin communities in Indonesia, see, for example, Bruinessen (1995) and Sujuthi (2001).

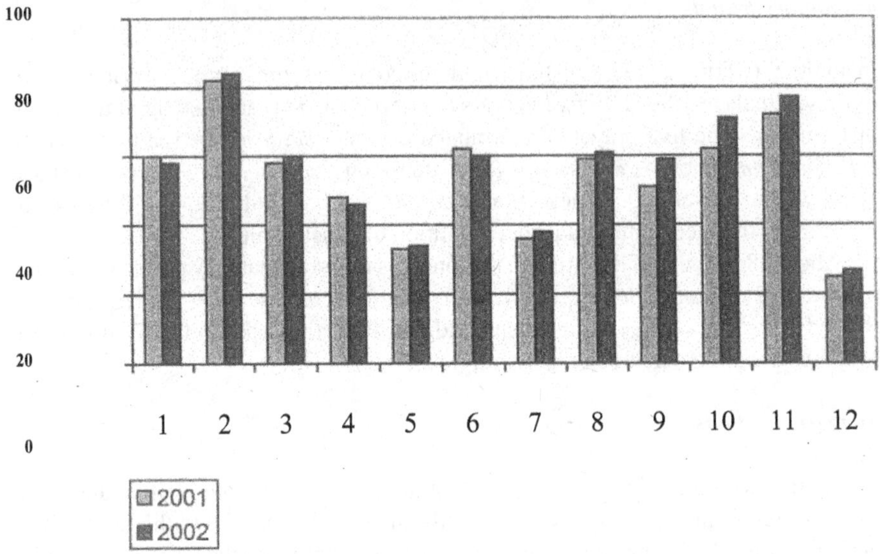

Figure 20.5 Intensity (very or quite frequently) of performance of various suggested and Nahdliyin rituals (%)

Note: 1 = reciting the Qur'an; 2 = praying outside mandatory rituals; 3 = collective prayer; 4 = suggested prayer; 5 = suggested fasting; 6 = go to religious classes; 7 = ask for kiai prayer; 8 = tahlilan; 9 = khaul; 10 = seven-day ceremony for the dead; 11 = charity; 12 = going to burial shrine.

often believed to have charisma and such spiritual power that he has a closer relation with God than ordinary Muslims.

In Indonesia, visiting a burial shrine (*makam wali/ziarah*) is another kind of ritual in the community. It is believed that the dead can spiritually communicate with and assist people who try to come to him or her.[8] About 26 per cent of the survey respondents stated that they visit burial shrines very or quite often.

Tahlilan, a collective ritual in which the greatness of God is praised repeatedly, is also found, most commonly among NU members.[9] About 60 per cent reported that they participate in the *tahlilan* ritual very or quite often.[10] A *tahlilan* is usually held by a community member who has a particular purpose, a prayer for the well-being of a family member who has passed away, for example. It is led by a religious authority. Participants are members of the community or neighbourhood, and food and beverages are served.

A more specific ritual associated with the *tahlilan* is the annual commemoration of the death of a family member, called *khaul* (see Fananie and Sabardila 2001;

8 Regarding *makam wali/ziarah* among Indonesians, see Jamhari (2001), Bruinessen (1996, 1995), and Sujuthi (2001).

9 Regarding *tahlilan*, see Fananie and Sabardila (2001).

10 Geertz (1960) started his description of *The Religion of Java* with an analysis of the *slameta*. For the Javanese, the *tahlilan* is part of the *slameta*.

Bruinessen 1995). Family members of the dead commonly invite *kiai* and community members to pray for the well-being of the deceased in the hereafter. About 55 per cent of respondents reported that they perform a *khaul* very or quite often. The seven-day ritual (*tujuh harian*) for the death of a family member is also found among Indonesian Muslims and, like the *khaul*, is commonly associated with NU members. About 66 per cent reported that they perform the seven-day ritual very or quite often.

In Islamic orthodoxy or orthopraxy, as mentioned above, the mandatory and suggested rituals are distinct. Those who perform the mandatory do not necessarily perform the suggested as well. In Indonesia, the Nahdliyin rituals are performed mainly by NU members. Most Muhammadiyah members do not perform these rituals. For this reason, I differentiate the Nahdliyin rituals from the other two types. According to a confirmatory factor analysis, these three distinct dimensions of Islamic rituals are valid. The analysis also suggests that the measures of Islamic rituals are consistent.

Islamic Social Capital

As stated earlier, Islam is not measured by ritual intensity alone but also by involvement in community life and by attachment to particular Islamic organizations. The former is networks of Islamic civic engagement; the latter is Islamic social identity. In Indonesia, Muslims are involved in many social organizations. In the surveys, two items were constructed to measure involvement in Islamic social organizations or the networks of Islamic civic engagement.

First, respondents were asked about voluntary membership in religious organizations at the national level such as NU, Muhammadiyah, Persatuan Islam and others. About 21 per cent of Muslim respondents reported that they were active members of an organization. A larger proportion (about 47 per cent) reported that they were active members in smaller religious groups in their local community such as religious study groups (*majlis taklim*) or the mosque youth association (*remaja masjid*).

NU and Muhammadiyah are well known as the first and second largest Muslim organizations in the country. A significant proportion of respondents (about 48 per cent) reported that they felt very or quite close to NU, and a smaller proportion (about 18 per cent) reported that they felt very or quite close to Muhammadiyah.

Islamist Political Orientation (Islamism)

An Islamist political orientation is believed to be crucial in defining the extent to which a Muslim is an Islamist. Students of Muslim societies such as Lewis and Gellner, and of political science such as Huntington and Kedourie, have even claimed without qualification that an Islamist political orientation is universal among Muslims.

How can we measure the Islamist political orientation? One way to do so is to first specify how Islamist ideologues define Islam as a socio-political ideology. We can then verify their definition empirically by seeing the extent to which ordinary Muslims replicate their interpretation. For example, Islamist ideologues such as Mawdudi, Qutb and Khomeini claim that Islam recognizes divine sovereignty rather

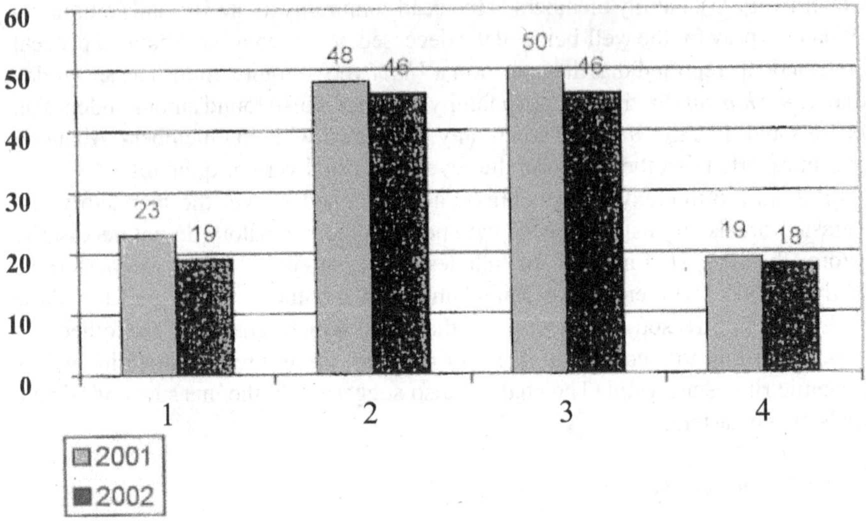

Figure 20.6 Islamic social capital: networks of Islamic engagement and Islamic social identity (%)

Note: 1 = active member in national Islamic organization; 2 = active member in local Islamic organization; 3 = feeling very or quite close to NU (NU identity); 4 = feeling very or quite close to Muhammadiyah (Muhammadiyah identity).

than popular sovereignty. Liberal Muslims, on the contrary, claim that God has given mankind autonomy and sovereignty for worldly political matters.

The Islamist tendency is much larger (about 63 per cent) when the concept is measured by whether the respondent agrees or not with the idea that Islamic governance, based on *shari'ah* and under the leadership of an Islamic authority, is the best for a nation like Indonesia (Figure 20.7). Related to this measure is an attitude toward state involvement in *shari'ah* enforcement. A still larger proportion (about 66 per cent) agrees with the idea of state enforcement. This large Islamist proportion significantly decreases (to about 50 per cent) when the concept is measured by support for Islamist movements such as the Islamic Defender Front (FPI), the Jihadi Militia and Darul Islam, which fight for the implementation of *shari'ah* in the society. These Islamist movement organizations are known to be very active in demanding implementation of the *shari'ah*. Support for Islamism declines further when it is gauged by agreement with the idea that Muslim voters should elect Islamic authorities to represent them (46 per cent). A still smaller proportion supports the idea that the party system should include Islamic parties only (about 22 per cent).

Islamist theoreticians interpret the concept of *shura* or consultation as a procedure for decision-making. They also understand the implementation of *shura* to include the party system through which Muslims channel their political interests. However, they argue that in an Islamic polity the party system should prohibit non-Islamic parties.

All of the evidence indicates that the general idea of Islamic governance and the *shari'ah* are problematic when they touch solid empirical ground. The majority of Indonesian Muslims agree with the idea of Islamic governance, based on *shari'ah* and under the leadership of Islamic authorities, and with state enforcement of the *shari'ah*. However, when these ideas are linked to implementation, the old Islamist majority opinion disappears. A new moderate majority (about 62 per cent) even disagrees with the idea of limiting the party system to Islamic parties.

This inconsistency between the general or abstract and the specific or implementational is also found when the concept of *shari'ah* is made more concrete. Islamism is unique in its view of women's social and political rights. Women are often the primary targets of Islamist regimes in power. In the surveys, some questions related to women's rights were asked to gauge Islamist orientations.

A significant minority of respondents (about 40 per cent) agree with the idea that the state should enforce the obligation for Muslim women to wear a veil (*jilbāb*). Verses in the *Qur'an* (Q, 33:59; 24:31) indicating that women must wear a veil have often been referred to by Islamist preachers and activists as important norms.

Among Indonesian Muslims, the form of veiling has changed substantially. Women used to wear a veil that only covered their hair or was draped about their shoulders. Since about the late 1970s, the most common veil has more tightly covered the head. The term *jilbāb* has also been redefined to mean a cloth that covers completely a woman's body. Nonetheless, many Indonesian Muslim women do not wear a veil.

When their failure to do so is condemned as un-Islamic by the Islamists, they struggle to find Islamic norms to support their behaviour. The Islamist claim is criticized as inaccurate historically and even in terms of the *Qur'an*. The works of Fatima Mernissi, Riffat Hasan and other internationally known Muslim scholars have helped Indonesian Muslim gender equality activists to defend their behaviour against the Islamist challenge.[11]

Muslim gender equality activists believe that the veil is only a medieval tradition that does not need to be followed by modern women. The *Qur'anic* verses examined historically and sociologically also reveal a holistic moral spirit or ethos in which man and woman are equal before God.[12]

An interesting example of this struggle for Islamically based gender equality is a volume entitled *Ulama Perempuan Indonesia* (Female *Ulama* of Indonesia) (Burhanudin 2002). The word *'ulama* commonly refers to 'male Islamic scholars'. Female *'ulama* do not have a significant presence in Islamic intellectual history. However, gender equality activists reinvented the history, creating female *'ulama* to counter the dominant image in Muslim society, including intellectual circles, that the female is inferior to the male.

Apart from the struggle for gender equality, wearing the veil is a growing public issue in Indonesia. It has become a part of the *shari'ah* enforcement movement

11 Fatima Mernissi, a Monacan sociologist, has written several books on women in Muslim society. *The Veil and the Male Elite* and *Islam and Democracy* have been translated into Indonesian.

12 See, for example, Umar (2002) and a volume edited by Munhanif (2002).

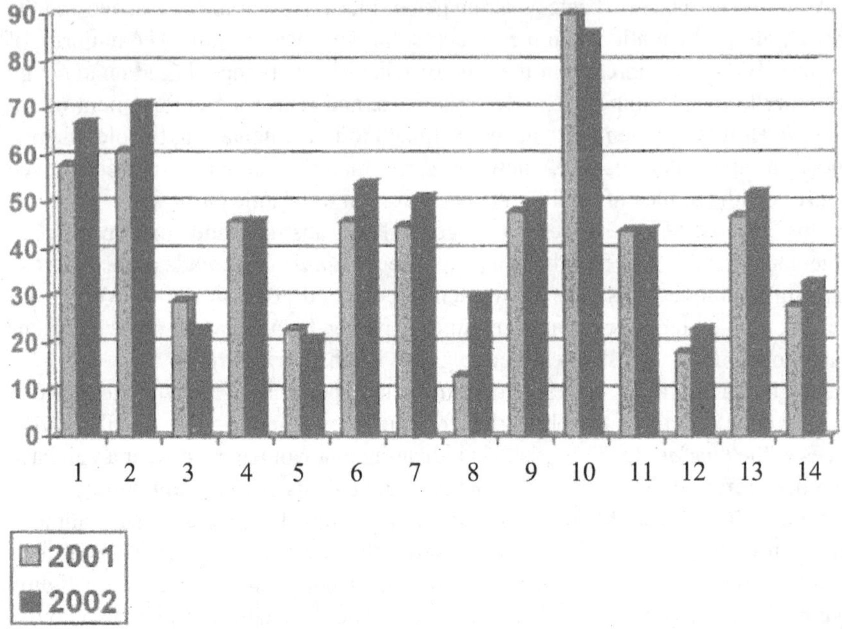

Figure 20.7 Support for Islamism (%)

Note: 1 = Islam is the best political system; 2 = the state must enforce Islamic law (shari'ah); 3 = hand amputation penalty; 4 = support for Islamic authorities; 5 = support for Islamist party; 6 = support for Islamist movement; 7 = woman's travel without her kin *(muhrim); 8 = police enforcement of the Ramadan fasting; 9 = superiority of male over female; 10 = woman's right to become a Member of Parliament; 11 = unequal right for education between son and daughter; 12 = woman is too weak to be a judge; 13 = unequal inheritance rights between son and daughter; 14 = God's sovereignty.*

which has been taken up by local governments in some districts and municipalities such as Cianjur, Tasikmalaya, Garut and Serang. The provincial government of Aceh is also responsible for the implementation of *shari'ah.* In each of these areas one of the first *shari'ah* enacted required veiling.

It is not an exaggeration to argue that in Islamist polities, women are often the first object of concern of the *shari'ah*-minded. Indeed, a simple way to figure out whether a polity is Islamist or not is through observing women's behaviour. In the Islamic Republic of Iran, Saudi Arabia and Afghanistan under the Taliban, for example, one can sense easily what an Islamist polity is through women's behaviour in public spaces. In the most extreme form, as practised by the Taliban, women were not allowed to have a career or a modern education, not to mention to be active politically (Gohari 2000).

A literal reading of the *Qur'an* uncovers several verses referring to female behaviour. The most cited is Q, 4:34, 'man is superior over woman'. An Islamist is expected to have an attitude toward women's activity in public service reflective of these passages. In order to explore these attitudes, a set of women's issue items were asked in the surveys.

First, respondents were asked about their attitude toward the perception that 'man is superior over woman in most things'. The percentage of positive responses is approximately 49 per cent. Related to the issue of gender-based leadership, Islamists are expected to oppose careers for women, such as a Member of Parliament or judge. The proportions 'for' and 'against' these issues should be similar to the general proposition that men are superior to women. However, according to the surveys, the percentage of Islamist attitudes is relatively small. Only about 5 per cent of the people opposed a woman's right to be a Member of Parliament, much smaller than the proportion of those who agree that she may (about 88 per cent). When asked whether they agree with an Islamist belief that a woman cannot be a judge because she is weak, about 21 per cent agreed. This proportion is larger, but still much smaller than that of support for Islamic government, as mentioned above (63 per cent).

There are other measures of Islamist attitudes toward women: a *Qur'anic* verse (Q, 4:11) states that the right of daughters to inheritance is half that of sons. Islamists commonly accept the verse literally, ignoring the socio-historical context. In Indonesian society, this is a persistent issue. Munawir Sjadzali, a former minister of Religious Affairs, once suggested that the verse should be understood within the socio-historical context of Arabia in which it was very progressive for its time (Sjadzali 1988). In that society, having a female baby was often thought to be a disaster. A story is told that in pre-Islamic Arabia, to bury alive a female baby was a common tradition (Mernissi 1991, 12). In the modern era, Sjadzali said that it is unjust to apply the verse literally. He suggested that the spirit of the whole *Qur'an* – justice – should be applied to understanding the verse. This idea raised a huge controversy among Muslims in the 1980s. Many Muslim authorities condemned the minister, claiming that the idea was dangerous to Islam (Saimima 1988).

In the surveys, respondents' opinions on the issue were split. About 50 per cent agreed with the idea that sons are superior over daughters in the inheritance matter. The controversy, between Sjadzali and other liberal Islamic scholars on the one hand, and the Islamists on the other, probably reflected mass opinion at the time.

The surveys included another item which was expected to reveal the Islamist orientation on gender. Respondents were asked if sons should be given priority in education, in a situation in which a family is able financially to support only one of the children. Responses to this issue were similar to those on the inheritance issue: about 44 per cent of the people agreed that educational priority of education should be given to a son.

The Islamist orientation toward woman can also be seen in more specific attitudes that are found in many Muslim societies, for example, the prohibition for a woman to make a long trip unaccompanied by a close kin member (*muhrim*).[13] About 48 per cent of the Indonesian Muslim respondents still accept this norm.

The *Qur'an* (Q, 21:3) also stipulates hand amputation for thievery. Islamists understand the verse literally and demand its implementation. However, many

13 *Muhrim* is a person who is related by blood and to whom the woman may not be married, such as parents, brother, sister, child and so on.

Muslim scholars, again through historical criticism, argue that the spirit underlying the verse is to create order and security in society. In medieval Muslim society, hand amputation was probably an effective and acceptable instrument to create social order. In modern society, other instruments such as prisons are believed to be more humane and educative and therefore an appropriate Islamic substitute for amputation (An-Na'im 1996, 208).

Indonesian Muslim authorities also debate this issue, probably reflecting a range of mass opinions. The surveys indicate that about 31 per cent of Indonesian Muslims agreed and 52 per cent disagreed that amputation should be carried out by the Indonesian state.

The Islamist tendency to involve government in religious affairs can be measured by many items, including obligations specifically prescribed in the *Qur'an* and *Sunnah*. Most Muslims everywhere would agree that they are obliged to implement the five pillars of the faith. The daily five prayers and the Ramadan fasting are two of the pillars. The Islamist idea is that government must be responsible for enforcement of the pillars. In the 2001 survey, the respondents were asked if they agreed that the police should arrest a Muslim who does not perform the daily five prayers or the Ramadan fasting.[14] Only about 14 per cent agreed. In the 2002 survey, the respondents were asked if they agreed that police must keep watch over (*mengawasi*) whether Muslims perform the Ramadan fasting. About 30 per cent agreed. In other words, a majority of the people disagree with state enforcement or supervision of their ritual obligations.

I would now like to summarize the many items described individually above into the larger components of mandatory rituals, suggested rituals, Nahdlyin rituals, networks of Islamic civic engagement, NU identity, Muhammadiyah identity and Islamism. On the basis of the first component, mandatory rituals, a large majority of Indonesian Muslims, above 80 per cent, are religious.

A significant proportion performs not only the mandatory but also the suggested rituals. If the scores of the seven suggested ritual items are added to constitute a four-point scale, the mean for these items is 3.15, indicating substantial performance.[15] A large number of Indonesian Muslims are also active in Islamic associations and identify themselves with NU or Muhammadiyah. However, they are neutral – either strongly anti- or pro-Islamist – on Islamist political orientation.[16]

14 Indonesian Islamists often demand that the government close restaurants or prohibit public entertainment during Ramadan to respect the fasting month. In the 2002 survey, the prayer item was dropped, while the fasting item stayed. However, the wording was different from that of the 2001 survey. The results are also different.

15 The four-point scale is constructed from the seven items of the intensity of suggested rituals, in which 1 = never; 2 = rare; 3 = quite frequently; and 4 = very frequently. Reliability of the scale (alpha) is .81.

16 The Islamist items were added to constitute a five-point scale of Islamist political orientation, in which 1 = non-Islamist; 3 = neutral; and 5 = very strong Islamist. The mean of this scale is 3.0, meaning that the people are about neutral on the issue. The veil and women's right to become a Member of Parliament were not included in the scale construction as they have negative correlations with some of the other items. The reliability coefficient (alpha) of the scale is .75.

These findings lead me to conclude that Indonesian Muslims are pious judged by their performance of their mandatory and suggested ritual performance. A significant proportion is also active in Islamic social organizations. However, their attitude toward Islamism is neutral. There is no indication that they reject or support the idea.

Democratic Values

In addition to Islam, democratic values also have potential to explain political tolerance. Students of political tolerance argue that the more committed to democratic values a person is, the more likely he or she is to be tolerant (Marcus et al. 1995; Sullivan, Pierson and Marcus 1982).

In this study, democratic values following Gibson, Duch and Tedin's study (1992) were gauged through several items. These included: allowing political views different from those of the majority; allowing minority groups to have demonstrations; supporting equality before the law; freedom to join any political organization; protection of mass media by law; allowing citizens to participate freely in economic activity; agreeing or disagreeing that competitive elections do harm to the country; and that competition among political parties in elections will improve how government works. The average proportion of support for the eight items of democratic values is about 71 per cent, meaning that a substantial majority of the people have positive attitudes toward democratic values.[17]

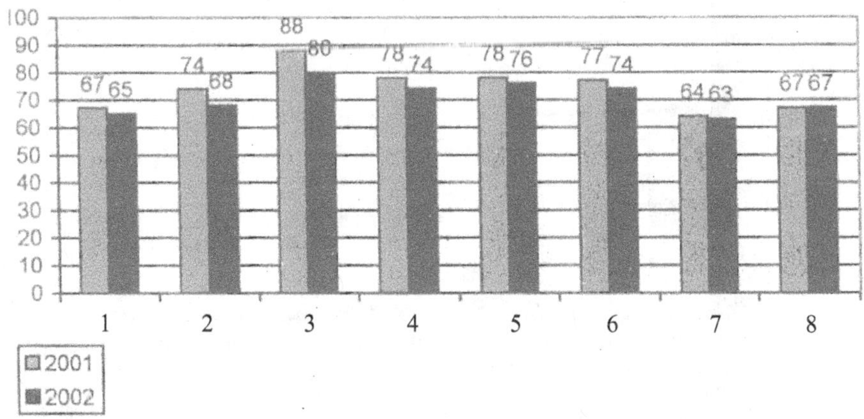

Figure 20.8 Some indicators of support for democratic values (%)

Note: 1 = disagree that minority should not have different view from the view of majority; 2 = disagree that minority should not be allowed to have demonstrations against majority; 3 = support equality before the law; 4 = free to join any political organization; 5 = free mass media; 6 = free enterprise; 7 = disagree that free elections harmful to national unity; 8 = competitive elections good for government performance.

17 The eight items of support for democratic values are added to constitute a five-point scale of support for democratic values, from not supportive at all (1) to very supportive (5). Cranbach alpha of the scale is .73.

Civil Society

In addition to democratic values, civil society is believed to be a crucial factor for political tolerance. It provides structures in which citizens of various social backgrounds work together for a collective interest. This feature of civil society helps build mutual understanding among the participants (Schmitter 1997). Therefore, the more engaged one is in civic associations, the more likely one is to be tolerant.

In the two surveys, respondents were asked to describe the intensity of their voluntary activities. Specifically, they were asked to report whether they were active members, non-active members, or non-members in a range of non-religious civic associations such as the *arisan* (rotating credit association), sports clubs, cooperatives, and so on. Figure 20.9 shows the percentages of people who reported that they are active members in various civic associations.

Figure 20.9 reveals that a significant number of respondents (39 per cent) are engaged in *arisan* or rotating credit associations, an association that Putnam (1993) takes as an exemplar of civic association believed to be important for democracy.[18] Most people are engaged in at least one civic association, but the number of those who reported that they are not engaged in any association is quite significant

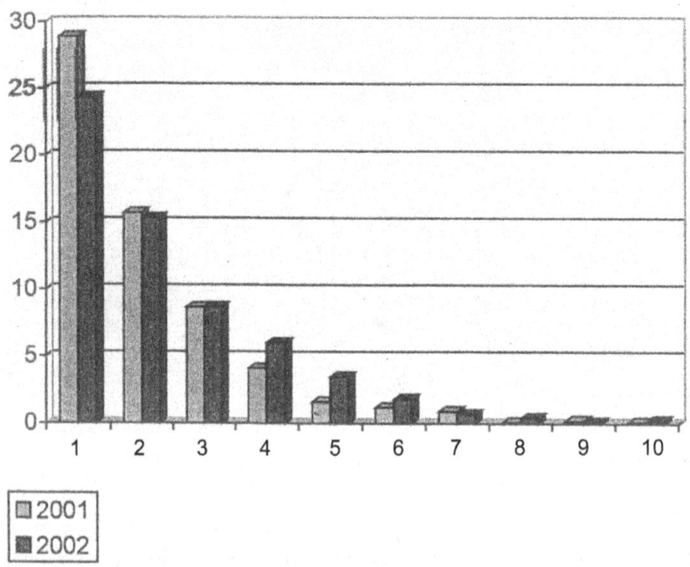

Figure 20.9 Proportions of active membership in various civic associations among Indonesians (%)

Note: 1 = arisan; 2 = village association (village council, village youth association or karang taruna); 3 = union/farm/fishery association; 4 = cooperative; 5 = sports club; 6 = cultural club; 7 = animal lover club; 8 = Red Cross or Boy Scouts; 9 = professional association; 10 = LSM or new social movement.

18 For discussion of the rotating credit association, see Geertz (1962).

(38 per cent). Only about 13 per cent of the people were active in sports clubs, which are believed to have an impact on political engagement (Putnam, 1993); only 7 per cent in cultural clubs; and only about 4 per cent in the Red Cross or Boy Scouts. Seen from the number of associations in which a citizen is engaged, only about two out of ten citizens were active in two civic associations.

Education

In addition to civil society, education is believed to be an important variable to explain political tolerance. The more educated one is, the more likely one is to be tolerant (McClosky 1964; Sullivan, Pierson and Marcus 1982; Marcus et al. 1995). The logic underlying this positive relationship is that feeling tolerant toward the disliked is not easy for most people. Knowledge about democratic values and pluralism is socialized through (modern) education. Education also helps to link these abstract values to concrete life (Prothro and Grigg 1960). Democratic beliefs and habits are not a state of nature, but are acquired through learning, including formal education (McClosky 1964).

Knowledge or information about democratic values is a crucial element which links education to tolerance. However, knowledge is not restricted to that acquired through formal education. It may also be shaped by contemporary knowledge acquired outside school (Marcus et al. 1995; McClosky and Zeller 1984). Following political news through mass media and through discussion may provide a critical information base for many people. An assessment of the information produced by the mass media becomes crucial to understanding how information shapes political tolerance.

Analysis

Table 20.3 displays how various dimensions of Islam, democratic values and secular civil society, controlling for socio-economic status and demographic variables, simultaneously affect the two forms of tolerance.[19] Islamism is the only component of Islam which has a negative, significant and stable relationship with tolerance toward Christians. Mandatory rituals and suggested rituals also have a negative, albeit unstable and weak, relationship with tolerance toward Christians. Regardless of demographic, socio-economic and democratic culture variables, Islamism decreases tolerance toward Christians. Even Muslims with better education and support for democratic values are likely to be intolerant toward Christians if they are Islamists.

19 In the analysis, independent variables which do not have significant correlations in bivariate analysis were excluded.

Table 20.3 Multivariate analysis of political tolerance (standardized regression coefficients)

Tolerant attitudes / Religion and nation	Demonstration	Hold public office
Islam		
Indonesia	14% (1704)	20% (1708)
Azerbaijan	0.7 (1907)	0.7 (1935)
Bangladesh	43.8 (1320)	36.0 (1349)
Bosnia-Herzegovina	4.4 (1136)	1.4 (1153)
Catholicism		
Argentina	13.8 (989)	7.0 (996)
Brazil	17.5 (1054)	7.7 (1061)
Spain	(1143)	2.7 (1167)
The Philippines	4.2 (1179)	3.6 (1190)
Venezuela	5.3 (1154)	6.0 (1153)
Orthodox Christianity		
Georgia	6.5 (2378)	4.7 (2410)
Russia	5.9 (2390)	2.2 (2447)
Hindu	11.3 (1840)	4.0 (1897)
India		
Confucianism	9.7 (1706)	7.7 (1727)
China	-	11.0 (1373)
Taiwan	13.9 (691)	17.5 (708)
Protestantism		
Sweden	30.3 (903)	9.4 (922)
Switzerland	6.3 (1079)	4.4 (1071)
USA	24.6 (1457)	14.4 (1467)
West Germany	19.4 (963)	6.3 (975)

Note: **P≤ .01, *P≤ .05.

It must be stressed, however, that these findings only partly confirm Huntington's claim about the intolerant nature of Islam. If Islam is defined by other components of Islam, especially Islamic civil society, his claim is unsupported by the data. Moreover, Islamism is not identical with Islam. To be more engaged in Islamic activity is not necessarily to be an Islamist. Therefore, specification of what we mean by Islam is necessary to understand more accurately the nature of its relationship to political tolerance.

Unlike Islamism, secular civic engagement has a positive and significant impact on tolerance toward Christians. Regardless of the Islamic factor, democratic values and education, secular civic engagement increases tolerance. The hypothesis that civil society helps build tolerance is supported by the evidence of Indonesian Muslims.

When defined by general political tolerance or tolerance toward the least liked group, political tolerance does not have a significant relationship with secular civic engagement. There is also no significance in the relationship between tolerance and almost all components of Islam. Only mandatory rituals and Islamic civic engagement have a significant relationship, but in opposed directions, and very weak.

A Muslim who frequently performs the rituals is likely to be intolerant toward the least liked group. The more engaged a person is in Islamic association, conversely, the more likely he or she is to be tolerant toward the least liked group. Civic association perhaps functions as theories of civil society predict, to help build tolerance. This association is the only variable in the multivariate analysis which has a positive and significant impact on tolerance.

A surprising piece of evidence is the negative and stable impact of support for democratic values on tolerance toward the least liked group. Another surprising finding is the negative impact of education on tolerance toward the least liked group. More educated citizens are more intolerant.

The negative relationship between support for democratic values and tolerance toward the least liked group requires further explanation. It is mainly communists as the target group that produces this result. It is still surprising, however, because support for democratic values is believed to be a strong and positive predictor of political tolerance. Why are Indonesian democrats not tolerant toward communists?

One possible answer has to do with the reliability and validity of the measures of political tolerance applied in the survey. Future surveys with better measures may help to minimize this problem. Another possible answer is related to the nature of communism in Indonesian society and politics. Most people probably perceive communists as a more dangerous group, relative to others, that threatens the society and polity. Perceived threat is believed to be a crucial factor which affects political tolerance (Marcus et al. 1995; Sullivan, Pierson and Marcus 1982). To be a democrat in Indonesia does not necessarily imply tolerance toward a group that the respondent thinks is a threat.

Communism and Political Tolerance

Further study to verify this hypothesis is required, since the two surveys do not provide information about threat perception of the target group. However, some description and hypothetical explanations may help to understand why Indonesian democrats are not tolerant toward communists.

Communists have a unique place in the history of Indonesian society and politics. Communist politics in the country emerged prior to independence in the early twentieth century (McVey 1965). International communist activists brought communist politics to the country from Europe. They helped to found unions, whose many members were active in the largest Islamic movement organization, Sarekat Islam (SI; Islamic Association), established in 1911. The influence of communism within the SI was strong and gave rise to white (Islamic) and red (communist) factions within the elites (Noer 1973). Their ideological conflict grew until the communists quit the SI and established the PKI (Indonesian Communist Party) (McVey 1965).

The SI under the leadership of the white faction continued, but became weaker. The colonial authorities banned the PKI in 1928 as it threatened its rule. PKI leaders were arrested and sent to the concentration camp of Boven Digul in far-off New Guinea.

At independence in 1945, the PKI revived under the leadership of Musso. In 1948, Musso's PKI rebelled against the central government in the town of Madiun in eastern Java (Van Der Kroef 1965; Hindley 1964). The government, crying treason, and anti-communist parties reacted with force against the PKI. At the time, Indonesia was facing a serious threat from the Dutch, who had not recognized Indonesian independence. The PKI rebellion took place in this situation and was felt by many to be traitorous, a thrust from behind. Many political and especially armed forces leaders have never trusted the PKI since then (Crouch 1988; Noer 1987).

The PKI soon revived, proclaiming its commitment to the democratic process rather than rebellion. Now under the leadership of D.N. Aidit, the PKI participated in the 1955 national election and received a significant number of votes (16 per cent). As parliamentary democracy declined and President Soekarno took over the government in 1959, he dissolved two important political parties, the Muslim-based Masjumi (Majlis Sjuro Muslimin Indonesia, Indonesian Muslim Consultative Council), which was the second largest party, and a social democratic party, the PSI (partai Sosialis Indonesia, Indonesian Socialist Party). The three other large parties, the PNI (partai Nasional Indonesia, Indonesian National Party), the NU (at that time, unlike today, a political party as well as a social and educational organization) and the PKI, were allowed to continue to participate in national politics.

Under Soekarno's Guided Democracy (1959–66), national politics was mainly dominated by three political forces, the army on the right, President Soekarno in the middle, and the PKI on the left (Crouch 1988). The sharpest confrontation occurred between the army and the PKI, then at the peak of its power and influence. President Soekarno was known to be sympathetic to Marxism and the idea of social revolution. The PKI seized the opportunity to ally itself with Soekarno.

At the national level, the PKI's main political opponent was the army under the leadership of General Ahmad Yani and General A.H. Nasution. At the grass-roots level were local landlords, many associated with the NU (Noer 1987). A series of 'one-sided actions' (*aksi sepihak*) by the PKI to implement the government's land reform programme caused extensive conflicts between PKI supporters and local landlords. Class conflict was intensified by religious sentiment, the pious Muslims of the NU against the nominal Muslims who supported the PKI.

In urban areas, conflict erupted between the PKI and its enemies, especially the army, liberal intellectuals, middle-class Muslims and Muslim university students. The communists appeared to have the upper hand. The PKI was the second largest communist political party in the world, after the Chinese Communist Party. PKI leaders and their opponents all believed that the party needed only one step forward to take over the government.

It never happened. Instead, on 1 October 1965, a political tragedy occurred in which six generals were abducted and killed. There has never been a clear answer as to which political force was responsible for the killings. The army, now under the leadership of Major General Soeharto, attempted to convince the public that the PKI was responsible. The PKI's friends countered that the army under the leadership of Soeharto was behind the tragedy.

Following the killings, the army under General Soeharto took over the national leadership from President Soekarno through a military coup in the name of the recovery of social and political order.[20] This new leadership, supported by anti-communist elements, particularly from the devout Muslim community, eliminated the communists as a political force. Anti-PKI protests mushroomed. The PKI members and leaders were chased, arrested and killed. In only one year (1965–66), several hundred thousand communists were killed, and hundreds of thousands of others were sent to prison (Cribb 1990; Crouch 1988).[21]

Anti-communism was a central pillar of Soeharto's New Order government. The opinion was trumpeted throughout the country that the PKI was dangerous and a threat to the very life of the nation. The New Order government established the BP7 (Badan Pusat Pengkajian, Pendidikan, Pengamalan, Penghayatan, dan Pemurnian Pancasila, Central Body for the Study, Implementation, Internalization and Dissemination of *Pancasila* Values), whose main aim was to institutionalize *Pancasila* values in society and polity. Civil servants, students and voluntary association members were trained via the P4 (pedoman, Penghayatan, dan Pengamalan Pancasila, Directives for the Internalization and Implementation of *Pancasila* Values). Communism was proclaimed one of the most serious threats to those values.

The extent to which this training or indoctrination gave rise to anti-communist sentiment among the people is uncertain. However, a major anti-communist effort was undertaken and billions of rupiahs were spent. It is probable that, at the very least, the massive anti-communism programme of the regime heightened the existing anti-communist sentiment among the people.

Social or student movements sympathetic to Marxism periodically emerged during the New Order. Leftist activists tried to distinguish Marxist from PKI doctrines, because of the bad image of the PKI constructed by the regime and the fear of state terror against the PKI. However, their activities were mostly underground. Marxist sympathizers were often sent to prison without trial. On one occasion, student activists went to prison only because they read Marxist works.

The regime censored books, mass media and film, and monitored many societal groups to preserve the polity and society from communist influence. *Penghianatan G30S PKI* (Treason of G30S PKI) is a popular film that demonstrates the brutality of Indonesian communism against the army prior to the coup. Under the New Order, this film was broadcast by state television every 30 September as part of the state's anti- communism campaign (Sen 1988).

The regime developed an anti-communism curriculum for schools and universities (Bourchier 1997; Leigh 1991). Anyone who wished to work for the government or to run for public office had to be screened by the military for communist connections. Any family member or descendant of a communist was denied his or her civil rights.

20 Regarding the coup, see, for example, Crouch (1988).

21 There has never been an exact estimate of the number of communists who were killed. Sources estimated the number, with a very large margin, as between 70,000 and two million; see Cribb (1990).

The New Order has fallen, but anti-communist sentiment has probably remained pervasive. Today, anti-communist terror comes not only from the state but also from society itself. In this post-New Order era, many leftist or Marxist works have been published and are sold in public bookstores. This would never have happened in the New Order era. However, some Muslim groups have campaigned against the publications, confiscated the books from bookstores and burned them. The police could not stop this action because the works are still formally illegal. The anti-communism campaign's success may be measured by the fact that there is no significant group that can convince the government or the public of communism's right to exist. Abdurrahman Wahid, as president in 2000, proposed that the anti-communism decree made in the late 1960s by the MPR-S (Majlis Permusjawaratan Rakyat Sementara, Interim People's Consultative Assembly), the highest state institution in the country, be dissolved. This proposal was rejected by the DPR (Dewan Perwakilan Rakyat, People's Representative Council, or The Council), and probably by the people in general. A faction in the DPR had even reacted against the proposal by threatening to impeach President Wahid (*Republika*, 4 April 2000).

The Council (DPR) is currently debating a new election bill. One clause in the draft states that communists or anyone associated with communism are prohibited from running for presidential office. Leaders of the Golkar party, the state party during the New Order period, have persuaded other parties to pass the law. They argue that communism is still a threat to the nation (*Koran Tempo*, 21 April 2003). However, the PDI-Perjuangan of President Megawati has attempted to convince The Council that former communist supporters, family or sympathizers are Indonesian citizens, and therefore have the same political rights as other Indonesians (*Koran Tempo*, 22 April 2003).

One aspect of the current debate is that communism has become a political resource. In addition to human rights considerations, the move by some parties to rehabilitate the political rights of former communists may help to enlarge their constituency. The communists were strong on Java, and among lower-class voters. The constituents of President Wahid's party, PKB, are mostly Javanese, and therefore the effort to rehabilitate the communists or anyone related to communism may be politically strategic for PKB.

This strategic reason may also drive the PDI-P to restore the political rights of communists. PDI-P is a continuation of the old PNI, which was once close to the PKI. President Soekarno, the founder of the PNI, was quite sympathetic to the ideals of the PKI. So it is not surprising if the PDI-P attempts to rehabilitate former communists or anyone related to communism.

Nonetheless, anti-communist sentiment is probably still pervasive among the people. The New Order's anti-communist jargon that the party is a latent threat to the nation is still powerful. This sentiment is reflected in an anti-communist sentiment expressed by a religious figure in a village to the author (16 October 2002):

> I came to this village in the early 1960s when communism was strong in national politics. Communism was very strong also here, and the people here rarely go to the mosque. The mosque was empty and not cared for. I believe that communism never dies. It is in the

hearts of its proponents, and can materialize at any time. So, we have to be careful with communism.

In post-Soeharto Indonesia, a new-leftist party, the PRD (partai Rakyat Demokratik, Democratic People's Party), participated in the 1999 election. Its leader, Budiman Sujatmiko, had been sent to prison by the Soeharto regime as a communist suspect. In post-Soeharto Indonesia, politics has been much more open, and the establishment of the party was possible. However, it could not legally state that it is ideologically communist or Marxist. The party received fewer than 100,000 votes in an electorate of more than 100 million. Its failure may to some extent reflect the pervasive anti-communism found in our surveys.

This short story about anti-communism may help explain why a majority of respondents are intolerant toward communists, regardless of democratic commitment and level of education. If political tolerance as measured by tolerance toward the least liked groups is essential to democratic values, those Indonesians who claim to support democratic values are likely to be majoritarian democrats only, that is supporters of democracy minus political tolerance (cf. Duch and Gibson 1992). This characteristic of Indonesian democrats is probably unique, a product of a specific historical context, the long history of anti-communism in society and the polity.

Does generation matter to anti-communist sentiment? It is possible that the post-1960s generation is more tolerant toward communists, as this younger generation did not directly experience the bloody political conflicts of the 1960s. The 2002 survey data, however, indicates that the generation difference does not matter. Instead, it is probable that the New Order regime has been extremely successful in its anti-communism campaign. Regardless of generational difference, Indonesian democrats are intolerant toward communists. A 'deviant' relationship between support for democratic values and political tolerance has been found in other cases as well, such as in Germany and Luxembourg (Duch and Gibson 1992). In the case of Russia, democratic values do not have a significant relationship with political tolerance (Gibson 1998a; 1998b). In the cases of Germany and Luxembourg, democratic values have a negative and significant relationship with tolerance toward fascists (Duch and Gibson 1992). The Indonesian case which reveals a negative relationship between democratic values and political tolerance should also be understood within its political context, especially the specific place of the PKI in the polity.

Conclusion

I have explored the extent to which Islam is inimical to the political tolerance which is believed to be crucial for democratic consolidation. I would like to restate some important findings to conclude this work.

First, the claim made by Huntington that Islam is an intolerant religion is only true if Islam is defined as Islamism and tolerance is defined as tolerance toward Christians. Mandatory rituals and suggested rituals indicate some negative impact on tolerance, but are inconsistent and very weak. Other components of Islam – Nahdliyin rituals, Islamic civic engagement, NU identity and Muhammadiyah identity – do not have a significant relationship with intolerance. Therefore, we must narrowly define Islam as Islamism in order to support the claim that Islam produces intolerance toward Christians.

Second, almost all Islamic components do not have any association with political tolerance defined as tolerance toward the least liked group. Mandatory rituals are the only exception, but the relationship is weak. Islamic civic engagement does have a positive and significant impact on tolerance, but it is safe to conclude that, overall, Islam does not produce intolerance toward the least liked group.

Third, democratic values and secular civic engagement have positive and significant impacts on political tolerance defined as tolerance toward Christians. These patterns confirm many findings about tolerance.

Fourth, democratic values and education surprisingly have negative impacts on political tolerance defined as tolerance toward the least liked group. This pattern deviates from many findings about political tolerance. This deviation should probably be understood locally. A majority of Indonesians select communists as the least liked group. Communism in Indonesian politics has a bad image, produced by its opponents who have been dominant in society and the polity since the fall of the Indonesian Communist Party in 1965. Communism is still today an illegal ideology and political force. The phenomenon of democrats intolerant toward communists should be understood in this specific context.

References

An-Na'im, Abdullahi A. (1996), *Toward an Islamic Reformation: Civil Liberties, Human Rights, and International Law* (Syracuse, NY: Syracuse University Press).

Biro Pusat Statistik [Central Bureau of Statistics] (2000), *Population Census* (Jakarta: Biro Pusat Statistik).

Bourchier, David (1997), 'Totalitarianism and the "National Personality": Recent Controversy about the Philosophical Basis of the Indonesian State', in Jim Schiller and Barbara Martin-Schiller (eds), *Imagining Indonesia: Cultural Politics and Political Culture* (Athens, Ohio: Ohio University Center for International Studies).

Bruinessen, M. van (1995), 'Shari'a Court, Tarekat and Pesantren: Religious Institutions in the Banten Sultanate', *Archipel* 50, 165–200.

Bruinessen, M. van (1996), 'Kurds, Turks and the Alevi Revival', *Middle East Reports* 200, 7–10.

Burhanudin, Jajat (ed.) (2002), *Ulama Perempuan Indonesia* (Jakarta: Gramedia Pustaka Utama).

Cribb, Robert (ed.) (1990), *The Indonesian Killings of 1965–1966: Studies from Java and Bali* (Clayton: Monash University).

Crouch, Harold (1988), *The Army and Politics in Indonesia* (Ithaca, NY: Cornell University Press).

Dahl, R.A. (1971), *Polyarchy: Participation and Opposition* (New Haven, CT: Yale University Press).

Denny, F.M. (1994), *An Introduction to Islam* (London: Macmillan).

Dhofier, Z. (1982), *Tradisi Pesantren: Studi Tentang Pandagan Hidup Kyai* [The pesantren tradition: a study of the view of a traditional Muslim religious scholar] (Jakarta: Lembaga Penelitan).

Duch, Raymond M. and Gibson, James L. (1992), '"Putting Up With" Fascists in Western Europe: A Comparative, Cross-Level Analysis of Political Tolerance', *The Western Political Quarterly* 45, 237–73.

Fananie, Zainuddin and Sabardila, Atiqa (2001), *Sumber Konflik. Masyarakat Muslim NU-Muhammadiyah: Perspektif Keberterimaan Tahlil* (Surakarta: Muhammadiyah University Press).

Geertz, C. (1960), *The Religion of Java* (Glencoe, Ill: Free Press).

Geertz, C. (1962), 'The Rotating Credit Association: A "Middle Rung" in Development', *Economics, Development and Cultural Change* 1: 3.

Gibson, J.L. (1998a), 'A Sober Second Thought: An Experiment in Persuading Russians to Tolerance', *American Journal of Political Science* 42, 819–50.

Gibson, J.L. (1998b), 'Putting Up with Fellow Russians: An Analysis of Political Tolerance in the Fledgling Russian Democracy', *Political Research Quarterly* 51, 37–68.

Gibson, J., Duch, R. and Tedin, K. (1992), 'Democratic Values and the Transformation of the Soviet Union', *Journal of Politics* 54: 2, 329–71.

Gohari, M.J. (2000), *The Taliban: Ascent to Power* (Oxford: Oxford University Press).

Hindley, Donald (1964), *The Communist Party of Indonesia 1952–1963* (Berkeley: University of California Press).

Huntington, S. (1997), *The Clash of Civilizations and the Remaking of World Order* (New York, NY: Touchstone).

Jamhari (2001), 'The Meaning Interpreted: The Concept of *Barakah* in *Ziarah*', *Studia Islamika* 8, 87–128.

Leigh, Barbara (1991), 'Making the Indonesian State: The Role of School Text', *Review of Indonesian and Malayan Affairs,* July.

Lewis, Bernard (1985), *Muslim Discovery of Europe* (New York: W.W. Norton).

Lewis, Bernard (2002), *Arabs in History* (New York and Oxford: Oxford University Press).

Lipset, S.M. (1994), 'The Social Requisites of Democracy Revisited', *American Sociological Review* 59, 1–22.

Marcus, George E., Sullivan, John L., Theiss-Morse, Elizabeth and Wood, Sandra L. (1995), *With Malice Toward Some. How People Make Civil Liberties Judgment* (Cambridge: Cambridge University Press).

McClosky, Herbert (1964), 'Consensus and Ideology in American Politics', *American Political Science Review* 58, 361–82.

McClosky, H. and Zeller, J. (1984), *The American Ethos: Public Attitudes Toward Capitalism and Democracy* (Cambridge, MA: Harvard University Press).

McVey, Ruth (1965), *The Rise of Indonesian Communism* (Ithaca, NY: Cornell University Press).

Mernissi, Fatima (1991), *The Veil and the Male Elite: A Feminist Interpretation of Women's Rights in Islam* (Cambridge, Mass: Perseus Books).

Munhanif, Ali (ed.) (2002), *Perempuan dalam Literatur Islam Klasik* (Jakarta: Pustaka Gramedia Utama).

Noer, D. (1973), *The Modernist Muslim Movement in Indonesia 1900–1942* (Kuala Lumpur: Oxford University Press).

Noer, Deliar (1987), *Partai Islam di Pentas Nasional 1945–1965* (Jakarta: Grafiti Pers).

Prothro, J. and Grigg, C. (1960), 'Fundamental Principles of Democracy: Bases of Agreement and Disagreement', *Journal of Politics* 22, 276–94.

Putnam, R.D. (1993), *Making Democracy Work: Civic Tradition in Modern Italy* (Princeton, NJ: Princeton University Press).

Saimima, Iqbal A. (ed.) (1988), *Polemik Reakstualisasi Ajaran Islam* (Jakarta: Pustaka Panjimas).

Schmitter, Philippe C. (1997), 'Civil Society East and West', in Larry Diamond (ed.), *Consolidating the Third Wave of Democracy* (Baltimore: Johns Hopkins University Press).

Sen, Krishna (1988), 'Filming "History" under the New Order', in Krishna Sen (ed.), *Histories and Stories* (Clayton: Centre for Southeast Asian Studies, Monash University).

Sjadzali, Munawir (1988), 'Reaktualisasi Ajaran Islam', in Iqbal Abdurrauf Saimima (ed.), *Polemik Reakstualisasi Ajaran Islam* (Jakarta: Pustaka Panjimas).

Stouffer, S.A. (1955), *Communism, Conformity, and Civil Liberty* (Garden City, NJ: Doubleday).

Sujuthi, Mahmud (2001), *Politik Tarekat. Qadiriyah wa Naksyabandiyah Jombang* (Yogyakarta: Galang Press).

Sullivan, J., Pierson, J. and Marcus, G. (1982), *Political Tolerance and American Democracy* (Chicago: Chicago University Press).

Umar, Nasaruddin (2002), *Qur'an untuk Prempuan* (Jakarta: Jaringan Islam Liberal dan Teater Utan Kayu).

Van Der Kroef, Justus M. (1965), *The Communist Party of Indonesia. Its History, Program, and Tactics* (Vancouver: University of British Columbia Press).

Appendix

Methodology

The data used in this study were produced by two mass surveys of the Indonesian population in October 2001 and October 2002. Budget and physical accessibility determined how the samples were drawn.

In the 2001 survey, the population was restricted to 16 provinces: Jakarta, Banten, Jawa Barat, Jawa Tengah, Yogyakarta, Jawa Timur, Sumatra Utara, Sumatra Selatan, Sumatra Barat, Lampung, Riau, Jambi, Kalimantan Selatan, Kalimantan Timur, Nusa Tenggara and Sulawesi Selatan. The population of these provinces is about 87 per cent of the total national population (Biro Pusat Statistik [BPS] 2000). Because of budget constraints, Papua (formerly called Irian Jaya) was not included. The population of Papua is only about 1 per cent of the national population (BPS 2000). Moreover, it is scattered throughout that vast island and mostly cannot be reached by ground transportation.

The Maluku islands were also excluded. The population is about 1 per cent of the national population. In 2001, local warfare, albeit calmed down considerably from the previous year, still occurred. It was impossible to conduct a survey in the war atmosphere. Sulawesi Tengah, Kalimantan Tengah, Kalimantan Barat and Aceh were also excluded from the survey for security reasons. Ethnic- and religion-coloured wars were ongoing in these provinces.

Sulawesi Utara, Nusa Tenggara Timur and Bali were excluded because the non-Muslim population is quite significant, if not predominant, in these regions. The intent of this survey was to explore Muslim political attitudes, not those of other religious groups.

Sulawesi Tenggara, Gorontalo and Bengkulu are remote and the population is very small: about 2 per cent of the national population (BPS 2000). Kepulauan Bangka Belitung is a new province, and in the survey it was part of Sumatra Selatan.

In the 2002 survey, the budget constraint was removed and we were able to draw a sample covering the whole national population.

In both surveys, the population was defined as citizens who are 17 years of age or older, or who are married. The interviewees were selected from the population according to a multi-stage random sampling procedure. First, the national population was stratified according to gender proportion, rural–urban residence, and province.

According to the national census data (BPS 2000), the ratio of males to females in the population is 100.6. In the surveys the ratio is rounded to be 100, and therefore the proportion of male and female in the sample is equal.

Rural–urban residence is defined by the national population of rural and urban residence: 52 per cent rural, 48 per cent urban (<http://www.bps.go.id/sector/population/Pop_indo.htm>). However, the rural–urban proportion varies by province. Therefore the number of rural and urban respondents was selected proportionately in each province based on the primary sampling unit, that is *desa* (rural administrative unit) or *kelurahan* (urban administrative unit). The BPS provides a list of *desa* and *kelurahan* in each province. The number of *desa* and *kelurahan* selected as the primary sampling unit was based on the rural–urban population breakdown in each province.

The number of respondents in the two surveys was set according to a calculation of typical sample size in scientific surveys, on the one hand, and budgetary restrictions on the other. For a large population, a sample between 2,000 and 2,500 is common. To achieve a figure within that range, first a number in a primary sampling unit was arbitrarily set at eight respondents. In the 2001 survey, 276 *desa* or *kelurahan* as the primary sampling unit were then randomly selected, according to the proportion of population and rural–urban residence from the 16 provinces. The sample size was therefore 2,176. In the 2002 survey, based on the same considerations and procedures, 311 *desa* or *kelurahan* from all the provinces were selected. Therefore, the sample size was 2,488.

How were the eight respondents selected in each *desa* or *kelurahan*? Interviewers went to the office of the selected *desa* or *kelurahan*, and asked for the list of RTs (Rukun Tetangga, neighbourhoods, wards or hamlets) in the *desa* or *kelurahan*. If the list was not available, interviewers, assisted by a local official, drew a map of the RTs in the *desa* or *kelurahan*. Four RTs were then randomly selected from the list.

Two *kartu keluarga* (household cards) were then chosen randomly from the list of households in the selected RT. This list was provided by the RT official. In cases where the list was not available, the interviewers, helped by the official, drew the map and listed the households in the RT. In each selected household, a member of the household who was 17, older, or married was chosen using a Kish Grid. The selected person, male or female, was interviewed.

The Principal Investigator (PI), helped by the PPIM, recruited 38 persons and trained them in how to conduct face-to-face interviews. These persons helped the PI to recruit and train interviewers in the provinces. They became field coordinators. In the 2001 survey, the PI, assisted by the coordinators, recruited and trained 138 interviewers. In 2002, the number of interviewers was 311. The interviewers were mostly university students in the respective provinces.

The field coordinators were responsible for obtaining permission from local administrators and for spot-checking the interviews. The Maluku islands (32 respondents) were not accessible for the interview because of security reasons. The spot-checking was conducted on 25 per cent of the total sample selected randomly. No significant errors were found.

Having cleaned the questionnaires, 2,012 (92 per cent) of the 2001 survey and 2,321 (93 per cent) of the 2002 survey were judged valid for analysis. The rest were non-responsive and defective questionnaires. The author was directly involved in all stages of the two surveys, from recruiting and training of field coordinators and interviewers, pre-tests, spot checks, cleaning, coding and data entry.

Chapter 21

Civil Society and the Media in Indonesia

Philip Kitley

Let me begin with a puzzle about the media and civil society. Since the end of the New Order government, which we can date in a formal sense as 21 May 1998, media diversity in Indonesia has increased significantly. The unexpected but welcome changes introduced by Minister Yunus Yosfiah opened up the print and electronic media in Indonesia very significantly. His simplification of licence application procedures and requirements led to the establishment of thousands of new radio stations, magazines and newspapers, and also to the establishment of five new, national, free-to-air television stations: MetroTV, TransTV, TV Global, TV7 and Lativi. The commercial television stations established in the 1990s are still operating, although some are experiencing financial difficulties, and there have been major changes in management personnel and operational style.

The new *Broadcasting Law No. 32*, enacted on 28 December 2002, opened up opportunities for even more diversity with provision for the establishment of regional television stations. Regional stations are planned for Bali, Lampung, Riau, Surabaya and Ujung Pandang. A small number have been established, funded by large media organizations such as the Jawa Pos group. The regional television sector remains, however, largely undeveloped. Four cable TV providers operate in Jakarta, delivering international programming to hotels and a relatively small number of subscribers. Indonesia's slow recovery from the economic crisis of 1997, compounded by political uncertainty, has inhibited the development of Pay TV (Television Asia 2002/2003).

International agencies such as Internews, the Ford Foundation, the Friedrich Ebert Organisation, the Friedrich Naumann Organisation and UNESCO, and Indonesian non-government organizations (NGOs or, in Indonesian, LSM) such as ISAI and SET Workshop have been active in developing training in journalism and campaigning for a more responsible public television and radio service. Universities have increased the number of communications and media studies courses on offer.

In short, media production and education, and training for media personnel, have expanded rapidly (albeit from a low base) and there is a more lively, more diverse mediascape in Indonesia than ever before. I say 'more lively' because even before May 1998, the print media especially, and the electronic media to a lesser degree, became more outspoken and overtly critical of the New Order government. An increased number of current affairs programmes, chat shows, news reports and interactive services provided Indonesian audiences with an up-to-the-minute coverage of major political developments and reflections on the growing criticism of public affairs that was coming from students and other activists.

Recent Indonesian publications which discuss the Indonesian media are aware of the developments in the media sector and comment on the expansion of the public sphere that the reform period has introduced. The contribution that civil society and a range of media have made to expanding public spheres[1] and dismantling established patterns of dominance and governmentality are also acknowledged and discussed in the press and in scholarly books and articles (*Komunikasi* 1998, I; 1999, IV; 2000, V; 2001, VI; Yasraf 2000; Abar 1997; Panjaitan 1999; Suroso 2001; Hidayat et al. 2000; Ishadi 2002).

The Black Hole of the Media and the Public Sphere

What is puzzling, however, is that the growing Indonesian civil society literature virtually ignores the concept of the public sphere and the intersection of civil society and the media. My survey of four articles in a special edition of *Paramadina* focused on civil society (Kitley 2000, 1, 2) and of 13 books published between 1996 and 2001 shows that the public sphere is mentioned briefly only in Culla (1999, 19, 77) and Hikam (1999), and the relationship between the media and civil society is raised briefly only in Hikam (1999, 152).[2] This suggests that Indonesian media scholars are convinced of the close dependency of civil society and the public sphere on processes of mediatization, but that civil society scholars have either underestimated the significance of the media–civil society relationship, or have a different view of the relationship between civil society and public debate and political process. If the latter is true, we need to ask:

- Whether this is a reflection of the history of state–media relations in Indonesia (Kitley 2002; 2001);
- Whether the lack of interest in media relations reflects LSM's long-established habits of keeping a low media profile (Eldridge 1995);
- Whether it signifies a civil society perspective which looks to a close relationship between state and society and disavows public contestation of state–society relations (Rahardjo 1999);
- Whether it reflects a tendency to adopt the concept of civil society without intensive exploration of its practical political implications (Baso 1999).

Not that this lack of attention is peculiarly an Indonesian problem. The British political scientist John Keane has noted that 'few detailed analyses of the relationship

1 In writing of 'public spheres' rather than the public sphere, I follow Keane (1998) who argues that the idea of a unified public sphere is obsolete and that today we deal with a 'mosaic of differently sized, overlapping and interconnected public spheres that force us radically to revise our understanding of public life and its "partner" terms, such as public opinion, the public good and the public/private distinction' (Keane 1998, 169).

2 See, for example, Azra (1999); Baso (1999); Boestam et al. (2000); Budiman (1990); Culla (1999); Efendi (1999); Eldridge (1995); Hikam (1999); Hikam (1996a); Hikam (1996b); Fakih (1996); Mitsuo, Siddique and Bajunid (2001); Rahardjo (1999): Setiawan (2000); Sufyanto (2001); Widodo (2000).

between civil society and "the public sphere" exist' (Keane 1998, 157), and in a workshop convened by the Royal Dutch Academy of Sciences in 2001, researchers working on 'The Making of Civil Society [in Indonesia] in Historical Perspective' also overlooked the significance of the media for civil society (Schulte-Nordholt and Abdullah 2002). But the gap between the political aspirations and activities of civil society and the media is an urgent issue because so much of contemporary politics and social transformation is constructed in and through the media. This is the way the British media scholar Roger Silverstone characterizes the significance of the media, and the need for media studies:

> We study the media because we are concerned about their power: we fear it, we decry it, and we adore it – the power of definition, of incitement, of enlightenment, of seduction, of judgement. We study the media because of the need to understand how powerful the media are in our everyday lives; in the structuring of experience; on the surface and in the depths. And we want to harness that power for good rather than ill (Silverstone 1999, 143).

I would add to that an additional point about the globalization of the media, and the need to understand that 'our media' (Indonesia's, Australia's) are always already somebody else's. The nation as the frame and point of reference for political action and change, and as a frame for media operations, has been supplanted by the 'space of flows', to use Castells' phrase. Just as civil society can be understood as a transnational phenomenon which explains in large measure its mobilization in Indonesia and in many other regions of the world, media relations in Indonesia are no longer restricted to a national frame of reference, and the intersection of civil society and the media in Indonesia must be understood as part of a global flow of ideas and models for political action and social reform (Kitley 2003).

Indonesian Ideas of Civil Society

While the concept of civil society is deeply rooted in Western political philosophy, it has been historically dynamic and speaks to a wide variety of political formations in the contemporary world. The concept of civil society has been important in informing and mobilizing social transformation in Eastern Europe, in Latin America, in South Korea, Japan, the Philippines and Indonesia.

In Indonesia, the concept is understood and deployed in contemporary political discourse in different ways. The most distinctive Indonesian perspective is the analogy drawn between (some) Western ideas of civil society and the character of the small-scale polity or city-state established by the Prophet Muhammad in 622 CE in the Yatsrib district near Medina (*Madinah*), 350 kilometres north of Mecca. The historical character of this polity is understood in part from the Medina Charter agreed between the local population and the immigrants from Mecca led by Muhammad. The Charter is understood to have established a pluralistic, tolerant society where Muslim followers of Muhammad, Jews, Arab Christians and others whose traditional beliefs were monotheistic or polytheistic lived together in peace under the authority of Muhammad and an agreed, public, codified set of basic laws

(Rahardjo 1999, 152). This historical political formation, known as 'Medina society' (*masyarakat Madinah*) is understood as analogous to the idealized model of the Greek city-state described by Aristotle as 'political society or community', where a diverse population lived together as an 'organized, solidary body of citizens capable of totally unified action' under a common ethos (Cohen and Arato 1992, 84).

Masyarakat madani is best understood, then, not as a *translation* of a Western concept but as a resonant historical analogy or parallel social formation which exhibited more or less the same political structure and ethos as the Greek model which is understood as the foundation of the Western tradition of civil society. The value and relevance of this normative historical model for post-New Order Indonesia is championed by high profile, modernist Islamic scholar-activists such as Nurcholish Madjid (2001) and Dawam Rahardjo (1999). Madjid injects a special intensity into the signification of *madani/Madinah* by suggesting that in Arabic *madinah* means civil or civilized, and further that *madani* in Arabic may be translated as 'city' or 'urban'. This cluster of significations preserves the association between a particular space, time and way of life, and extends it by catching up the idea of an urban society living according to a common code which is understood as inherently civilized and superior to the way of life of others 'beyond' *Madinah.* In Madjid's perspective, *masyarakat madani* is thus an intensely normative concept, a sign of a superior way of life and far more than a description of an historical polity (Madjid 2000).

The idea of an organic solidarity has resonances in Indonesia beyond its Islamic roots. The notion of an integralistic state drawn from Spinoza, Hegel and Adam Müller was discussed at length in the Japanese-sponsored committee established in 1945 to draft an Indonesian constitution. The eminent customary law expert Supomo described an integralistic state as a social-political formation where there was an organic unity between all groups and in which there was no need for any separation of powers, no need for political rights, indeed no distinction between state and society. While Supomo failed to convince his colleagues that this idealization of a unitary state was the model for an independent Indonesia, his idea of the *negara integralistik* surfaced in the late New Order period and was represented as fundamental and grounded in Indonesian traditional culture. The supposedly indigenous concept of the organic state became the warrant for New Order ideologues to argue against Western ideas of rights, state–society dichotomies and the 'divisive' idea of checks and balances on government policies and authority (Bourchier 1996).

Rahardjo rejects the organic unity of the state idealized in the historical *masyarakat Madinah* and in the New Order revival of the concept of the integralistic state. He argues that civil society organizations, especially religious organizations, were active prior to the establishment of the Republic, and that these organizations were crucial in the creation of the Republic. Civil society, that is to say, was prior to state formation, and the state is a dependent outcome of civil society action. Nevertheless, in Rahardjo's view, the state has an important role in empowering civil society, but state authorities need to understand in turn that their decisions, policies and actions must be open to critical analysis advanced by civil society. Rahardjo dispenses with the glorious vision of the Medina society and describes a somewhat tense and uneasy unity between the state and civil society which he characterizes as a union of 'working partners' (Rahardjo 1999, 133ff).

The relevance of the *masyarakat madani* construction for contemporary Indonesia may be questioned on a number of grounds. The small scale of the historical city-state (perhaps no more than a few hundred citizens) has implications for processes of communication. Mass media are crucial in communicating with a population as large and dispersed as Indonesia's. Issues of media ownership and regulation, freedom of speech and the free circulation of information are vital in facilitating the development of civil society discourses, as the media are both a means and a factor in participative democracy. Civil society's access to the media, its trust of the media, and its input into the governance of the media is a complex, fundamental issue that demands detailed examination. We need go no further than to think of the loss of public confidence in news reporting that has developed following the practice of 'embedding' journalists with the Coalition forces in the 2003 Iraq war, and recall the controversy over the BBC's claim that intelligence reports about Iraq's capacity for launching weapons of mass destruction were embellished, to understand how trust in the media has been eroded. Communication practices and relations are shot through with all sorts of competing agendas in contemporary commercial environments and require sophisticated, specialized understanding.

Secondly, we might ask whether a normative ideal which looks back to a very different time, place and scale of society can provide sufficient guidance for the day-to-day conduct of a large, complex, globalized society? Is the *masyarakat madani* discourse an inherently inward-looking, culturally conservative exercise which aims primarily to show that there are indigenous parallels to Western notions of civil society and democratization? Does it overlook the derived character of *masyarakat Madinah*, privileging one cultural tradition and historical trajectory over another, rather than examining more fundamental political and social principles that civil society – however understood – presents for discussion? As I understand it, this is the essence of the critique advanced by Ahmad Baso when he argues that *masyarakat madani* discourse adopts the concept of civil society uncritically, treating it as a convenient 'ready-to-wear' (*siap saja, siap pakai*) ideological construct which in the process becomes more transcendental than transformative (Baso 1999, 323, 329). Baso argues that we should begin with the assumption that civil society has no relevance and presents no solution for Indonesian democratic transition or the empowerment of society without demonstrating its value through a prior critical examination of the realities of Indonesia's situation, making sure that we take into account religious traditions, socio-economic factors, culture and Indonesia's intellectual traditions or system of reasoning (Baso 1999, 325).

Thirdly, is the *masyarakat madani* paradigm best understood as a model for personal, moral renewal for Muslims rather than as a model for social and political transformation? If it is, what communicative practices will be important in this programme of renewal? Are the public processes of the mass media appropriate for achieving normative change, or is this more a matter of communicative relations in the private, family and community sphere? Does this more atomistic, small-scale community model go some way towards explaining the apparent lack of interest in the public sphere and media–society relations in the work of advocates of *masyarakat madani*?

On the other hand, if the ideals of *masyarakat madani* are not only for Muslims, but have a general, society-wide application in a social formation where Islam is understood as just one belief system among many, are the mass media the most appropriate channels of communication for reaching the national, culturally diverse audience? Nurcholish Madjid's focus on the ancient texts and scriptures, which are the foundation resources for understanding *masyarakat madani*, present significant communicative challenges in a secular society and a media environment largely driven by entertainment values (Madjid 2001).

A.S. Hikam's Secular Theory of Civil Society

The prominent intellectual and former minister in the Wahid government, Muhammad A.S. Hikam, has written extensively about civil society after submitting his doctoral dissertation on the topic at the University of Hawaii. While closely involved in the Islamic organization Nahdlatul Ulama (NU), Hikam outlines a secular theory of civil society which he believes will be conducive to democratization. In opposition to Nurcholish Madjid's 'particularistic' contention that Islam is the foundational culture of Indonesia, and in opposition to the relegation of religion to the private sphere, Hikam argues that Islam should be understood as a public religion in debate with other faiths and paradigms:

> The role of Islam in empowering Indonesian civil society in the future will be determined by the ability of the proponents of the third [secular] approach in mobilising support not only from within the *ummah* [community of Muslim faithful] but also, and more importantly, from outside it. For, it is primarily in the interest of the larger Indonesian society that this inclusive approach prevails. Otherwise the nation will have to face intermittent tensions in society caused by sectarianism and particularism. If this happens, then any effort to democratise the existing political system will have to face a similar problem in other Muslim countries, namely a fundamentalist temptation (Hikam 1996b, 37).

Hikam prefers not to translate 'civil society', as in his view *masyarakat madani* has been co-opted by state authorities much in the way as 'Pancasila society' was once part of the state's cultural project. He remarks that civil society is probably best rendered into Indonesian as *masyarakat sipil*, but because of sensitivities associated with the civil role of the military during the New Order, the phrase is best left untranslated and treated as a neologism to be adapted but not assimilated into contemporary Indonesian social and political realities (Hikam 1999, 80). Second, Hikam argues that understood as *masyarakat madani*, civil society has lost its general applicability and has become monopolized by Islamic thinkers and groups (Hikam 1999, 77).

Hikam's own understanding of the concept is eclectic but is informed primarily by the Tocquevillian perspective of the vital role of voluntary social solidarities that are bound by community values, self-generating and self-supporting, mature and independent in their relations with state authorities (Hikam 1996b, 3). Civil society is as much a *process* of public discourse as a social structure and depends for its proper functioning on an unfettered dialogue between interest groups in a free public sphere. Hikam assumes that civil society in a complex, pluralist, modernizing society such as Indonesia will be 'inherently conflictual', but takes the view that civil society provides an arena and a 'mechanism' for managing conflict in an even-handed way (Hikam 1999, 78). The mechanism is multifaceted and comprises the rule of law, a powerful but responsible state and a watchful, active society which provides checks and balances against domination by the state and military forces. Hikam looks to intellectuals, the NGO sector, an expanding middle class and the active participation of farmers and workers as the driving force for the realization of civil society and the democratization of Indonesia.

In contrast to the idealized unitary state imagined in the *masyarakat madani* social formation, A.S. Hikam's concept of civil society differentiates state and society and sees each bound to the other in a watchful, mutually constructive relationship. Hikam understands that the watchful relationship must necessarily be transparent and played out in a free public sphere. He does not elaborate on the modes of publicness which characterize state–society and internal social debates, but there is little doubt that he has modern processes of mediatization in mind.

It is regrettable that he does not explore how the sectors which in his view will drive or empower civil society will gain media access and develop the skills and resources required for effective utilization of the media. This is a matter which cannot be left to technicians, public relations consultants or the media sector itself. It must become a central plank in civil society theory, planning and action. In an Asia-wide survey of media regulation, Kitley and colleagues found that television, the most pervasive and most popular of all media, is heavily compromised in ownership and regulation, and is not hospitable to the kind of debate and discourse that Hikam presents as vital for the empowerment of civil society and transition to a more democratic society (Kitley 2003). It is only in countries where authoritarian political regimes have been publicly and sometimes violently contested as a part of more general social unrest (Korea, Thailand, Indonesia) that regulatory bodies and systems of nomination to those organizations make formal acknowledgement of the public and civil society.

In modern Western political philosophy, civil society is premised on a clear distinction between the government and non-government spheres. In many Asian countries, this assumption does not hold. The 'public interest' is not an empirical category at all – states define the public interest largely in terms of their own political and cultural aspirations. The public interest is represented as an emergent category to be addressed once the challenges of nation-building are in hand. Conveniently, this defers an adequate response to the unruliness of multi-ethnic, pluralist societies indefinitely, and has favoured the creation of state-dominated, centrally managed television systems. Where commercial television has been introduced, state authorities tend to create clientelistic relationships with broadcasters and trade-off access to advertising revenues for general support of state objectives and ideological priorities.

Such relations are often managed in an undercover, non-transparent way, as both parties know that their cosy relations are maintained at the cost of the public interest. Clientelistic relations are tense and are characterized by practices which are understood by all parties as against the public interest and the rule of law. A good illustration of this kind of cronyism was former President Soeharto's unprecedented attempt to get Parliament to change sections of the *Broadcasting Act No. 24* (1999) in a way that would make it more acceptable to commercial broadcasters – most of whom were family members. Another illustration of the principle, this time from the broadcaster's perspective, was their willingness to ignore the strict letter of the law forbidding them to produce their own news broadcasts, by developing so-called 'soft-news' or 'current affairs' bulletins as a way of building audience share.

It was also obvious from our survey that the regulation of the media is contested and that across the region there is a range of practices which broadcasters use to skirt or disengage from formal regulation. This finding suggests that in most of the countries studied, the rule of law, particularly as it applies to the public/private distinction, is relatively weakly developed. In Indonesia, the indifference which commercial TV stations expressed over the requirement that they pay a proportion of their advertising revenues to the state broadcaster was a clear sign of their impatience with formal regulation. The state regulatory authority at the time, the Department of Information, was equally reluctant to enforce its own regulation because of the clientelistic relations that existed between it and the commercial television stations, which were all owned by either family or close friends of President Soeharto.

The complexity and criss-cross of power relations evident in these few examples suggests that, while acknowledging the significance of the public sphere for the construction and maintenance of civil society, Hikam needs to go further in his discussion of the relations between social solidarities, the media and the public sphere, so that the free, undistorted and fearless debate that Hikam sees as central to the functioning of civil society can be realized.

Civil Society and New Media Relations

In this brief review, I have examined two influential theorizations of civil society in Indonesia. I suggest that whichever interpretation of civil society is favoured, the *masyarakat madani* model, or the secular civil society perspective represented by A.S. Hikam, the role of the media and the nature of state–society–media relations needs urgent consideration – both from a theoretical point of view, and from the point of view of the specific training, resources and activities that voluntary associations need to develop in order to achieve their social goals through the transformative effects of civil society. In short, there needs to be more *mediani* in both *masyarakat madani* and *masyarakat sipil*.

State hegemony during the New Order period was buttressed by a wide range of formal and informal practices and, in Hikam's evocative metaphor, created a bonsai civil society in Indonesia (Hikam 1996b, 247). To dismantle these entrenched and widespread patterns of governmentality and to empower civil society will require a sustained effort. This is as true for the *masyarakat madani* concept as for the more Tocquevillian model. *Masyarakat madani* understood as a normative ideal depends on the promotion and acceptance of a particular way of life. Such a transformation depends ultimately on creating persuasive communicative relations which are grounded in the assumption that the persuader and audience share a common cause. This assertion is equally true for Hikam, whose secular vision is inclusive but inherently fragmented. In this case, it is vital that social solidarities believe that they will be heard and treated with respect, and that they have relatively equal opportunities to advance their cause and persuade the audience of its value.

Media Forums and Civil Society

It is vital that media–society relations are characterized by formally constructed processes of accountability. Given the differential in power between corporatized media and differentiated and shifting civil society solidarities, there is a need to reinforce and draw attention to civil society's stake in media practice. I suggest that legislation establishing media forums is one way of doing this. For most of the time, civil society will maintain a 'watching brief' on its broadcasters, but at other times will need to be on 'high alert' and use its rhetorical skills to bring concerns about the mediatization of significant political issues before the public and their prolocutors whom they rely on to serve them in a trustworthy manner. These educative and informative forums must be a legislated, regular part of media discourses, and must not be shoved off into other less influential venues and public sphericules such as town hall meetings, street marches or the internet.

The mode of interaction between the media and its audiences needs to be educative to be effective. It is only in that mode that each side can cash in their stake in their ongoing relationship. It will also be important for the forums to be truly public in the sense that they must represent the contested character of the society, and not simply publicize matters in the weak sense of public. Media forums will be part of every television channel's monthly schedule, and will be primarily and self-consciously concerned with the processes of mediatization in contemporary society, rhetorical practices and the construction of trustworthiness in public communication.

The requirement that media forums should be established by legislation, and that their operations must be part of the responsibilities of an independent broadcasting authority, introduces an element of coercion into the communicative environment. My justification for this is based on three considerations. The asymmetry in the power which commercial organizations and fragmented social solidarities can exert in lobbying for programming time, let alone prime-time exposure, is very great. Given powerful commercial calls on programming time, and civil society's much weaker financial resources, civil society's access to television schedules must be written into commercial broadcasters' licence and operating conditions. Second, civil society must be afforded the protection of state public institutions and processes, as it is only under these conditions that the pluralism and antagonisms which are an inherent feature of civil society can flourish without being subject to intolerant and possibly violent attack. Third, as I noted above, in many Asian countries, the prospects for civil society access to television are not promising. In many countries, state regulation and institutions are not hospitable to the aspirations of civil society and make little attempt to provide civil society with regular access to the media. In some countries where institutional arrangements do apparently support the mediation of civil society's concerns, co-option and collusion between state authorities and domestic operators undermine apparently progressive relationships (Kitley 2003). Under these circumstances, state protection for the mediation of civil society activities is a fundamental or 'transcendental-logical condition of democracy' (Keane 1998, 64).

The media forums I envisage will function not just to open up the media to civil society and other solidarities. Ideally, that sort of interaction will be a part of regular programming, although achieving that objective will be immensely challenging, as I have suggested. Media forums are educative in the sense that they are dialogic, reflexive, and concerned primarily with a democratic conversation about communicative practices and rhetoric. Media forums, that is to say, are about the construction, understanding and appreciation of communicative competencies in social and cultural life. The forums are powerful in that they are grounded in the fundamental interests of all parties in the mediatization of political discourse. They will be equally demanding on the media as on civil society, but the attention each pays to their mode and practices of communication will be crucial in understanding, appreciating and realizing the dynamic role of civil society in Indonesia's democratic transition.

References

Abar, Akhmad Zaini (1997), 'Televisi Swasta dan Keterbukaan Komunikasi Publik', in Deddy Mulyana and Idi Subandy Ibrahim (eds), *Bercinta Dengan Televisi: Ilusi, Impresi, dan Imaji Sebuah Kotak Ajaib* [In Love with Television: Illusion, Impressions and Images from the Magic Box] (Bandung: Remaja Rosdakarya).

Azra, Azyumardi (1999), *Menuju Masyarakat Madani: Gagasan, Fakta dan Tantangan* [Towards Civil Society: The Concept, Facts and Challenges] (Bandung: Remaja Rosdakarya).

Baso, Ahmad (1999), *Civil Society Versus Masyarakat Madani: Akeologi Pemikiran 'Civil Society' dalam Islam Indonesia* [Civil Society versus Masyarakat Madani: Archaeology of 'Civil Society' in Indonesian Islam] (Bandung: Pustaka Hidayah).

Boestam, Ambia B., van Kesteren, C.E., van Sandick, R.A. and de Meyier, J.E. (2000), *Kahmi, Reformasi dan Civil Society* [Islamic Students' Alumni Association, Reform and Civil Society] (Jakarta: Majelis Nasional KAHMI).

Bourchier, David (1996), 'Lineages of Organicist Political Thought in Indonesia', PhD dissertation, Monash University.

Budiman, Arief (ed.) (1990), *State and Civil Society in Indonesia* (Clayton, Victoria: Monash University Press).

Cohen, Jean L. and Arato, Andrew (1992), *Civil Society and Political Theory* (Cambridge, MA: MIT Press).

Culla, Adi Suryadi (1999), *Masyarakat Madani: Pemikiran, Theory, dan Relevansinya Dengan Cita-Cita Reformasi* [Civil Society: Thinking, Theory and Relevance in Aspirations for Reform] (Jakarta: RajaGrafindo Persada).

Efendi, Firdaus (1999), *Membangun Masyarakat Maḍani Melalui Khutbah dan Ceramah* [Building Civil Society Through Sermons and Lectures] (Jakarta: Nuansa Madani).

Eldridge, Philip (1995), *Non-Government Organizations and Democratic Participation in Indonesia* (Oxford: Oxford University Press).

Fakih, Mansour (1996), *Masyarakat Sipil Untuk Transformasi Sosial: Pergolakan Ideologi LSM Indonesia* [Civil Society for Social Transformation: Upheaval in Indonesian NGO Ideology] (Yogyakarta: Pustaka Pelajar).

Hidayat, Dedy N., Effendi, Gazali, Harsono, Suwardi and Ishadi, S.K. (2000), *Pers Dalam Revolusi Mei: Runtuhnya Sebuah Hegemoni* [The Press in the May Revolution: The Collapse of Hegemony] (Jakarta: Gramedia Pustaka Utama).

Hikam, Muhammad A.S. (1996a), 'Islam and the Empowerment of Indonesian Civil Society', *Indonesia Quarterly* 1, 24.

Hikam, Muhammad A.S. (1996b), *Demokrasi dan Civil Society* [Democracy and Civil Society] (Jakarta: LP3ES).

Hikam, Muhammad A.S. (1999), *Islam, Demokratisasi dan Pemberdayaan Civil Society* [Islam, Democratization and the Empowering Civil Society] (Jakarta: Erlangga).

Ishadi, S.K. (2002), 'Pratek Praktek Diskursus Di Ruang Pemberitaan RCTI, SCTV, Indosiar: Analisis Kritis Proses-Proses Produksi Teks Berita Menjelang Berakhirnya Pemerintahan Soeharto Mei 1998' [Discourse Practice in the Newsrooms of RCTI, SCTV and Indosiar: A Critical Analysis of the Process of Production of News Texts Towards the End of the Soeharto Government May 1998], dissertation, University of Indonesia.

Keane, John (1998), *Civil Society: Old Images, New Visions* (Stanford: Stanford University Press).

Kitley, P. (2000). 'Reformasi, Vulnerable Values and the Regulation of Television in Indonesia', *Asia Pacific Media Educator* 8, 132–48.

Kitley, Philip (2001), 'After the Bans: Modelling Indonesian Communications for the Future', in Grayson Lloyd and Shannon Smith (eds), *Indonesia Today: Challenges of History* (Singapore: Institute of Southeast Asian Studies).

Kitley, Philip (2002), *Konstuksi Budaya Bangsa Di Layar Kaca* [*The Construction of National Culture on Television*] (Jakarta: LSPP and ISAI).

Kitley, Philip (2003), *Television, Regulation and Civil Society in Asia* (London and New York: RoutledgeCurzon).

Madjid, Nurcholish (2000), 'Kedaulatan Rakyat: Prinsip Kemanusiaan dan Musyawarah dalam Masyarakat Madani' [Popular Sovereignty: Principles of Humanism and Consultation in Civil Society], in Usman Widodo (ed.), *Membongkar 'Mitos' Masyarakat Madani* [Deconstructing the 'Myth' of Civil Society] (Yogyakarta: Pustaka Pelajar).

Madjid, Nurcholish (2001), 'Potential Islamic Doctrinal Resources for the Establishment and Appreciation of the Modern Concept of Civil Society', in Nakamura Mitsuo, Sharon Siddique and Omar Farouk Bajunid (eds), *Islam and Civil Society in Southeast Asia* (Singapore: Institute of Southeast Asian Studies).

Mitsuo, Nakamura, Siddique, Sharon and Bajunid, Omar Farouk (eds) (2001), *Islam and Civil Society in Southeast Asia* (Singapore: Institute of Southeast Asian Studies).

Panjaitan, Hinca (1999), *Memasung Televisi: Kontroversi Regulasi Penyiaran di Era Orde Baru* [Banning Television: Controversy Over Broadcasting Regulation in the New Order] (Jakarta: Institut Studi Arus Informasi).

Rahardjo, M. Dawam (1999), *Masyarakat Madani: Agama, Kelas Mengenah dan Perubahan Sosial* [Civil Society: Religion, the Middle Class and Social Change] (Jakarta: LP3ES).

Schulte-Nordholt, Henk and Abdullah, Irwan (2002), *Indonesia in Search of Transition* (Yogyakarta: Pustaka Pelajar).

Setiawan, Bonnie (ed.) (2000), *Perjuangan Demokrasi dan Masyarakat Sipil: Reposisi dan Peran ORNOP/LSM di Indonesia* [The Struggle for Democracy and Civil Society: The Repositioning and Role of Non Government Organisations in Indonesia] (Jakarta: International NGO Forum on Indonesia Development).

Silverstone, Roger (1999), *Why Study the Media?* (London: Thousand Oaks).

Sufyanto (2001), *Masyarakat Tamuddun: Kritik Hermeneutis Masyarakat Madani Nurcholish Madjid* [Hermeneutic Criticism of Nurcholish Madjid's Concept of Civil Society] (Yogyakarta: Pustaka Pelajar).

Suroso (2001), *Menuju Pers Demokratis: Kritik Atas Profesionalisme Wartawan* [Towards a Democratic Press: A Citique of the Professionalism of Journalists] (Yogyakarta: LSIP).

Television Asia (2002/2003), *Satellite and Cable Annual Guide 2002/2003* (Singapore: Reed Business Information).

Widodo, Usman (2000), *Membongkar 'Mitos' Masyarakat Madani* [Deconstructing the 'Myth' of Civil Society] (Yogyakarta: Pustaka Pelajar)

Yasraf, Amir Piliang (2000), 'Public Sphere dan Cyber-Democracy' [The Public Sphere and Cyber-Democracy], *Demokrasi dan HAM* [Democracy and Human Rights] 1: 2, 101–23.

Chapter 22

Indonesian Islam and Democracy: Ways Ahead

Wayne Hudson and Azyumardi Azra

Many Westerners who comment on the relationship between Indonesian Islam and democracy are more interested in democracy than in Islam. This is a bias which we wish to contest in this concluding chapter.

This volume makes it clear that there is a will to embrace democracy on the part of many Indonesian intellectuals. It has also shown that Indonesian intellectuals are sensitive to their specific geography, and to the unique political trajectory that their country has followed since independence. Indonesians are not sentimental about the brutal governments which have come to power in their country. Nor are they slow to note the pervasive culture of corruption which continues to subvert the potential of the country from within. On the other hand, they note, with justified pride, the contributions which Islam and Muslims have made to the development of democracy in the largest Muslim country in the world. This suggests, we believe, that a critically informed pride in Islam, and in its inherent rationality and universality, offers the best foundation for democracy in Indonesia (Azra 2006). On the other hand, Western political theory is an outstanding resource upon which Indonesians can draw in their process of renewal, as the chapters in this volume by Zifcak, Maddox, Patapan, Stokes, Thompson, Hindess, Kane, Crowder and Camilleri demonstrate.

Our view of the need to rethink how rationality, democracy, citizenship, the rule of law and pluralism should be understood in political and legal contexts in Indonesia follows from this. In Indonesia, rationality needs to be understood in complex and sometimes plural ways, and with reference to diverse religious traditions. Rational approaches need not be secular, nor need they be insensitive to religious pluralism and individual freedom.

The issue of *democracy* is often discussed in Indonesia in over-idealized terms – terms which map poorly onto institutions and practices on the ground. Once, however, it is accepted that Indonesian Islam and democracy are compatible in principle, there is much to be said for recognizing that the struggle for democratic institutions is difficult in Islamic societies, as Bahtiar Effendy implies in his chapter in this volume. Actual political practice in Indonesia, as in other states, does not meet the high standards set by the Islamic call to justice, and more detailed and independent Islamic political thought is needed, as well as actual institutions that give this thought adequate expression.

Here, Indonesia could learn from the institution-building of non-Anglo-Saxon nations such as Germany and Sweden. Looking wider afield is compatible with inculturating at home. And precisely because, as Ahmad Syafii Maarif argues in this volume, Islam remains on the whole a positive force in the democratization process in Indonesia, better institutional models from around the world could make it possible to make better use of Islamic principles within Indonesia itself.

The case of *citizenship*, in comparison, is relatively straightforward. In contrast to the exclusivist statist understandings of citizenship which prevailed in recent centuries in the West, citizenship in Indonesia can be plural and reflexive, and take full account of emerging and historically innovative forms of citizenship, including religious and sexual citizenships (Hudson and Kane 2000; Hudson 2003; Hudson and Slaughter 2007). The need to thoroughly think through religious citizenship leads to conclusions which frighten some Western secularists, while the issue of sexual citizenship can be rather challenging for conservative Muslims. How, for example, does Indonesian Islam deal with the rights of gay and lesbian couples? These are tough questions, but an Islam which tries to address them may prove compatible with the multiple lifestyles found in technologically advanced societies.

In the area of *pluralism*, Indonesians can learn, like everyone else, from the work of Isaiah Berlin on the irreducible heterogeneity of moral values. Nonetheless, building such pluralism into Indonesian society will require concrete institutions, the adequacy of which will need to be evaluated by both particularist and universalist principles. Only institutions which capture the actual grain of Indonesian history and social patterns are likely to really work. Meeting both particularist and universalist criteria will not be easy, especially since there are many universalisms and particularisms to contend with, and will require exactly the subtlety and flexibility in which Indonesians excel. In Indonesia, the views and values of Christians and other non-Muslims need to be respected and protected by concrete arrangements. This also means, however, that what works best in Indonesia may differ from what would work well in other parts of the Islamic world. In some cases, it may simply be a matter of following an international precedent; but in others, more complex and gradual mediations will be required.

As far as *human rights* are concerned, it seems clear that Indonesian Muslims will be able to embrace most of the purport of Western universalist claims in ways which respect their traditional values, even if the boundaries may prove difficult for some time. Here, as Fadhil Lubis argues in chapters in this volume, the rich political, legal and philosophical heritage of Islam provides important precedents. There is also much to be said for the view that Muslims who are nervous about human rights need to be better educated in the complexities and nuances of Islamic traditions. These complexities and nuances arguably moderate arguments which are over-dependent on narrow-minded trajectories, just as they challenge potentially complacent ethno-nationalist accounts of particularities of the Indonesian case. Among Indonesians, there is a tendency at times to lean too heavily on idealized and over-uplifting accounts of the history of Islam in the archipelago, or on Romantic claims about the unique trajectory of the Indonesian republic. A degree of nationalism here is probably healthy, but also needs to be moderated in due course. For related reasons, over-simple contrast between Indonesia and the Middle East should also be treated with caution, and it could be argued that, in a range of cases, Indonesian Islam can still learn much from the historical experiences of Arabs, Persians and

Turks. Manifestations of Islam deserve study wherever they are to be found, from North Africa to China.

The *rule of law* may be difficult to implement on the ground in Indonesia. Hence there is a need to make sure, as Brian Galligan argues in this volume, that the rule of law is understood in thick political and ethical terms, and with reference to particular political arrangements rather than merely as a set of legal rules. The notion of *civil society* has particular and profound pertinence to Indonesian developments, even if the rather special nature of civil society in Indonesia (most civil society institutions are Muslim) needs to be respected. As Philip Kitley argues in this volume, the historically specific intersections of civil society and the media in Indonesia make it possible for Islam to play the role of a public religion in a variety of cultural contexts, and this public Islam dimension could be developed further in ways which would help alleviate the concern of some Muslims that the country will fall into some form of American secularism. Indonesia is not, and should not be, secular in the American sense, although, like other modern states, it can explore forms of legitimate secularity in a range of political and social contexts. This approach is further strengthened once *multiculturalism* and the need for *inter-faith dialogue* are taken into account. In both these areas, Indonesia has learnt much from Western societies and in particular from Australia, its close neighbour.

Overall, this volume suggests that there are fewer differences in principle between the best-informed Islamic thought emerging in Indonesia and Western political thought than might have been imagined. The major obstacles to Indonesia critically assimilating Western political concepts (in areas where it wishes to do so) are the relative weakness of Indonesian political institutions and the pervasive presence of corruption in particular domains and practices. Other obstacles include simplistic understandings of Islam on the part of some sectors of Indonesian society, and the short-sighted foreign policy adopted by Anglo-Saxon countries, including Australia, in the Middle East, which motivates some Indonesians to be hypercritical of Western values and lifestyles.

In the longer term, it is likely that the way forward lies in better institutions and arrangements, including both integrity regimes to counteract corruption and the development of a richer public sphere in Indonesia, in which major issues can be critically debated in informed and discursively rational ways. Islam itself is not in our view a problem but, on the contrary, has the capacity to be a part of the solution if it is creatively developed in ways which are informed by a deep knowledge of Islamic traditions as well as contemporary Western political thought. Of course, such a sentiment may seem pious and impractical to Western scholars who have read too much Hobbes. However, it has tremendous resonance on the ground with both the administrative intellectuals and the ordinary people whose support and help is needed if democracy in Indonesia is to work.

References

Azra, A. (2006), *Indonesia, Islam, and Democracy: Dynamics in a Global Context* (Jakarta: Equinox).

Hudson, W. (2003), 'Religious Citizenship', *Australian Journal of Politics and History* 49: 3, 425–9.

Hudson, W. and Kane, J. (2000), *Rethinking Australian Citizenship* (Melbourne: Cambridge University Press).

Hudson, W. and Slaughter, S. (eds) (2007), *Globalisation and Citizenship* (London: Routledge).

Index

Notes: Italic page numbers indicate tables & graphs; numbers in brackets preceded by *n* are footnote numbers.